Abraham Cahan

Twayne's United States Authors Series

Nancy Walker

Vanderbilt University

TUSAS 670

ABRAHAM CAHAN. PHOTO PORTRAIT BY SPACHNER AND BERGER, FROM AN ARTICLE ON CAHAN IN A SERIES, "INTERESTING PEOPLE," BY JOSEPH GOLLOMB, *AMERICAN MAGAZINE* 74 (OCTOBER 1912): 673.

Abraham Cahan

Sanford E. Marovitz

Kent State University

Twayne Publishers
An Imprint of Simon & Schuster Macmillan
New York

Prentice Hall International
London • Mexico City • New Delhi • Singapore • Sydney • Toronto

Twayne's United States Author Series No. 670

Abraham Cahan
Sanford E. Marovitz

Twayne Publishers
An Imprint of Simon & Schuster Macmillan
1633 Broadway
New York, NY 10019

Library of Congress Cataloging-in-Publication Data

Marovitz, Sanford E.
　　Abraham Cahan / Sanford E. Marovitz.
　　　　p.　　cm. — (Twayne's United States authors series : TUSAS 670)
　　Includes bibliographical references and index.
　　ISBN 0-8057-3993-9 (cloth)
　　1. Cahan, Abraham, 1860–1951—Criticism and interpretation.
　2. Jews—United States—Intellectual life. 3. Jews in literature.
　I. Title. II. Series.
　PS3505.A254Z8 1996
　813'.4—dc20　　　　　　　　　　　　　　　　　96-27133
　　　　　　　　　　　　　　　　　　　　　　　　　　　　　CIP

10　9　8　7　6　5　4　3　2　1

Printed in the United States of America.

To the Marovitz Family,
the first of whom to arrive in America
passed through the doors of Castle Garden in 1888,
six years after Abraham Cahan

Contents

Acknowledgment

Without the kindness and assistance of many people—publishers and editors, colleagues, friends, and family—this book might not have come into being. I am grateful to the editors of *American Literary Realism, 1870–1910,* for permission to use materials from the Cahan bibliography compiled by Lewis Fried and myself, *ALR* (Summer 1970). Selected passages on Jewish American realism were published by the University of Delaware Press in my chapter on that subject in *American Realism and the Canon* (1994), edited by Gary Scharnhorst and Tom Quirk, and I thank the editors and publisher for allowing me to present them in revised form here. I am also grateful to the Jewish Publication Society for their permission to draw heavily from *The Education of Abraham Cahan* (1969), the English translation of volumes 1 and 2 of Cahan's Yiddish autobiography, *Bleter fun mayn lebn,* translated by Leon Stein, Abraham P. Conan, and Lynn Davidson; to Dover Publications for allowing me to quote as necessary from their excellent text *Yekl and The Imported Bridegroom and Other Stories of the New York Ghetto* (1970), edited by Bernard C. Richards; and to the Family History Library, Church of Jesus Christ of the Latter-Day Saints, Salt Lake City, Utah, for giving me access to important records concerning Cahan's naturalization.

In addition, I should like to thank again the individuals who have been helpful in many special ways: Dini Hansma and Gloria Cronin, who provided invaluable assistance in locating Cahan's immigration records in the Family History Library; Albert J. von Frank, Wes Mott, and Joel Myerson for helping me track down an unfamiliar quotation from Emerson; Lee and Connie Shneidman, who guided me on a walking tour of the Lower East Side; Dan Walden, whose knowledge of Jewish American literature seems endless; Louis Harap, a model of integrity and scholarly devotion in American Jewish letters; Ellen Schiff for her confidence and sustained interest in this project; "Fishl" Kutner for his timely advice on Yiddish; David Guralnik for his expertise and sage guidance on transliteration; and Joe Landis for supporting my work on Cahan in many ways.

x ACKNOWLEDGMENT

I am also grateful to valued colleagues at Kent State University: Gene Wenninger, former Director of Research and Graduate Studies, and Fred Schwarzbach, Chair of English, for granting me the blocks of time necessary for research and writing; Mike Cole and the interlibrary loan staff, who gave me access to essential items otherwise unavailable in Kent; Herb Hochhauser, Director of Jewish Studies, who assisted me with Yiddish titles and phrases during the early stages of this study; Tom Davis and Lew Fried for their continued support and encouragement; Christine Shih and Ray Craig for helping me through problems with my computer; and Kathleen Ward for early bibliographical aid.

Moreover, the assistance I have received from the editorial staff at Twayne has been invaluable. To Nancy Walker I owe my deepest thanks for guiding me through the problems in writing the original manuscript, suggesting improvements toward its revision, and patiently answering questions along the way. I also thank Mark Zadrozny, senior editor at Twayne, for his sound advice and his compassion in gaining additional time for me when I found it impossible to meet the original deadline. Reading the manuscript with pencil in hand, India Koopman has enabled me to tighten and clarify my prose throughout by virtue of her sensitivity to language and her skill in employing it without imposition, for which I am most grateful to her. My thanks go, also, to Impressions Book and Journal Services, Inc. for their courteous help on questions related to the page proofs.

Finally, I wish to express my deep appreciation to my sweet, patient wife, Nora, who has been sharing our home for the past several years not only with her husband but also with the spirit of Abraham Cahan, and she has never once complained. Her love and confidence are as much a part of this study as my thoughts and words.

Preface

A century ago at this writing, Abraham Cahan published his first story in English. Entitled "A Providential Match," it appeared in a small literary magazine called *Short Stories* in February 1895. The title proved fortuitous, for it led to Cahan's finding a "providential match" of his own—but in a literary rather than a matrimonial sense. When the story was brought to the attention of William Dean Howells, then still the predominant figure in American realism, it became a link between the two authors, who had briefly met a few years earlier. No sooner had Howells recognized Cahan's kinship in realism than he renewed their association and encouraged the younger writer to continue in the same vein of literary authenticity. Cahan did, of course, and Howells provided the support that eventuated in Cahan's bringing out not only several volumes of fiction over the next twenty-two years but also a considerable number of journalistic articles, essays, and sketches—all in English.

Yet the bulk of Cahan's writing, surprisingly enough for those unfamiliar with his life and work, was done not in English but in Yiddish, his *mame-loshn,* or native language, for he was born in a small Lithuanian village in the Pale of Jewish settlement during the reign of Czar Alexander II. When he immigrated in mid-1882 he knew no more English than he had been able to acquire with a bilingual dictionary during his trans-Atlantic voyage to the United States. Although it was almost at the last moment that he decided to come to America at all rather than remain a radical in Europe, helping to bring down the czardom, once his decision was made, he was determined to acculturate quickly and leave the Old World of his past behind for good.

The extent of his transformation is chiefly apparent in his English publications, in which many of his fictional characters are torn between their European Jewish traditions and their new American environment, generally the Lower East Side of New York City. Cahan's Old World ties were also visible in his career as a Yiddish-speaking Jewish journalist, socialist, and voice for labor in the New York ghetto—jammed with tenements and littered streets, sweatshops and pushcarts. The connection was inevitable, and Yiddish in itself constituted the nexus. How could he disengage from the past when he continued to depend on his *mame-loshn* to carry the word to his fellow immigrants, to cajole and enlighten them in their mutual tongue? Cahan was immersed in

Yidishkayt, the culture of Yiddish that dominated the East Side, and it was this very immersion that infused his English fiction—from "A Providential Match" to his final grand achievement, *The Rise of David Levinsky,* twenty-odd years later—giving it the vitality and authenticity that Howells so much admired.

To be sure, Abraham Cahan warrants a place among the writers in Twayne's United States Authors Series on the basis of his English journalism and fiction, but it would be shortsighted to disregard his extensive contributions to American culture on the broader scale of his pronounced social influence among Jewish immigrants from Eastern Europe. He was a force for Americanization, and his chief vehicle was the Jewish daily *Forward,* the newspaper that he cofounded in 1897 and, after a problematic on-and-off relationship at the beginning, edited for nearly fifty years. As many leading voices in American letters have testified—not all of them Jewish—the *Forward* became not only the most successful Yiddish daily in the world, with its circulation of approximately a quarter million in the 1920s, but it was also a model of what an outstanding ethnic newspaper could be.

This critical study is the first full-length work on Cahan since the publication of Jules Chametzky's *From the Ghetto: The Fiction of Abraham Cahan* (1977), a perceptive scholarly analysis of the fiction, now almost twenty years old. His emphasis on matters of language complements Theodore Marvin Pollock's more comprehensive earlier account, "The Solitary Clarinetist: A Critical Biography of Abraham Cahan, 1860–1917," a valuable Columbia University dissertation of 1959 that was never published beyond the standard UMI microfilm format. A third study deserving mention in this context is by Ronald Sanders, *The Downtown Jews: Portraits of an Immigrant Generation* (1969), a work that centers on Cahan, to which the present volume is deeply indebted; whereas Chametzky gives particular attention to the fiction, Sanders traces the intricacies of Cahan's relations among socialists, journalists, and a variety of other controversial figures who had fled the pogroms of Eastern Europe for the internecine altercations of Lower Manhattan.

Cahan emerged from this disputatious, factionalized milieu as a towering figure in support of four major goals: the expansion of socialism and organized labor; the Americanization of the immigrant East European Jews, especially those from the Russian Empire; the establishment of a popular Yiddish daily for the common reader; and the promotion of literary realism. His ultimate realization of all four aims might have been anticipated by a perceptive observer, for Cahan had begun making a name for himself in East Side meeting halls within a few weeks of his arrival in the United States. By the time he took over the *Forward* as permanent editor in 1903, he had already published two volumes of fiction and half a dozen uncollected stories in English. Two more novels would follow. Emerson, whom Cahan quoted in an article of 1903 on the Jewish massacres in Russia, wrote in "Self-Reliance": "An institution is the lengthened shadow of one man." If Cahan's "institution" may be considered a composite of his great Yiddish daily and his acclaimed realistic fiction, which both fostered and illustrated the rapid Americanization of the Russian Jew, his success in this endeavor is a splendid example of Emerson's point.

In the present study I have integrated the information and insight drawn from the principal works on the period of mass East European Jewish migration, especially biographical and critical studies of Cahan, with my own understanding of his English writings, chiefly his fiction. I have explored these in the context of Cahan's life and culture as well as on their own terms, both aesthetic and moral. Personally, Cahan was a confrontational, recalcitrant man with more than a trace of arrogance. But he was also an individual with a streak of genius, multiple talents, and high aspirations, a man who seems now to have been nearly indefatigable.

If he had done no more than guide the *Forward* to success and maintain it thus for decades, it would have been enough. If he had done no more than promote improvement in the lives of his Jewish *landslayt* (Jews from the homeland) and facilitate their acculturation, that, too, would have been enough. But he complemented both by crowning his literary career with *The Rise of David Levinsky*, a major work of naturalistic fiction and perhaps the best immigration novel yet written in the United States. His life and accomplishments simultaneously fulfilled his own American Dream, vaguely formulated before he left Europe, and exemplified the possibilities vested in it for all those hopeful immigrants who followed him.

Note on the Yiddish Transliteration

In transliterating Yiddish words and titles, I have attempted to follow the YIVO standard. Also, I have transliterated largely according to the Germanized Yiddish spelling of words used around the turn of the century in Cahan's day rather than the modernized spelling in our own. To avoid confusion over transliteration, whenever feasible I have used the Anglicized versions of familiar Yiddish words now considered naturalized into English and included without foreign designation in one or more of the current academic English dictionaries listed below. The English orthography of these words varies among the lexicons. In the Glossary, naturalized words and phrases appear without italics. The spelling of proper names and words in direct quotations is necessarily that of the originals.

The principal lexicons consulted for this study were *Webster's New World Dictionary of the American Language,* second edition (1980); *The American Heritage Dictionary of the English Language,* third edition (1992); and *Merriam-Webster's Collegiate Dictionary,* tenth edition (1993). For assistance with Yiddish definitions, pronunciation, and transliteration, I have turned to Alexander Harkavy, *English-Yiddish Dictionary* (1891) and *Yiddish-English Dictionary,* twenty-second edition (1898), and to Uriel Weinreich, *Modern English-Yiddish Yiddish-English Dictionary* (1977), which includes the YIVO guidelines.

Although I received much valuable advice on transliteration in this study, ultimately I depended upon my own judgment. Therefore, I assume full responsibility for any errors that may appear.

Chronology

1860   Abraham Cahan born 7 July in Podberezy, Lithuania, a shtetl in the Pale of Jewish settlement.

1865–1866   Moves with family to Vilna, fourteen miles away.

1870   Enrolls in Jewish public school without father's knowledge.

1873   Celebrates bar mitzvah in July; brother, Isaac, born soon afterward.

1874   Enrolls in public Jewish gymnasium; withdraws from yeshiva after losing interest in Talmud study.

1875   First reads a forbidden socialist pamphlet.

1876   Matriculates in Vilna Teacher Training Institute for Jewish students during summer.

1879   Associates with radical movement.

1881   March, Czar Alexander II's assassination by Will of the People Party followed by anti-Semitic pogroms beginning at Easter. Graduates from Teacher Training Institute in June; visits St. Petersburg; travels in August to Velizh to begin first teaching assignment.

1882   Shortly before Passover, police search Cahan's room twice for radical publications, and he flees. Docks at Philadelphia 6 June; 7 June, at Castle Garden, officially admitted into U.S. as immigrant. Attends first socialist meeting and presents first talk in the United States 27 July. In an important innovation, gives the first socialist speech in Yiddish 18 August.

1883   Begins teaching English in fall to immigrants at Young Men's Hebrew Association.

1885   Marries Aniuta (Anna) Bronstein, from Kiev.

1886   Works during autumn with Henry George mayoral campaign.

1887   Formally joins Socialist Labor Party in December.

1888 With Morris Hilkowitz (Hillquit), helps establish United Hebrew Trades 9 October.

1889 Essay "Realism" published in *Workmen's Advocate* on 15 March. In Boston during the autumn; delivers his first socialist lecture outside New York.

1891 Becomes naturalized citizen 8 June. Named delegate to Second International European Congress. Edits socialist *Arbeter tsaytung* (through 1895).

1892 Meets William Dean Howells.

1893 In Europe for Third International Congress; sees parents for last time, his only visit with them since 1881.

1894 Serializes *Rafael naritsokh* in *Arbester tsaytung*. Edits *Di tsukunft* (through early 1897).

1895 "A Providential Match," first story in English, published in *Short Stories* in February.

1896 First English novel, *Yekl, A Tale of the New York Ghetto*, published by D. Appleton.

1897 First issue of the *Forward*, Yiddish socialist daily, cofounded and edited by Cahan, published 22 April; Cahan resigns during summer. Made full-time reporter for *New York Commercial Advertiser* (through 1901).

1898 Houghton Mifflin publishes *The Imported Bridegroom and Other Stories of the New York Ghetto*.

1899–1901 Six stories published in five popular magazines, November 1899 through August 1901.

1902 March, returns to editor's chair of *Forward*; resigns again in September.

1903 Kishinev Massacre in Easter season. Returns to *Forward* in summer as permanent editor.

1905 *The White Terror and the Red* published by A. S. Barnes.

1910 Forward Publishing Co. brings out volume 1, *From the Old World to the New One*, of his projected multivolume *History of the United States with Details Concerning the Discovery and Conquest of America*.

1911 Fire at Triangle Shirtwaist Factory 25 March kills 146 workers, mostly young Jewish and Italian women.

1912   *Discovery Journeys after Columbus,* volume 2 of Cahan's
        Yiddish *History of the United States,* is published. Cahan
        meets Nikolai Lenin in Europe during summer.

1913   Undergoes surgery in March for intestinal ulcer; April
        through July, *McClure's* publishes "The Autobiography
        of an American Jew," early serialized version of *The Rise
        of David Levinsky.* Leo Frank case begins.

1915   Leo Frank case climaxes with Frank's lynching.

1917   Harper & Brothers publishes *The Rise of David Levinsky.*

1925   Visit to Palestine stirs Cahan's sympathy with Zionism.

1929   Second visit to Palestine.

1946   Suffers severe stroke and releases most of his control
        over Forward to associate.

1947   Anna dies 2 May at 86.

1951   Cahan dies 31 August at 91.

Chapter One

The Life: From Russian Student to American Man of Letters

Not yet through his twenty-first year when he arrived in the United States on 6 June 1882, Abraham Cahan was already a man of two worlds. Standing on the deck of the *British Queen* as the vessel approached Philadelphia after its thirteen-day crossing from Liverpool, the young Lithuanian immigrant was for a moment overcome on seeing America, "this magic land," before him.[1] It was not more than a couple of months earlier that the vision of his future had suddenly been transformed when a chance conversation with a new acquaintance shifted his attention and aspirations from Europe to the United States. From that moment, America became his destination (*Education,* 187).

By then he was already a fugitive, fleeing the Czar's police, who sought to connect him with the underground Nihilist movement then gaining strength in Russia. A series of pogroms had commenced immediately after the assassination of Alexander II in March 1881, and as a Jew Cahan was increasingly vulnerable to the anti-Semitic brutality of government and peasantry alike. So he fled one night from his lodging and set out for the border with no certain plans beyond escape. A liberated intellectual with a strong commitment to social reform, Cahan was stifled as well as endangered in his homeland. Before he crossed the border into Austria, however, his new direction was clear: "I paced my room in a fever. America! To go to America! To re-establish the Garden of Eden in that distant land. My spirit soared. All my other plans dissolved. I was for America!" (*Education,* 186–87).

Early Life in the Pale

Although most of Abraham Cahan's early years were spent in the city of Vilna, he was born in Podberezy, a shtetl, or small Jewish community, located about fourteen miles from that city. His birth date was 7 July 1860, but in his autobiography he notes it only with reference to the Hebrew calendar as the seventeenth of Tammuz [in the year 5620]. For

Jews, this date traditionally begins a three-week period that memorial-
izes the days on which the First and Second Temples of Jerusalem were
destroyed by the Babylonians and Romans in 586 BCE and 70 CE respec-
tively. According to tradition, it was also on the seventeenth of Tammuz
that Moses broke the tablets on his return from Mt. Sinai when he saw
his people worshiping the golden calf. Cahan provided no reason for
specifying his birth date on the Hebrew rather than the Gregorian calendar now commonly used, but the fact that he did so suggests his
awareness of the catastrophic changes thought to have occurred among
the Hebrews on that day in history, and perhaps he felt, as he drafted his
autobiography in the 1920s, that it marked him to become an agent of
change for the Jewish people in another era of darkness.

Podberezy and Vilna were situated in the Pale of Jewish Settlement, a
vast area of Eastern European land under the control of Russia to which
Jews were confined by law; it incorporated twenty-five western
provinces between the Black Sea and the Baltic.[2] If the Russian Jews
were limited predominantly to shtetl life in the Pale during these years,
so at the same time were their religious traditions largely protected from
change by external forces. Indeed, poor as it was, the shtetl was a small,
isolated world of its own. This is the type of community and life that
were idealized and romanticized in *Fiddler on the Roof* (1964), the popular
Broadway musical adapted from the Yiddish stories of Sholem Aleichem.[3]

It is surprising to learn that as Cahan was composing his five-volume
autobiography, *Bleter fun mayn lebn* (Pages from My Life, 1926–31), he
recalled experiences that he had undergone even before his third birthday, such as falling into a torn sofa at about eighteen months. A more
striking recollection, though a grim one, materialized as part of the setting over thirty years later in Cahan's first extended work of fiction in
English, *Yekl, A Tale of the New York Ghetto* (1896). He was only three
years old when he traveled with his mother from Podberezy to Vilna,
and along the road he noticed several gallows standing out amid a field
of cabbages. On them hung the bodies of men "wrapped in white gowns
that fluttered in the wind" (*Education,* 4), the remains of Polish landown-
ers executed after their unsuccessful rebellion against Russian control.
The opening pages of Cahan's autobiography are literally punctuated
with repetitions of the phrase "I remember" followed by details of incidents, places, and people: a boot dropping from one of the hanging
corpses; a small gift of grits and a pan from his Aunt Fayge; the fright-
ening sound of the name Khovanski, a high Russian official feared for

his taking Jews from their families for twenty-five years in the Czar's army; the faded portrait of his paternal grandfather, Reb Yankele, "the pride of our family and the people of Podberezy" for his great learning (*Education*, 5). Those vivid recollections of his childhood are testimony to the depth and extensiveness of his memory, which served him so well as a journalist and fiction writer during the course of his long career. In a few telling descriptive passages, Cahan effectively portrays his family. From the portrait of his father, Shakhne, readers familiar with Abraham Cahan's life may easily recognize marked attributes that the two shared. His name—*Cahan*—connotes that Shakhne was a *koheyn,* or *koyen,* a descendant of Aaron, the brother of Moses, and therefore a select member of the priestly tribe of Judaism. Heavily influenced by his "fanatically religious" Uncle Ezrial (*Education*, 33), Shakhne earned his living in Podberezy as a *melamed,* a teacher of beginning Hebrew to children, respectful toward orthodoxy and piety.

Yet he was at least equally attracted to secular learning; he read philosophy in Hebrew more than he did the Talmud (Rabbinic commentary on Hebrew law) and had no wish to prevent his son from acquiring knowledge of the Gentile world beyond the physical confines of the shtetl. In fact, he fostered it, with results that were soon to alienate father from son as well as dramatically alter Cahan's life and entire future. Until he was fourteen or fifteen, the young Cahan was strongly inspired by his father, admiring Shakhne's respect for both Judaic tradition and secular learning, a duality appreciated by few others in the family. At one point, Cahan suggested that were it not for their Orthodox family and friends, his father might have become a freethinker (*Education*, 33). Yet Shakhne insisted that the boy maintain his faith: "I will hire tutors to teach you Russian, German, French and how to play the violin. But you must also be a pious Jew" (*Education*, 34). He learned the languages and the clarinet but not the violin.

The tongue of the shtetl was Yiddish.[4] As a child, however, Cahan was told, "A prayer in Yiddish was a mock prayer," and God would not hear or heed it (*Education*, 27). Although Shakhne Cahan himself was not repulsed by Yiddish in this way, his awareness that languages were the tools by which one could develop intellectually and culturally beyond long-established confines was passed on to Cahan in the boy's early years. His father "loved the Hebrew language and often read it aloud," Cahan recalls. "The beauty of the language would make his eyes sparkle with excitement" (*Education*, 34). This devotion was not lost on the young Cahan, whose impassioned dedication to the study and application of languages proved instrumental in the rapid blossoming of his career in New York City.

Like Shakhne, Cahan's mother, Sarah, was a teacher, but she taught reading and writing to young girls while maintaining a traditional Jewish household. Like all other married Jewish women in the shtetl, she always kept her hair covered in public, either with a wig or kerchief, silk for the Sabbath and cotton for weekdays. On the Sabbath, she read from her Yiddish prayer-book. In *Bleter fun mayn lebn,* Cahan describes the family Sabbath in Vilna with great clarity—including his walk back from shul (the synagogue) with his father and the dinner table with its holiday candles aglow—as if the past had been vividly restored in his imagination: "All of this was more than half a century ago," he later recalls, "all so very far away and yet so clear, like the memory of a treasured song, a godly song" (*Education,* 38). Deeply pious, Sarah was more forceful and practical than her husband, whose "idealism and vague longings . . . disturbed his peace" (*Education,* 54). She shared his affection for language, however, and wrote both Russian and German as well as Yiddish, an unusual attribute for a Jewish woman in the shtetl. Generally speaking, girls were taught only Yiddish, not even Hebrew, and it was Yiddish that they spoke in the home, first to their parents and later to their own children. For this reason, Yiddish was called the *mame-loshn,* the "mother tongue," and Hebrew was the *loshn-koydesh,* "the language of holiness."

Cahan was an only child until shortly after his bar mitzvah (ceremonial initiation into adulthood at thirteen), when he gained, in addition to his manhood, a baby brother, Isaac.[5] At the age of about four and a half years, Cahan attended his first *kheyder,* or Hebrew elementary school, but he recalled his two earliest teachers more as eidolons than tutors of flesh and blood. As Cahan portrays them in the early section of *The Rise of David Levinsky* (1917), his last and most important work of fiction, the *kheyder* teachers were notorious for acts of cruelty toward their young pupils; pinching, pulling ears, jabbing with thumbs, rapping hands with rulers, and other such torturous practices were evidently commonplace. If Cahan commenced his education in the *khadorim* of Podberezy, however, he received little of it there; within the year, his family moved to Vilna, where he would live for the next sixteen years.

Surely, nowhere in the Russian empire at that time could a Jewish youth gain a better education in Talmud and scripture than in the city of Vilna, known as "the Jerusalem of Lithuania" because of the Hebrew sages who had studied, written, and taught there for more than two centuries.[6] As a boy receiving a Jewish education in Vilna during the late 1860s and early 1870s, young Cahan was inevitably affected by both the Talmudic and Hasidic traditions.[7] As with the Podberezy period, Cahan clearly remembered many childhood experiences in Vilna that are illuminating with respect to his early religiosity and the imaginative work he published several decades later. His eye for detail and the clarity with which he recalled it is at times astonishing. For example, he refers to his many imaginative daydreams as a seven-year-old: "On the back of my bench I can see the ocean. Huge ships are crossing. . . . In one of my daydreams I suddenly saw that the flies that plagued our home were really transmigrated souls. Some were accursed evildoers; others were tsaddikim, righteous men. The two groups were in constant warfare. Of course, the tsaddikim always won." "I translated the historic stories my father told me. In my fantasies, butterflies, bees and birds re-enacted the deeds of heroes" (*Education, 23*).

Soon after arriving in Vilna, where Shakhne worked in a tavern owned by Sarah's uncles, Cahan was sent to his first *kheyder* in that city. Over the next seven years or so, until shortly before his bar mitzvah, when his father enlisted him in a yeshiva (a seminary for Talmudic studies), he passed through a series of five such preliminary schools, each taking him to a higher stage of his Hebrew education. When he was only eight he began his earliest study of Talmud, and two years later he entered his fifth and apparently favorite *kheyder,* where he remained for three years. Although his teacher, like most others, wielded the lash, Cahan respected him as hard working and honest, and he acknowledged knowing this *kheyder* "like a home" (*Education, 53*).

During the early part of his three years of study there, two incidents occurred in and around Vilna that generated extended reverberations for Cahan, one ominous for the Jewish people in Russia and the other a foreshadowing of what lay ahead for countless thousands of those who would immigrate to the United States during the next half century. The first took place a few miles from Vilna, where a Jewish family was attacked, murdered, and robbed in an inn by a group of Gentiles, one of whom grabbed and brutally killed an infant by smashing its head against an oven. The atrocity frightened Vilna's Jewish community, whose members had not forgotten the sporadic acts of anti-Semitic hostility and riots in the history of their city and others in the Russian empire, though in this case the bandits were apprehended (*Education, 49*).

The other incident was the importation of the first Singer sewing machines to Vilna (*Education*, 60). Those who learned to use the machines in the Old Country would gain a great advantage in New York, which rapidly became home to the largest producers of ready-made garments in the world. Eastern European Jews and their Singers took over the fledgling industry late in the nineteenth century.

But for young Abraham Cahan at eleven and twelve, these developments were still well in the future. Over the few years that he spent acquiring a basic familiarity with Talmud he felt the "greatest religious fervor" of his young life. During the "Days of Awe" between Rosh Hashana (marks the New Year and anniversary of the Creation) and Yom Kippur (Day of Atonement), the market square outside the court-yard where the Cahans lived became a "preachers' market," to which famous Hebrew preachers from other Jewish communities came and declaimed to all who would listen. Cahan said that he heard every one of them in autumn 1872, though he admitted that he did not always understand what they said (*Education*, 62).

Meanwhile, Shakhne continued to work in the tavern, which Sarah's uncles had left for him to run. When he could no longer earn a living from it, he let it go to serve as a bookkeeper, but eventually he became a *melamed* again. Although the family undoubtedly suffered financial hardship, their poverty was not as severe as it was among many Jews in the Vilna ghetto.

Nevertheless, the scarcity of money led Shakhne to attempt to apprentice his son to a woodcarver so that the boy could learn a trade. Cahan found the carver despicable for several reasons and detested the idea of leaving school to become a common tradesman, especially as an apprentice to so crude and immoral a craftsman. After persuading his parents that he would under no circumstances go back to the carver's shop, he returned to the yeshiva. It was located in the Jewish sector of the city at the base of a hill and had a typical shtetl atmosphere, though at the top of the same hill, only eighteen steps up, was the modern part of the city with lawns, gardens, and a new railroad station (*Education*, 60–61). In the yeshiva the living conditions for the students and the approach to learning "had not changed in a thousand years" (*Education*, 69–70). The medieval and the modern nineteenth-century worlds were virtually juxtaposed, separated only by a flight of stairs.

For Cahan, the head of the yeshiva, Reb Elya Itkhe, embodied the truth that "ambition can make a man learned but not necessarily quick-witted" (*Education*, 61), and the dissatisfied student did not remain there long. By this time, he had celebrated his bar mitzvah and despite his short period of spiritual excitement a little earlier, had lost his interest in Hebrew study altogether. With the ceremony behind him that marked the end of his childhood, Cahan suddenly realized that he "was another person" (*Education,* 64). The influence of his father's inclination toward Gentile learning, his brief stay at ten in a secular public school, and his fascination with languages other than Yiddish and Hebrew undermined his earlier attachments to Jewish tradition and piety. He enrolled in a public gymnasium for Jewish students and after briefly attempting to attend both the yeshiva and the public school, left Talmud study behind him. Cahan's father seemed to have expected it and said nothing to dissuade him. During the following decade, however, relations between father and son continued to deteriorate, and by the end of the decade, the two were no longer on speaking terms.

Not until Cahan left for Velizh would the gap between them be bridged; later, although a personal reconciliation had occurred, the spiritual break was reinforced by the physical distance between them. Although he wrote to his parents from New York, Cahan would not see either of them again until they met by arrangement at a cousin's home in Vienna in the summer of 1893, when he was a Socialist delegate to the Second International in Zurich. Cahan's parents died within a few years of each other in the first decade of the new century, and his brother, who had immigrated to the United States in 1892, succumbed to pneumonia early in 1909 at age thirty-five (Sanders, 155, 390).[8]

Now in his midteens and dedicated to secular studies, Cahan decided to make teaching his career; he had no intention of becoming a *melamed* like his father but wished instead to teach in a public school: "Four years of study and then a petty official post, a teaching position, brass buttons and a frock coat, a cap with a cockade—what better career was there for a boy of my circumstances?" (*Education,* 76). Although one may sense here a glimmer of self-derisive humor in Cahan's assessment of his aims and possibilities half a century earlier, the statement includes less irony than truth, for even as a teenager, he would have been aware of the limitations he faced in his choice of career as a Jew in Russia. A new teacher-training institute for Jewish students had opened in Vilna a few years earlier, and Cahan intended to apply for admission to its four-year program when he was old enough. But first he needed to prepare for the entrance examinations, which would take him two years.

During these preparatory years, Cahan acquainted himself with heretofore unfamiliar Russian authors, including Turgenev, all of whose works he read, taking special pleasure from "the beauty of his language" (*Education*, 97). Nearly two decades later, he would reverse his admiration for Turgenev in favor of Chekhov, whose realistic stories were widely acclaimed in Russia. He also attempted to learn drawing, a pastime he had relished as a child but had never developed into an art. His interest in drawing is evident in most of his writing—both the journalism and the fiction—which is strikingly graphic; the intrinsic visual qualities of his verbal art are particularly evident in his characterizations, which often become startlingly alive by virtue of only a few distinctive details that individualize the portraits.

As Ronald Sanders observes in *The Downtown Jews*, Cahan "had a remarkable talent for providing vivid illustrative examples" (64), and he employed it to great advantage. Early in *Bleter*, for instance, he describes his new neighbors, among the poorest inhabitants of the courtyard where he lived, whom he met soon after moving to Vilna from Podberezy: "One was our blond ritual slaughterer[9] and his brunette wife. He limped and she stammered and he was quiet and she was fun-loving. . . . [Living near them] were also Schmaltz, the scribe who praised my penmanship, a young man who sold geese and absentmindedly shrugged his right shoulder" (*Education*, 20). In like detail, he limns the "famous Jewish writer Isaac Meyer Dick," who "would stroll about the courtyard in bedroom slippers, a flat hat on his head, a pipe in his mouth, a sardonic smile on his lips and a melancholy air all about him" (*Education*, 45).

Several of his teachers at the institute are similarly individualized and caricatured in only a few lines. All of these miniportraits represent people Cahan had known over half a century earlier, but his power of recalling and reproducing details about them enabled him to render them imaginatively with restored vitality. Sanders suggests that as the son of Shakhne, Cahan was "a born *melammed*," with "a mind that naturally thought in concrete examples" (104), and for him those details were most effectively tied to people. Cahan may not have known Emerson's understanding of the past, yet *Bleter* is a dynamic illustration of his statement "There is no history; only biography."[10] The same might be said for much of Cahan's journalism—and his fiction. His representation of reality always highlights individuals and specific details by which they can be identified.

At about the same time Cahan developed his youthful interest in drawing, he suffered from an eye infection that endured for a few weeks and left him with crossed eyes, a disfigurement he accepted for many years until a German ophthalmologist in New York advised him that minor surgery could quickly correct it. During his years as a student before and after his entrance to the institute, however, he was self-conscious about his crossed eyes, which caused him embarrassment and confusion in the company of girls. As he remembered his early years, he occasionally made a fool of himself over the girls who visited the students at the institute, and his uneasiness led him to shy away from them. This left him at times with a sense of isolation: "There were hours when I ached with melancholy, with longings and sadness" (*Education,* 135–36). Such sentiments often appear in his fiction, from the early stories through *The Rise of David Levinsky,* though they are then merged with the feelings of alienation and loneliness-suffered by immigrants unable to adjust to the New World. Although Cahan himself adapted successfully, it is likely that he, too, felt estranged during his first years in the United States.

Meanwhile, he studied for his examination and passed it easily. In the summer of 1876 he became a student at the Vilna Teacher Training Institute for Jewish students, where he remained at government expense for the next four years (*Education,* 76, 104–5). Although Yiddish was forbidden at the Institute, the Jewish students did not resent this prohibition because, like Cahan, most of them were eager to divest themselves of their Hebraic background in favor of a secular lifestyle. At one point Cahan admitted that he envied Jewish youths who had no knowledge of Yiddish. Ironically, he carried this disaffection for Yiddish with him to America a few years later and sustained it in the United States despite his dependence on it initially as an outspoken socialist and later as editor of the Jewish daily *Forward.* This seeming anomaly can be explained by his belief that the immigrants' dependence on Yiddish for communication precluded rapid acculturation and assimilation, which Cahan recognized as essential if Jews were to ascend social and economic ladders in the United States, a possibility that did not exist for them in most of the Russian Empire.

Teaching at the institute was traditional, and although Cahan had been eager to enter and learn, he was soon disappointed with the methods and expectations there. Memorization was the standard method of learning, and independent thinking was considered rebellious. Neither a top student nor a poor one, Cahan did reasonably well. Like most of his classmates, he was more concerned with grades than with learning (*Education,* 114, 123–25), and he was often bored with the classes.

Eventually, Cahan grew disgusted with the institutional life as a student, one to which he would be subject later as a teacher in what now appeared to him a dull career. He decided to flunk out in his third year and devoted little time to study. Shortly before the examinations were given, however, Cahan's father came to the institute to inform him that he had been called up for military service—twenty-five years in the Russian Army. Cahan had forgotten that possibility and quickly understood that the only way he could avoid entering the military, which held no promise for a young Jew from the Pale, would be to remain at the institute and enter government service as a teacher after graduation. With the alarming thought of army duty to motivate him, he injected new vigor into his studies. After assiduous effort, he passed the exams. It is worth noting that the timely draft notice Cahan received as a student altered his future at least as radically as a spilled bottle of milk was to transform that of his fictive industrialist, David Levinsky. This early experience confirmed for Cahan that life cannot be realistically represented without coincidence, a lesson he was to apply in his fiction more than once.

A New Social Conscience

Even before matriculation into the Vilna Teacher Training Institute, Cahan had perceived undertones of dissatisfaction with the dictatorial impositions and restrictions of the Czarist regime, and he was aware that clandestine groups of dissenters had formed to provoke either reform or revolution. But he was still a boy in his early teens, and gaining access to a forbidden pamphlet or broadside was more thrilling for its secrecy and implicit danger than for any revolutionary information or argument it might provide—much of which he was still too young to understand. Cahan and a few friends, most a little older than he, met regularly to read books of mutual interest and discuss them; as a meeting place they had a small, hidden room they called "The Goosery" in one of the courtyards where geese were sold. Secretly given a socialist proclamation by another Jewish boy one day, they were frightened because they knew it was forbidden reading and did not know what to make of it.[11] The innocuous-seeming leaflet had been printed in Yiddish on one side, Hebrew and Russian on the other.

Not long afterward, they read Nikolai Chernishevsky's radical utopian novel *What Is to Be Done?* (1863), which eventually would appeal to Lenin, though Cahan found it dull on his first reading (*Education*, 101–2). In fact, from an aesthetic perspective, Theodore Marvin Pollock considers it "[p]ossibly the worst novel . . . in the history of world literature." He sees its importance to Russian youth at the time as residing not in its "preposterous love story, badly related," but in its "auctorial asides" on the coming new era of social justice, a communist economy, and women's equality (Pollock, 37n1). Four years later, when he had greater command of the issues, Cahan would be more sympathetic toward the novel and, like Lenin, he would be more attentive to Chernishevsky's call for revolutionary action through a committed brotherhood than to his vision of a utopian socialist future. Although Cahan continued to recognize the aesthetic limitations of *What Is to Be Done?* he knew that its author had been exiled to Siberia for his radical activities, and for anyone at that time aspiring to reform or overthrow the czardom, "every word of Chernishevsky's was holy" (*Education,* 144).

Hardly conspirators during their "Goosery" years, Cahan and his companions achieved a sense of intimacy from their small group meetings in a "secret" room. This early experience constituted an introduction to the frame of mind and pattern of behavior that would characterize the underground movement with which Cahan was to become familiar, though his role would be more that of a marginal figure than radical participant. Nevertheless, he was involved closely enough with it that he could adapt his limited experience with underground conspirators and publications to produce two decades later what may still be the best novel written on prerevolutionary activities and fears in Russia, *The White Terror and the Red* (1905). Cahan indicates that being given a subversive pamphlet (which he does not name), probably in 1879, marked "a turning point in [his] life. The pamphlet came from people who lived as brothers, who were willing to face the gallows for freedom" (*Education,* 142). His language here is almost identical to that of Clara, his idealistic revolutionary heroine in *The White Terror and the Red,* but the noble self-sacrifice it celebrates is more rhetorical than truly expressive of Cahan's willingness to become a martyr for the cause.

In fact, it is difficult if not impossible to determine what caused his radicalization. Jules Chametzky places little value on Cahan's reference to the life-changing effect of a pamphlet when he states that no particular circumstance or event motivated Cahan toward revolutionary activities. Instead, he believes that occasional, almost offhand remarks may have caught Cahan's attention and become etched in his mind; the messages conveyed were reinforced by a series of underground writings, including the unnamed one in *Bleter,* that Cahan came across shortly before and after he entered the institute for training to become a teacher under the very government that the socialists, nihilists, and anarchists

were attempting to overthrow.[12] Moreover, Cahan acknowledged that
when involved with the movement in his final two years or so at the
institute, he and many of the rest of the collaborators were still naive,
"inexperienced youngsters" (*Education,* 184). Perhaps this was true, but
not long after he became implicated with the amorphous "brotherhood"
against the Czar, he found himself in serious trouble.

Jews and Gentiles alike were involved in the revolutionary underground, though, like Cahan, most of the radicalized Jews had relin-
quished their faith and piety to the new religion of socialism. (To avoid
unnecessary complexity in this brief account of the background, the
word *socialism* as I use it here should be understood in the broadest possible sense to include the wide range of socialistic aims and ideologies
associated with the radicals.) Discussion of the most acceptable theories
and the best ways to implement them constituted the basis of meetings
and the illegal publications of the conspirators. Despite their quest to
achieve a liberated Russia for everyone, not all of the radicals had
divested themselves of the anti-Semitic attitudes that still seem to have
been endemic to much of Eastern Europe. Nonetheless, the more dedicated Jewish revolutionaries dismissed or minimized reminders of a
Russian history laden with centuries of anti-Semitic hostility and rampage, assuming that once the revolution had taken its course, Judaism
would disappear as the Jews were assimilated with the free, unified
Russian people (*Education,* 183). Within a few decades, of course, after
the revolutionaries had overthrown the Czar and established a totalitarian Communist regime in his place, time would prove them terribly
wrong.[13]

But first came the pogroms, which commenced in Elisavetgrad with
the assassination of Czar Alexander II in March 1881, a little over a year
before Cahan fled Russia. The violence and destruction they caused and
the popular support they generated led many naive Jewish radicals to
reassess their position; they found themselves liable to persecution as
Jews on the one side, secularized or not, and as revolutionary conspirators on the other. Hence after the riots in Elisavetgrad and in Kiev
shortly afterward, these putatively assimilated Jews, living on the mar-
gins of their Hebraic culture, suddenly made a turnabout and
returned—fearful, embarrassed, and humiliated—to the faith and people that they had all but shunned for much of their adult lives. In *Bleter,*
Cahan mentions an occasion at a synagogue in Kiev when one of a pair
of these prodigal children of Israel stood to acknowledge and apologize
for their "tragic . . . mistake. Yes," he said humbly to the astonished con-

gregation, "we are Jews" (*Education,* 182). As noted above, Cahan used much of this prerevolutionary experience as the basis for *The White Terror and the Red* a quarter of a century later.

In addition to fomenting the pogroms, Alexander III clamped down hard on the underground movement. Cahan was not directly involved with the assassination of the new Czar's father in St. Petersburg, and initially he was safe, though he had read much forbidden literature and maintained a correspondence with several radical friends, any of whom could implicate him under pressure. Still, he did not feel threatened. After graduation as a teacher in June 1881, he was assigned to a school in Velizh but did not have to report for duty until August. During the interim, he returned to his family in Vilna and spent three weeks visiting a wealthy uncle and his family in St. Petersburg.

After another short stay with his family, Cahan left for Velizh. A small provincial town, Velizh had little to offer him beyond the job. Jews there were of the Lubavich sect—the *Khabad* Hasidim. To his surprise, they welcomed him to shul (the synagogue), but it had been eight years since his bar mitzvah, and he did not read the Hebrew scripture well. Ill at ease because of it, he stayed away from shul after that. He seems to have made friends easily, however, and became associated with another group of socialist sympathizers. The school at which he taught was a new one; at first, he lived alone in a small room but later found more comfortable quarters where he wrote his first published article, an essay in Russian on the need for a technical school in Velizh. But Cahan was dissatisfied; he knew that Velizh did not offer the kind of life he sought, and his head continued to ring with the question: "How can I get out of here?" (*Education,* 170).

Early in 1882 the answer came to him when he received a veiled letter from his mother warning him that a friend had been arrested and imprisoned. Then came a second letter, this one from an associate, telling him that a member of his group living in Vitebsk had committed suicide in a Vilna prison after being arrested (*Education,* 171). Cahan sensed that he himself would be suspected by the police as a consequence of a vaguely incriminating correspondence he had sustained with this friend, now dead, and his hunch was soon corroborated when several police and other officials came to his room one day while he was in bed reading and searched for forbidden materials. Because he had taken the precaution of hiding such items and was clever enough to mislead them on others that were questionable, he was bothered no further at the moment, but a few days later, he was pulled from class, and his room was searched again. After finding several journals edited by Chernishevsky that he had bought in St. Petersburg, the officials questioned him in court, but freed him after warning him not to leave the city. Cahan knew then that if he did not leave Velizh fast, arrest was likely and imprisonment possible. Assisted by a Jewish family he had befriended in the city, he soon fled under the name of Lifshitz on a moonlit night with two men hired to row him down the Dvina River to Vitebsk. From there, he traveled by wagon to Orsha, crossed the Dnieper, and continued south by steamboat to Mohilev (now Mogilev), where he spent the Passover holidays, acquired a passport, and met Belkin, the ardent young emigrant to Palestine whose enthusiasm for colonization ironically turned Cahan not toward the Middle East but the United States. Uncertain where he was ultimately headed before meeting Belkin, Cahan was "a pro-American" (Education, 186) by the time he boarded the steamboat Marusia for a two-day voyage down the Dnieper south to Kiev. His passport was illegal, of course; Cahan's name was now Kruglansky, and the description included his crossed eyes for "authenticity."

He left Kiev on "the longest emigrant train ever to move out of Kiev"; indeed, he says, that was the Saturday night that "began the broad stream of Jewish migration that was to continue for almost two generations. It was to make America the major center of Jewish population. The course of Jewish history would be changed by it" (Education, 196). He was one of more than 13,000 Eastern European Jewish immigrants to the United States in 1882.[14]

Cahan was on the leading edge of the great transoceanic movement westward. On the way from Kiev to what was then the Austrian border and Brody, his train, now moving west and stopping at various cities along the way, continued to pick up additional passengers. Among them were idealistic members of different Am olam (Eternal People) groups from Odessa, Kiev, Vilna, and other cities, who were setting out to establish new colonies in rural and wilderness areas of the United States. Cahan briefly associated with one of them, the Balta Am olam, chiefly because he wanted to propagandize for the socialist cause, but he was disappointed in finding no dedicated socialists or communists among them; they were idealists, yes, but not ideologues. Still, Cahan admits that at the time, he was "[c]arried away with the excitement of debate" (Education, 207) and eager to serve as an advocate, though he was fully aware of his limitations as a theorist, having done almost no serious reading in doctrinal socialism. After humiliating himself over his impetuosity and tactlessness—"Who needs you?" they asked him—he made amends by contributing substantially to the group's small treasury and continued with them all the way to America.

But first their crossing into Austria had to be made with care. Cahan was still an "illegal" and subject to arrest by the Russian police. When safe in Austria, he traveled by horse-drawn cart to Brody. He was impressed there with the many marriages he saw among immigrants awaiting, sometimes for months, their turn to depart. Apparently, few of them relished the idea of settling alone in the New World, and weddings complete with fiddlers and dancing, even in the streets, were a common sight. "So they had banished the loneliness and the longing that gnawed at their hearts," Cahan said, in a line that would be appropriate in most of his stories written in America (*Education*, 208).

Travel by train through Poland and Germany brought no further problems; from Hamburg he sailed to England, where he was shocked in Liverpool by the poverty of the bootblacks. Knowing no English, he purchased an English-Russian/Russian-English dictionary there and used it well during the nearly two weeks he spent aboard the *British Queen* on his way to America.

In *Bleter*, Cahan glosses over the mundane problems of travel and emphasizes his trials in learning and using English. With the help of his dictionary, his careful observation of the lip and tongue movements of English speakers, and attentive tonal perception, Cahan began to acquire the rudiments of a language that heretofore had been completely foreign to him. He was assisted in his efforts by the steward, whom the steerage passengers called "Mister" all the way to Philadelphia because one of them had heard him addressed by that honorific title. Not only did Cahan constantly ask the steward for help with his pronunciation, but dictionary in hand, he also served as a mediator between the steward and the immigrants. They would speak to the steward in Russian or Yiddish, and Cahan would find the English definition in his Russian-English dictionary, or vice versa, with the steward speaking in English and Cahan communicating his message to the passengers after consulting the English-Russian half of his lexicon. Although many of the uneducated Jewish immigrants could speak some Russian, most preferred Yiddish, unlike the more sophisticated of them, who favored the language they had used in their secularized schooling. The interpretive polyglot interplay among the eager translator, the steward, and the passengers would constitute the experiential base for one of Cahan's few non-Jewish short stories, "Dumitru and Sigrid." By the time his ship docked in Philadelphia, English was no longer so foreign a tongue to Cahan.

A Greenhorn in America

After leaving the *British Queen,* Cahan set out almost immediately for Castle Garden, situated on the edge of Battery Park at the southern end of Manhattan Island. (The now-historic receiving station on Ellis Island was still several years in the future.) He was processed quickly at Castle Garden and was soon off to the Lower East Side, where the Jewish population of the city was concentrated.

Because Cahan was among the earliest immigrants of the mass exodus of Eastern European Jews between 1881 and 1924, the population density of the East Side Jewish district was still relatively low, though year by year the increase was dramatic. He noted that no Jewish cafés or restaurants existed there when he arrived, yet Hester Street was already a center for the garment workers (*Education,* 220) and would soon become a leading retail quarter as well. As Jews by the tens of thousands moved into the East Side tenements from the early 1880s through the 1890s, they settled largely in diverse sections of the district according to national origin: Hungarian, Galician, Romanian, Levantine, and Russian.[15] Before long the ghetto on the Lower East Side had become the largest in the world, and Hester Street was the heart of it.[16] East Broadway was a major thoroughfare that attracted professional people and the Russian intellectuals, while the stores and pushcarts on Grand, Hester, and Delancey Streets, among several others, drew the shoppers (Rischin 1962, 76–78). The thoroughfares were busy, the tenements were increasingly packed with renters and their boarders, and poverty was rife. Living conditions for many of the immigrants were dreadful, a replay of the worst of the shtetlekh in the Old Country, and under such circumstances, they cursed Columbus for discovering the so-called "golden land" that proved to be simply another broken promise.[17]

Andrew R. Heinze points out in a revisionist view of early Jewish life in the United States that if living conditions on the East Side were often deplorable, "the rapid flowering of retail commerce in the district would have been impossible without a population that upheld standards of consumption." He proposed that the society of mass consumption that characterizes American culture had a particular appeal to Jews, who were especially eager to acquire new commodities and move to better quarters in the "New Jerusalem" that attracted them. They embodied the "phenomenon of continually rising expectations" and the idea of "keeping up with the Joneses [in] an endless cycle of acquisition."[18] This may be so, but countless immigrants nevertheless were pressed for years to endure nearly intolerable circumstances. For them existence was bitter and their expectations unfulfilled, though certainly their children were better off on the East Side than in a city or shtetl of Eastern Europe, amid the pogroms and under conditions of deprivation that could well have been still worse.

Cahan was not one of the subjugated, despondent poor. He had little "cash" (a ubiquitous new word in the immigrant vocabulary), but he was young, educated, self-reliant, apparently tireless, and obligated to no one financially but himself, not at least before his marriage to Aniuta (Anna) Bronstein in 1885.[19] He first noticed Anna listening attentively to one of his early Yiddish speeches and occasionally saw her at meetings afterward because of their common social interests. She had emigrated from Kiev following the pogrom there and, like Cahan, had tentatively become associated with one of the *Am olam* groups. Also like her husband, she was bright, independent, and temperamental, though she was evidently more sophisticated aesthetically than he. Because she admired Cahan as both an intellectual and a fiction writer, she encouraged his imaginative work, and later she was distressed over the time and attention that his editorial duties and journalism took from it (*Education*, 306; Sanders, 75, 209, 227, 254–55). To a large extent, their marriage is said to have been a conflictive and essentially unfulfilling as well as a childless one, a relationship punctuated with informal separations, yet it lasted for sixty years, until Anna's death.[20]

More firmly than Anna, Cahan had committed himself to promoting some form of socialism in the New World, a commitment facilitated by his being strictly an urbanophile. "I felt strongly drawn to the life of the city," he recalls of his early days in New York. "My heart beat to its rhythms, and as the heart feels so thinks the head" (*Education*, 226). To earn a living, he first took a job stripping tobacco in the cellar of a cigar factory, but he did not stay there long. It was exploitative work for a pittance, and the owner knew that he could not keep workers after a modicum of experience had carried them beyond their "greenhorn" period. The new immigrants were called "greenhorns" because they were ignorant of American ways; it was used as a term of ridicule by earlier immigrants toward the naive and embarrassed newcomers, who wanted to outgrow its stigma as quickly as possible. Once Cahan left the tobacco-

stripping routine, he found work in a tin factory, where he stood all day
feeding small pieces of tin into a machine and operating a treadle with
his foot. The job was easy but dreadfully boring, and when his apathy at
the machine became evident to his employers, he was fired. These two
experiences made it clear to Cahan that over such tasks as he had been
assigned, "The worker was reduced to being a dead tool" (*Education*,
231). He was unsuited for such work, and he knew it. All of his life thus
far had been given to reading and study, so it was difficult for him to
adapt to manual labor in America.

For a while he was assisted by his socialist friends, but before long his
facility with languages allowed him to earn his bread by giving English
lessons to other immigrants. He had already been paying for his board
with lessons in Yiddish and Hebrew (though his knowledge of the latter
was poor; like many young men who had not gone beyond their bar
mitzvah training in Hebrew, he could read and pronounce the words but
not understand the text). Boarding in a house where a great deal of English was spoken, he persistently attended matters of pronunciation,
again noting the lip and tongue placement of the speakers. His friends
were amused over his facial gyrations as he attempted to duplicate the
sounds of correct English. One of his first actions after settling in New
York was to purchase a copy of *Appleton's Grammar,* which he studied
assiduously. With the steerage steward no longer available, he turned to
his landlord for assistance with pronunciation. During this first year in
America Cahan tried to deliver a socialist speech in English; it was a
noble attempt, but no one understood him. Nevertheless, he was convinced that by attending meetings at which English was spoken, his
familiarity with it would rapidly improve.

To enhance his speech and aural comprehension still more rapidly, he
entered a public school to study with adolescent boys and listen carefully to their native pronunciation, which he assumed was accurate and
correct. Teachers and pupils alike welcomed him in the class and supported his efforts to progress. Because he complemented his classwork
with his grammar text, he surpassed the other students within a few
months and left the school to continue studying on his own. From then
on, he carefully monitored his acquisition and development of English
to the extent that within two years he could perceive how his syntax and
vocabulary had improved and how his ability to think in his newly
acquired language had matured (*Education*, 240–41, 293).[21]

In fact, he had already begun teaching English for beginners in the
evening school at the Young Men's Hebrew Association (YMHA) in the

fall of 1883, earning a small salary and gaining valuable experience in language instruction. After passing the city's teaching examination in 1885 he left the YMHA in the fall and went directly to the public school on Chrystie Street, where he continued to teach for the next twelve years (*Education,* 262, 375).

Meanwhile during the days, he taught peddlers and other immigrants eager to learn the language. His frame of mind seems roseate and nostalgic in *Bleter* as he recalls the early 1880s as being "among the best years of [his] life in America." But he was not always as happy and confident in these years as his memory makes him appear. Melech Epstein quotes from a letter Cahan had written to a friend in 1883 or 1884, after he had begun to promote socialism in the United States. "It is a joke," Cahan had written; "I debate, I argue, I get excited, I shriek, and in the middle of all this, I remind myself that I am a vacant vessel, an empty man without a shred of knowledge, and I begin to blush. I am ashamed of myself."[22]

But he was still a sensitive young man in a new country, and success would soon reinforce his defenses against such occasional lapses of self-confidence. With Cahan's reputation as a tutor expanding, he acquired new students; Ronald Sanders credits him with "the born teacher's capacity to be at his best with material he was only just absorbing himself, to recapitulate for students the stages of his own understanding" (64). This ability proved highly advantageous, for he could both teach the language as he acquired a greater fluency in it himself and promote socialism as he gained a more subtle knowledge of it—a two-pronged endeavor and accomplishment. The success of his teaching, of course, enabled Cahan to avoid the laborious, mind-numbing jobs for which most of the newcomers had to settle, such as those he had already attempted and the more common trades on the East Side—peddling and sewing.[23]

Socialism as Religion

Despite his long, close affiliation with socialism, Cahan was neither a theorist nor a true revolutionary. His earliest memory of a socialist ethic may be his childhood recollection of a certain Friday on which all the Jewish inhabitants of Vilna sacrificed their traditional *Shabes* (Sabbath) dinner so that replacements could be purchased for military service with the money saved. Cahan writes: "[M]y father spoke emotionally of how wonderful it was for all to sacrifice equally for the good of the community—the rich no more privileged than the poor. . . . [W]hen I became a socialist, I often recalled that Sabbath and my father's words" (*Education*, 27). This incident had an enduring and pronounced effect on his life thereafter. Ultimately, he became more than an advocate; although Cahan was never a doctrinaire socialist and his viewpoint was increasingly conservative in the second quarter of the twentieth century, Moses Rischin aptly suggests that for Cahan "socialism was a religion" (Rischin, 1962, 166).

Cahan attended his first socialist meeting in the United States on 27 July 1882, less than two months after his arrival and only three weeks after his twenty-second birthday. It was held in a large hall that would soon become popular with organized labor, especially the Cloakmakers' Union. Like most of the audience, Cahan was well pleased with the first speaker, Sergius Schevitech, editor of the New York *Volkstsaytung* (People's Newspaper), who delivered his talk in aristocratic Russian. Afterward, Cahan arose and spoke, also in fluent Russian, in support of the revolutionaries in his homeland; on completion, he received "a storm of applause," which led him to regard himself as "the hero of the day" (*Education*, 236). According to Sanders, Cahan felt "a natural, populist's *mystique* . . . between himself and any group of workers before whom he stood up to speak" (73), a truth that was borne out by his experience time and again. Years later Cahan would acknowledge that his first speech had more rhetoric than content, but it led to his gaining favorable recognition, and that in itself was important for the young greenhorn.

Later on the same day of his opening talk in America, he discussed the meeting with several older acquaintances who had been present and suggested that future speakers address their audiences in Yiddish rather than Russian or German if they wanted to appeal to Jewish voters. His associates laughed at the idea and asked, What Jew does not understand Russian? "My father," Cahan responded (*Education*, 237). Immigrants from the large Russian cities did not realize that Jews from smaller communities, especially the shtetlekh in the Pale, often spoke nothing but Yiddish. As a result of this brief exchange, Cahan was challenged to give a speech in Yiddish, which he did about three weeks later on 18 August 1882. It was the first socialist speech in America delivered in Yiddish. He spoke on this occasion for two hours and again two weeks later for three hours. Although Cahan says nothing in *Bleter* about praise or applause (which was unusual for him), the audience remained to hear him out at both meetings. Again he admitted long afterward that he employed mostly "revolutionary platitudes," thus conforming with older, more experienced speakers of the time (*Education,* 237–38). But he successfully made his point about the value of Yiddish as a means of carrying the socialist message to the Jewish workers on the East Side. Theodore Marvin Pollock says that Cahan seldom planned speeches and "preferred to speak extemporaneously" (159); this practice made his native Yiddish especially suitable.

According to Melech Epstein, only after acquiring a little knowledge of English would a Jewish immigrant be able to wander beyond the boundaries of the ghetto, and at first, few had even this rudimentary familiarity. Consequently, despite their desire to find some way to earn a better living than the East Side offered, few of them left their homogeneous district during the 1880s and 1890s (Epstein 1969, 101). For decades that section of the city remained thoroughly Jewish, and Yiddish was the prevailing language. Nearly fifty years later, Alfred Kazin was reared under similar circumstances in Brownsville, the section of Brooklyn in which Jews of the first and second generations settled as later immigrants entered the country and earlier families moved away from the East Side. Kazin recalls his teenaged years in Brownsville during the Depression of the 1930s. His mother knew no English, and of the neighbors, he wrote: "All I knew was that my immediate world was Jewish, that everyone and everything was Jewish, Jewish all day long."[24] If this statement accurately describes Brownsville of the 1930s, one might intensify it many times over to imagine life on the East Side during the peak years of Jewish immigration.

Although he spoke with vigor at the early socialist meetings, Cahan still had little confidence in socialism itself as a viable means of bringing forth a more equitable society. This was largely because he was confused and perplexed over how it could be introduced and effected in the United States without violence, an attitude carried over, of course, from his experience in the Old Country. He saw himself more as an anarchist than a true socialist during his first few years in America. But he also worked for Henry George in New York's mayoral campaign in 1886 and recognized the inconsistency between his anarchist leanings and his democratic politics; his convictions at the time, he says, were "a mishmash of ideas" (*Education,* 255–57, 314). He also found it difficult to take politics seriously at first because he perceived that many Americans thought of it as "a kind of sport"—and not a very honest one at that (*Education,* 287). Buying votes and selling influence were ubiquitous political practices on the East Side, and Cahan knew that the immigrants had to be persuaded neither to condone nor to support such criminal activity if they intended to bring improvement to their Jewish neighborhoods.

Cahan's serious involvement with organized labor probably commenced with his efforts in the mayoral campaign, when he was pulled into the socialist orbit through his cooperation with the Jewish Workers' Verein (Union), a socialist-labor organization working toward the same end; in 1885 the Jewish Workers' Verein had combined two smaller groups of Jewish workers and rapidly become an influential force in organized labor. Once Cahan became committed to socialism as an effective means of organizing the workers into a massive influential body, he "grew into one of the most self-assured, spirited and aggressive leaders of the movement," according to Melech Epstein, and as time passed, "Cahan emerged as the most dominant figure in Jewish labor" (1969, 140–41, 147). On 9 October 1888, he and Morris Hilkowitz— later Hillquit—were central in establishing the United Hebrew Trades (Pollock, 128).

His first lecture outside of New York was delivered in Boston in autumn 1889, when he was invited by Jewish socialists there to speak one Sunday afternoon. On his way back to New York, he realized how limited was his knowledge of America and acknowledged in *Bleter:* "I was locked into a tiny little world of my own in this vast land" (*Education, 413–14*). A year later, he served as moderator and Yiddish interpreter in a labor controversy among union factions during a strike against the manufacturers. The workers were being led by a "charlatan"—as Cahan called Thomas Garside—to settle on unreasonable terms, but at the last minute they were requested by the charismatic Joseph Barondess—"King of the Cloak Makers"—to continue their strike, and under Cahan's guidance, they voted overwhelmingly to do so, whereupon the manufacturers succumbed, and Garside disappeared. At this point, Barondess was at the peak of his influence over the workers, but his authority soon began to wane, and as his star descended, Cahan's rose (Sanders, 118–22).

Despite his initial skepticism over politics as an avenue toward genuine reform in America, it did not take Cahan long to realize that anarchism was not the answer to social improvement, either. He was acquainted with Johann Most, who advocated the violent overthrow of any form of government in favor of absolute individual freedom, but Chicago's Haymarket Riot in May 1886 all but convinced Cahan that he was no anarchist.[25] Moreover, although Henry George lost his campaign for mayor later that year, he drew considerably more votes than had been expected, and Cahan had acquired a clearer sense of the possibilities for social advancement through politics by working vigorously on his behalf. Before committing himself to a socialist program, however, he wanted to be sure that this would be the appropriate direction for him, so he reread the principal works on anarchism and individualism by Proudhon, Bakunin, Kropotkin, and Herbert Spencer, and he read for the first time books by George Plekhanov and Karl Marx's collaborator, Friedrich Engels (*Education,* 332–36). He found the experience remarkably illuminating, and in December 1887, about a month after three of the convicted Haymarket anarchists were hanged in Chicago, Cahan formally joined the Socialist Labor Party. In the coming decade, he would serve as a delegate to the Second International European Congress in 1891 and the Third in 1893.

After his naturalization on 8 June 1891, Cahan traveled to Brussels, where he represented the United Hebrew Trades and the Jewish members of the Socialist Labor Party.[26] There he was bitterly disillusioned over the absence of the nonprejudicial, egalitarian social structure he had envisioned in Vilna and Velizh; indeed, he discovered that anti-Semitism was as endemic to European socialists as to the Christian masses in Russia. He wanted the congress to discuss the problems facing the Jews within the socialist groups, and he forced the hostile European delegates to put it on the agenda. Why were they opposed? Allegedly, they believed that explicit support for Jewish workers would give substance to the anti-Semitic view that socialism depends on Jews and promotes the Jewish cause, that is, that socialism itself is "a Jewish affair." Cahan wanted them to repudiate anti-Semitism altogether, but after extended argument they would do no more than state their opposition to both anti-Semitism and philo-Semitism so as to placate the Gentile members who held that the masses were being exploited by Jewish bankers. It was the old song, and Cahan was livid, so angry, in fact, that he refused to report this outrage in the *Arbeter tsaytung* (Worker's Newspaper), which he was editing, fearing that readers in the United States would cut their ties to socialism if they learned of the European hostility toward them (Epstein 1965, 68–71). Ironically, as Sanders observes, being in America evoked Cahan's latent sense of Jewish nationalism, which had been repressed in Europe by his strong socialist ideals (152).

During the early years of the Russian Revolution a quarter century later, Cahan enthusiastically supported the new Communist regime not only because of its socialist orientation but also because the Communists allegedly defended "Jewish life and honor" whereas the Czar's army continued to persecute the Jews. In this respect, his attitude was representative of Jewish feelings toward the revolution at the time. Within a few years, however, he completely reversed himself. Because of the regime's increasing use of terror as a means of control and because of the dreadful, pervasive hunger that it was allowing to decimate Russia, after 1922 he vehemently opposed the Communist dictatorship (Epstein 1965, 102–3). This turnaround is nowhere more evident than in his justification for it in a volume of short pieces he edited in 1934 in support of Democratic Socialism over Communism, *Hear the Other Side*. In an argument that echoes Tom Paine's approach to the American Revolution in *Common Sense,* Cahan's introduction emphasizes the use of facts and reason as weapons against the tyranny of Soviet Communism. The American propagandists for Communism had plenty of financial support from the Soviets, Cahan alleges in the essay he contributed to the volume, whereas his Socialist Party lacked the funding necessary to compete effectively against the Communist line. Cahan tries to present "the other side" by disclosing what life was actually like in Russia in the early 1930s, with people by the millions starving and dying in poverty. By this time, according to Sanders, Cahan had become firmly opposed not only to the Communists but to radical leftists of all kinds (445).

Cahan never believed that preaching socialism to the immigrants alone would effect the socialization of the United States. Because the workers of the East Side were more eager to assimilate and acculturate with the rest of American society than to promote a socialist ethic, proselytizers like himself would have to convince English-speaking Americans of all backgrounds to accept socialist principles. Furthermore, as Irving Howe notes, he knew that socialism could not remain static in America; if it helped the Eastern Europeans adapt to American life, it would have to change as well in order to be effective (112; also see *Education,* 412). To be sure, as much of Cahan's effort in his first half-century in the United States was directed toward effecting this transformation in socialism as it was toward helping the immigrants accommodate cultural practices in America that heretofore had been totally unfamiliar.

Meanwhile, of course, he was adapting as necessary himself. According to a recent portrait by David Engel, "Cahan's political convictions . . . evolved from the idealistic, utopian socialism of his youth toward a pragmatic, nondoctrinaire commitment to the labor movement and the gradual changes it seemed to promise. The *Forward* itself exemplified this political realism."[27] This is exactly the kind of social and ethical evolution toward practical socialism that Louis Harap and other ideological critics found so appalling in Cahan and that led to their charges of opportunism and hypocrisy against him.

By the late 1880s Cahan had brought out several English articles in the New York *Sun* describing East Side life; few Americans then, even in New York, knew anything about it, including the editor, but he admired Cahan's colorful details. Cahan was also writing both for the *Workmen's Advocate,* an English journal supported by the Socialist Labor Party, and, after 1890, for the Party's Yiddish weekly, *Arbeter tsaytung.* In the latter, he not only wrote under his own name but also used pseudonyms such as "Sotzius" for his fiction, "David Bernstein" for his translation of Tolstoy's *The Kreutzer Sonata,* and "Ben Shalom" for other writings (Chametzky 1977, 48; Pollock, 140). Late in 1891, about a year after the *Tsaytung* opened, Cahan became its editor (Sanders, 157), a post he held for three years, after which he accepted the editorship of *Di tsukunft,* a recently inaugurated Yiddish monthly devoted to science and socialism; under Cahan's guidance until 1897, *Di tsukunft* took a literary turn in conformity with his own developing interests as a writer. As Jules Chametzky suggests, after Cahan's first few years in the United States, his commitment to socialism was increasingly "cultural rather than specifically political"; for him, its values "had long been 'spiritual' and ethical rather than programmatic" (21–22).

Early in January 1897 a serious dispute arose over the leadership and policies within the association that published *Arbeter tsaytung,* and Cahan walked out with several like-minded associates. He had been opposed by the egocentric Daniel De Leon and his supporters, including the *Ovent blat* (Evening Sheet) staff, who had gained control of the Socialist Labor Party (Sanders, 179–80). The breach led to the founding of a new association—the Forward Press Association—supported by several unions and other labor groups, including some of those associated with the American Federation of Labor. Its published voice was a new daily called *Forwerts,* popularly known outside of the Yiddish-speaking world as the Jewish daily *Forward.* Cahan was selected to edit it, and under his control it would eventually become not only the leading Yiddish newspaper in the world but also "a party organ, an instrument for the building of labor unions and a popular university."[28] The inaugural issue, published on 22 April 1897, marked the opening of a new era in Yiddish journalism.

First Months of the *Forward*

Despite his prosperous future there, Cahan's beginning at the *Forward* was far from smooth. Only a few months after the first issue was published, he resigned from his editorial post over a disagreement that had divided the staff. On one side were those who wanted to use the newspaper as a weapon against their opponents at the *Arbeter tsaytung* and the *Ovent blat,* and on the other side, with Cahan, were those who wanted to develop a popular socialist organ uninfected by the polemical attacks and squabbles that characterized Yiddish journalism in America near the end of the century. Cahan was a cantankerous and demanding personality with more than a trace of arrogance; elected or appointed to a position of authority, he insisted on maintaining it in his own way, and to a large extent, that meant assuming full control. As an editor, he would accept no less, and when he could no longer have his way over policies, he resigned. To someone with less talent, intelligence, and imagination than Cahan one might say under such circumstances, "Good-bye, and good riddance!" But losing the leadership of Abraham Cahan could be a devastating loss indeed, as the staff of the *Forward* were soon to learn.

Of course, leaving his editorial post also meant the end of his salary, and Cahan had to find another source of income. He was not sorry about this except that, owing to his overt support of socialist candidates, he also lost his position teaching English and the salary that came with it when the school trustees decided against renewing his contract for 1907 (Sanders, 210).

Making His Way in English

Cahan had continued to work on his English, and by the mid-1890s he was on the point of writing fluent articles and short stories in his adoptive language. Moreover, by the time he left the *Forward,* he had already established himself as a promising new voice in American letters with short stories in the commercial press and his first English novel, *Yekl, A Tale of the New York Ghetto* (1896), which was warmly received, especially by the "Dean of American Letters" at the time, William Dean Howells. In fact, he had met Howells a few years earlier, when America's leading realist had come to the East Side to learn about Jewish socialism firsthand (Sanders, 190).

But Cahan could not depend on Howells's good will or his own fiction to provide a living for Anna and himself, so he turned again to the

New York dailies, the *Sun,* the *Post,* and particularly the *New York Commercial Advertiser,* the oldest continuously running newspaper in the United States. After he had published a few articles in the *Commercial Advertiser* in the fall of 1897, that paper hired a new city editor, Lincoln Steffens, who would become known nationally early in the next century as one of the country's leading "muckrakers."[29] Because Steffens was interested in making the *Advertiser* a model of journalistic excellence, not only for the depth and breadth of its coverage but also for the quality of its writing, he brought reporters with literary talent to his staff, and Cahan was hired before the year was out.

Return to the *Forward*

His four years with the *Commercial Advertiser,* along with his stint editing and writing for the *Arbeter tsaytung* earlier in the 1890s, provided Cahan with a decade of seminal, highly diversified journalistic experience in Yiddish and English. He would draw on it heavily when he returned to the *Forward* in 1902 to resume the editor's chair, with the absolute authority that he demanded. Apart from nearly a year's hiatus over another, similar squabble about policy between the summers of 1902 and 1903, Cahan remained with the *Forward* until his death in 1951, though a stroke he suffered in 1946 forced him to relinquish much of his editorial control.

Under his guidance, the circulation of the *Forward* increased so rapidly that the newspaper was soon in danger of bankruptcy again because the advertisements did not yet bring in enough cash to cover the costs of publication. But the adversity was overcome as its popularity expanded. Critics regarded Cahan as pandering to popular taste instead of disseminating the gospel of socialism, but Cahan insisted that socialism was as much a matter of learning how to live within a new community as a concern with ideology and polemics. He was then and he remained an ardent assimilationist.

Cahan understood that success in reaching his aim would inevitably diminish and finally destroy *Yidishkayt,* the traditional culture of Yiddish-speaking Eastern European Jewry that was supporting him and the *Forward* in the New World (Howe, 524, 641). This identifies a part of the paradox that led to the hostility and alienation that evolved between him and the more ideological Jewish radicals, those who attempted unsuccessfully to attract the immigrants to their own groups through Yiddish publications. With the immigrants in mind, Cahan believed fully in Israel Zangwill's famous concept of America as a "melting pot," introduced in 1908; this called for assimilation over "ethnic diversity," or "multiculturalism," as phrased in the jargon of the 1980s and 1990s. As Cahan gained experience and prominence with the daily *Forward,* his socialism became even less a matter of polemical issues than it had been when he took over as editor, and he gave increasing attention to social reform. Moses Rischin says that Cahan showed "almost a personal concern with all human problems and a deep sympathy for the miserable and oppressed of all lands, races, and creeds."[30] This view may be overstated, but it is doubtful that anyone is more familiar with Cahan's life and work than Rischin, and his assessment cannot be taken lightly. Before long, workers and organizers turned readily to the *Forward* for advice and support; nor is it going too far to say that they often depended on it, though, again, critics who remained committed to Communism complained that he was closer to the labor bureaucrats than to the workers,[31] an arguable view that may apply more to the decades following World War I than earlier. Eventually, the Socialists expelled him from the party for supporting Franklin Delano Roosevelt for president.[32]

During the first four decades of the twentieth century, a copy of the *Forward* could be found in most Jewish homes, not only in New York but in other cities across the country; with diversified publication sites, the paper covered not only national and international affairs but also local issues. As Rischin's comment suggests, Cahan empathized with ordinary people confronting personal problems, and he knew that his readers would be interested in them as well. The best illustration of this concern is evident in the famous *"Bintl briv"* ("Bundle of Letters") column that began to appear only a few years after he assumed the editorship of the paper. An antecedent of Ann Landers and "Dear Abby," Cahan's *"Bintl briv"* printed letters from people with problems who wrote for advice to the editor as if writing to a parent or a *tsadik,* a sagacious and upright man, one who can be depended on to convey the truth as if he were a holy seer.

The Fiction in English

Although he had been writing fiction in Yiddish since 1892, it was not until 1895 that Cahan published his first story in English, "A Providential Match." Howells's favorable impression of it led to the reacquaintance of the two men, which soon proved greatly to Cahan's advantage, for perhaps no one at the time was in a better position to assist him in gaining an audience than that highly influential author and critic then living in New York City. Howells's aid was employed a year later when Cahan published his first novel, *Yekl, A Tale of the New York Ghetto,* which was followed in 1898 by a collection of short fiction in English, *The Imported Bridegroom and Other Stories of the New York Ghetto.* By the end of the century, Cahan's English stories had found a ready market in such popular monthlies as *Cosmopolitan, Century,* and *Scribner's,* and he was earning as much as $50 apiece for them (Sanders, 210). Simultaneously, a cornucopia of his short pieces of journalism and fiction were being published in the *Commercial Advertiser* during the four-plus years he spent there as a reporter covering chiefly the Lower East Side.

His experience with the *Advertiser* gave Cahan the opportunity to develop a complementary method of writing by combining his predilection for imaginative composition with his journalistic skills, emphasizing one aspect or the other as the work at hand demanded. For example, his reportorial manner is readily evident in parts of his second English novel, *The White Terror and the Red,* through graphic descriptions of incidents, places, and people involved in prerevolutionary Russia. On the other hand, in a short expository piece of the same year—"The Russian Jew in the United States"—Cahan responds with imaginative rhetorical power to the cavalier treatment of Jewish strikers in the daily press:

> Would that the public could gain a deeper insight into these struggles than is afforded by newspaper reports! Hidden under an uncouth surface would be found a great deal of what constitutes the true poetry of modern life,—tragedy more heart-rending, examples of a heroism more touching, more noble, and more thrilling, than anything that the richest imagination of the romanticist can invent. While to the outside observer the struggles may appear a fruitless repetition of meaningless conflicts, they are, like the great labor movement of which they are a part, ever marching onward, ever advancing.[33]

Ironically, however, although Cahan's success as a fiction writer in his adopted language was clear, he published no English fiction in the monthlies between 1901 and 1913. By then Cahan was living in an uptown apartment on East 76th Street, and he was extremely busy with the *Forward.* It had nearly suffered bankruptcy in 1907, but he had brought it back so successfully that in 1913 and 1914 "[t]he *Forward* coalition, along with the politics that it represented, was now at the height of its power on the Lower East Side," and in the decade that followed, its circulation continued to increase. By 1923, with its local editions in eleven cities, the *Forward* could legitimately claim a daily circulation of approximately a quarter-million, equivalent to that of any other large American newspaper (Sanders, 413, 437).[34]

It was at the very time, then, that his daily was approaching its heyday that Cahan was asked by the editor of *McClure's Magazine* to contribute articles on a new phenomenon in the United States, the success of the Jewish businessman. Cahan wanted neither to refuse nor to devote much time to the project because this kind of work no longer had priority with him. Nevertheless, he wrote more than he had expected for the series, which developed into four consecutive installments that constituted a novel-in-progress, though he was not yet aware of what he had wrought. The work was published in *McClure's* between April and July 1913 under the title "The Autobiography of an American Jew: The Rise of David Levinsky."

The derivation of Cahan's title from that of Howells's *The Rise of Silas Lapham* (1885) is unmistakable, though ironic. In Howells's novel, Lapham's moral rise accompanies his financial descent in contrast to Levinsky's amoral acquisition of increasing wealth. Nevertheless, this titular parallel clearly betokens Cahan's appreciation for Howells's valuable acquaintanceship.

The Rise of David Levinsky was published in full by Harper & Brothers in 1917. It remains Cahan's most significant literary achievement, and it was the last work of fiction in English that he wrote. From then on, Cahan was no longer a short-story writer and novelist but the celebrated editor of the Jewish daily *Forward*. After reaching his sixtieth year, as Jules Chametzky observes, "the inner and private man . . . yielded to the public one" and thus surrendered the creative self that had nourished his fiction (Chametzky 1977, 145).

A Secular Jew with Zionist Sympathies

Long a secular Jew, Cahan gave little attention to the Hebrew faith per se after immigrating, though he bitterly resented anti-Semitism, especially as it had manifested itself among the European socialists. In the United States, nearly all of Cahan's associates were Jewish, and the *Forward,* printed in Yiddish, appealed only to a Jewish readership. From July 1913 to August 1915—that is, from the time that Leo Frank, a Jewish factory owner in Atlanta, was charged with murdering a thirteen-year-old Christian girl there to the time of his lynching—Cahan and the *Forward* were outspoken in attempting to gain a legitimate trial for him (Pollock, 364–69).

With regard to Zionism (a call for the dispersed Jewish people to return to Israel as their true homeland), J. C. Rich suggests that in the early years of the *Forward,* Cahan showed no support for it because he did not consider it a plausible solution to global Jewish problems. But after visiting Palestine twice, first in 1925 and again in 1929, he perceived the dynamic transformation occurring there and consequently developed a strong sympathy with the Zionist effort himself. As a result of the anti-Semitism he had observed among European socialists, in pogroms in Europe, and during his travels to the Holy Land, Cahan changed.

On his first visit, he spoke with several labor leaders there, including David Ben-Gurion, an ardent Zionist who had fled to Palestine from Poland, and he wrote of "the heroic fire that burns in them" (Cahan, quoted in Sanders, 441). After the Arab riots four years later, he visited again to see how the Jews had been affected by them; a few years afterward he brought out *Palestine* [Palestine] (1934), a volume on his travels and revised views. According to Sanders, Cahan never became a Zionist himself, but he did identify with the Palestinian Jews (441).[35] Epstein succinctly describes the slow emergence of Cahan's identification with Judaism since his arrival in America, by noting that in the late 1880s Cahan associated chiefly with American journalists and Jewish immigrant intellectuals but had little to do with the faith itself. Ultimately, however, Epstein says, Cahan understood that "his destiny . . . lay with his own people" (Epstein 1965, 66).

No matter how carefully the *Forward* was tended in the post-Depression years, as the first generation of immigrants gave way to the second, and the second in turn to the third, its popularity inevitably succumbed to the literally new world that had evolved for the Jews in America. Whatever reverberations of anti-Semitism they might have felt in America, they were minor compared with the life-threatening dangers they had faced in Eastern Europe. As the older generations passed on, so too did first the use, then the knowledge, of Yiddish—the *mame-loshn*—give way to English, which was no longer the adoptive tongue but the native one for all those Jewish children reared in American homes and educated in American schools.

Nevertheless, the *Forward* had not lost its appeal to thousands of older readers through the years of the *Shoah* (Holocaust) and World War II, and Cahan refused to relinquish the editorial position he had held for nearly half a century until a severe stroke at eighty-six forced him to pass much of his control on to a successor. He spent his final years residing at the Hotel Algonquin, famed for the legendary journalists who have congregated there. Frail and tired, Cahan was feted with a birthday celebration at ninety, one year before his death on 31 August 1951. More than ten thousand mourners packed the auditorium of the Forward Building and the area immediately around it to pay tribute to the man whom the *New York Times* called "the lower East Side's first citizen."[36] Following a secular service, Cahan's remains were interred at Mount Carmel Cemetery in Queens.

Chapter Two
The Journalism

In the 1920s, reviewing his formative years from the vantage point of half a century in his autobiography, Abraham Cahan found little direct evidence that pointed to a long career in journalism. His future as an author of fiction, perhaps, is connoted in the imaginative activities he recalled from childhood and adolescence—his fanciful dreams, his predilection for drawing, his fascination with the intricacies and emotive possibilities of language, even his attraction to music (later manifest in his "love of Italian opera" [Sanders, 71])—all of which imply an aesthetic sensibility and creative urge. As for journalism, Cahan's autobiography reveals a keen memory, certainly an invaluable attribute for a journalist, and a curiosity about the people and places around him that could be satisfied only through careful, persistent observation.

More than likely, however, his father's enthusiasm for language—indeed, Shakhne Cahan's sheer love of the rich sounds of words—inspired the same in young Cahan, though in his case a good part of the affinity for language resided in the power it carried. Early in life he realized how language could stir the emotions—the language of prayer and preaching, of czarist decrees and the name Khovansky "whispered in fear," of forbidden books and broadsides, of songs at home and chanted prayers in shul, of *pilpul* (analytical debate on complex Talmudic commentary) in the yeshiva and ideological debate among radical comrades in meetings, of folktales in Yiddish and fiction in Russian. All of these and more were subtly moving young Abraham Cahan toward working with language as his vocation, not as a teacher but a writer, though he could not have been aware of it until he arrived in New York. As far as we know, he had published nothing before that but an article on the need for a technical school in Velizh.

The Emerging Journalist

Once in the United States, Cahan seems almost immediately to have reasoned that the quickest, most effective way to promote his ideas—and simultaneously gain recognition for himself—was to disseminate them as widely as possible by speaking persuasively at socialist and labor meetings and by publishing in the English and Yiddish press. While teaching on Chrystie Street shortly after his arrival in New York, he was already beginning to establish his reputation as a vibrant journalist. Despite his limitations in English, he had already published his first article in that language on 28 May 1883. Entitled "The Crowned Criminals" and written in the form of a letter, it appeared on the front page of the *New York World* as a corrective response to current Russian propaganda on the affection that the new czar, Alexander III, was allegedly receiving from the masses (Chametzky 1977, 9–10). In this article, he vigorously denied the truth of such statements. Cahan admitted that the editor of the *World* had to make extensive corrections to his English before the article was publishable, but at that point its author had only begun to learn the language a year or so earlier.

Meanwhile, his work had also been appearing in Russian newspapers beginning in the early 1880s. From his vantage point in the 1920s, Cahan looked back with disappointment on these early Russian articles about the Lower East Side, feeling that he had failed to capture the vitality and color that characterized urban Jewish life in America at the time (*Education*, 292). Although Ephim H. Jeshurin's bibliography lists more than a dozen items in Russian written by Cahan, mostly newspaper articles published in the early 1880s, and a few others in collaboration with his wife, Anna,[1] nearly all of his written work in America was done in either Yiddish or English, the principal languages of the two worlds he straddled.

Of course, gaining access to the Yiddish press would not have been difficult for an intelligent, well-educated, ambitious young immigrant with a head full of reformist ideas and native fluency in the language. The problem was that in the early 1880s, when Cahan had immigrated, a Yiddish press barely existed in but one weekly that had begun less than a decade earlier. Not until 1885, three years after he arrived, did another edition of that paper begin appearing a few times each week under the title *Togeblat* (Daily Sheet). Thus commenced the turbulent period of Yiddish journalism in America, and Cahan was present as the door opened (Sanders, 97). A year later, Cahan and a friend made an unsuccessful attempt to begin their own socialist weekly, *Di naye tsayt* (The New Era), written in simple Yiddish so that anyone literate in that language could read it; it was a good idea, but the project failed after the third issue partly because there was not enough money to support it. In attempting to promote and sell the weekly, Cahan addressed prospective advertisers more as a propagandist for socialism than a circumspect businessman. Strange to say for a man who was so practical in other ways, he maintained this attitude for many more years until he finally realized that one cannot run a newspaper on fervent advocacy alone (*Education,* 308, 360). As can be seen from his editorship of the *Forward,* once he learned the lesson, he was implacable in carrying it out.

But the inauguration of the *Forward* was still more than a decade in the future, and after the premature collapse of *Di naye tsayt* Cahan gave diminishing attention to writing and speaking in Yiddish. Instead, he turned to the Henry George campaign for mayor of New York, working with members of the Socialist Labor Party, though he was not to join the party until late the next year. By then, most of his writing was being done in English. Between 1886 and 1889 he was a major contributor to the *Workmen's Advocate,* the English voice of the Socialist Labor Party. Indeed, Jules Chametzky says that Cahan's articles appeared "regularly—in almost every issue" of that weekly during those years. He cited two of Cahan's longer pieces of 1888 called "Social Remedies" that were reprinted and published as a pamphlet for the party (Chametzky 1977, 13).

Also near the end of this decade, Cahan wished to publish in the *New York Sun,* so he wrote a series of short sketches on East Side life and showed them to Erasmus Darwin Beach, who was reading submissions for the Sunday edition. After accepting Cahan's sketches for the next Sunday, Beach astonished him with the question, "What is a ghetto?" (*Education,* 355). He was also intrigued by what may now be called Cahan's *Yinglish,* a term recently popularized by Leo Rosten in *The Joys of Yinglish* (1989) to signify words and phrases created by combining Yiddish with English. A good example of such yoking occurs in *olraytnik* (from "all right"), a work coined by Cahan himself to identify an immigrant who had successfully acquired the money and security to live comfortably but still lacked the requisite "good taste" to accompany them (Howe, 138). In a more popular phrase from a third language, Cahan's *olraytniks* were the nouveaux riches. He generally portrayed them with a poignant mix of irony and sympathy—irony because they pretended to be more than they were, sympathy because one could not expect much else from people who came to wealth suddenly with little sense of its value but to spend and show. That a reader for the *New York Sun* did not know what a ghetto was in the late 1880s is remarkable because a large one existed not far from his office. His ignorance in that respect is representative of how little Gentile America knew of the burgeoning Jewish community—not only in New York but in other large U.S. cities as well.

The Yiddish Journalism

By January 1890, Cahan had returned to Yiddish journalism for the next seven years. The leading Yiddish newspaper at the time was the *Togeblat,* which would retain its popularity through the 1890s. But as an anti-socialist, anti-anarchist, and religiously conservative vehicle, it was definitely not a paper that would appeal to Cahan and his fellow travelers on the left (Howe, 519–20). Late in 1889, representatives of about thirty groups, including anarchists (whose own short-lived weekly, *Di varhayt* [The Truth], had recently failed), socialists, and labor organizations, met to discuss the possibility of beginning a new "coalition newspaper" from which they all could benefit with mutual support. The result of their discussion was the establishment of the Arbeter Tsaytung Publishing Association and its vehicle for expression, the *Arbeter tsaytung.* By the time of publication, the anarchists had angrily broken relations with the socialists over incompatible aims and policies for the new weekly, and the social democrats alone took it over (Sanders, 100–102).

Cahan's anonymous article in the first issue, published early in March 1890, was entitled "Two Worlds in the World"; the contrast of a world of wealth with a world of poverty makes it a Yiddish counterpart to Herman Melville's diptych of 1854, "Poor Man's Pudding and Rich Man's Crumbs." Cahan wrote it in the commonplace vernacular rather than in the more formal style that characterized Yiddish journalism, with its emphasis on ideology and polemics (Sanders, 107–8). The essay anticipates two aspects of Cahan's later writing, especially the fiction in English: first, it illustrates the double view that he often presents of people and situations, and second, it appeals principally to the common reader rather than the intellectual. In his later work, the double view would generate purposeful ambiguity, whereas in "Two Worlds in the World" the effect is chiefly and heavily ironic. From the date of that opening salvo, Cahan's journalistic career would be more or less stabilized until the end of 1897, though it certainly would not lack controversy.

The extraordinary success of the first issue of *Arbeter tsaytung* boded well for the future of the paper. Although Cahan did not assume the editor's chair until late the next year, he already had many ideas he was prepared to test as a means of increasing the *tsaytung's* circulation and therefore its influence. As Ronald Sanders points out, in "any given issue, he could be several things at once: poet, feuilletonist, popular-science writer, socialist theoretician, storyteller, reporter, and so on" (Sanders, 108). As one might expect of so imaginative and strong-willed a man as Cahan, he was constantly at odds with the first editor of the weekly, Philip Krantz, a recent immigrant from England, whom he had liked when they first met the previous year. But Cahan was ambitious, and Krantz was sensitive to the intense competition from his younger colleague, so the tension between them was constant, and neither one wished to defer to the other. When Cahan replaced him as editor, the move was smoother than it might have been because by then the Yiddish-speaking members of the Socialist Labor Party were on the eve of establishing a new national monthly, *Di tsukunft* (The Future), which was to focus on "popularizing socialist theory and scientific knowledge." Krantz, with his decided interest in socialist and economic theory, was chosen to edit it (Sanders, 156).

Also in the first issue of the *tsaytung* Cahan contributed an article that was to become the opening piece in a series under the title of *"Der proletarishker maged"* (The Proletarian Preacher). This was another attempt to gain popularity among the immigrants, who Cahan knew could be attracted to his socialist message if he approached them through their Jewish background. To be sure, this method was anathema to the doctrinaire socialists and directly opposed to the philosophy of the anarchists, who did all they could to dissociate themselves from any religious orientation. In fact, they went so far in promoting their break with religion as to schedule a "Yom Kippur Ball" annually on the holiest Jewish day of the year, a day of fasting and prayer meant to atone for sins committed against God over the past twelve months. But Cahan knew that only a small percentage of the Jewish immigrants would tolerate such heresies and that most by far wanted to maintain whatever traditional Hebrew associations they could. Hence by appealing to a Jewish readership through the religious device of the *maged* (preacher), not only did he successfully reach his immigrant readers but he also drew them in. The *maged* identifies himself as an Eastern European (like most of his readers) and presents the weekly *sedre,* that passage from the Torah which is read during the Sabbath service at synagogue each week; then he offers a sermon as a means of interpreting and commenting on the *sedre* from "a revolutionary socialist point of view" (Sanders, 109–11; Chametzky 1977, 18–19). Sanders also explains that the use of a *k* near the end of *proletarishker* signifies "a conscientiously lowbrow air," an obvious attempt on Cahan's part to appeal to an unsophisticated readership, though a hint of derogation is implied.

If Cahan was trying to proselytize for socialism here, he was also displaying the power of an imagination that was no less suited for writing fiction than exposition and exhortation (Chametzky 1977, 35). During his years with the *Arbeter tsaytung,* he wrote critical articles, drama reviews, and his own fiction as well as his Yiddish translations of novels and stories written by such contemporaries as Tolstoy, Hardy, and Howells. Even in the midst of such productivity, however, troubles were emerging among the socialists behind the Arbeter Tsaytung Publishing Association, partly attributable to doctrinal differences, partly to matters of policy, and partly to conflicting personalities. In *The Downtown Jews,* Ronald Sanders meticulously traces the intricacies of these controversies, and anyone interested in learning more about them would be well advised to turn to his enlightening analysis. Here, though, it is sufficient to note that a schism had developed over competitive unionization among various umbrella groups, including Samuel Gompers's growing American Federation of Labor (AFL), the United Hebrew Trades, and those members of the Socialist Labor Party who held firmly to the publishing association, which was becoming more rigid and bureaucratic as time passed. Cahan and others were increasingly at odds with the bureaucracy as they sided with a broad coalition comprising branches of the Socialist Labor Party from outside of New York. Late in 1893, the seething trouble erupted.

At that time Cahan's support was sufficient to see him elected to displace Philip Krantz once again, this time as editor of *Di tsukunft,* early in 1894, while he stayed on as editor of the *tsaytung.* Cahan held his office with the *tsukunft* until he was pushed aside three years later when he and his supporters were outmaneuvered by Daniel De Leon, who had gained control over the opposing faction of the Social Democrats. By that time, De Leon had become a formidable adversary who supported politicians and unions as long as they were committed to a totally socialist society. J. C. Rich describes him as "[o]ne of the most brilliant[—]and certainly the most malevolent bigot[—]among the radicals of the day" (11), and in 1934 George Tucker looked back on him as an egotist who actually retarded socialism to elevate his own stature.[2] In any case, Cahan and his associates were on the losing side this time, though while he was editing the monthly during those past three years, he had continued to write for both papers, thus fulfilling his journalistic obligations and nourishing his literary propensities simultaneously (Sanders, 162ff).

Because Cahan had had so much latitude to write and publish largely as he wished, he acquired invaluable experience during his *tsaytung-tsukunft* period, and he looked retrospectively on those years of the early and middle 1890s as among his most edifying (Chametzky 1977, 18). Together with the time he spent working for the *New York Commercial Advertiser* immediately afterward, under the guidance of Lincoln Steffens, his years with the *tsaytung,* as he later understood, had prepared him with the writing experience and practical knowledge that would prove essential when he returned to the *Forward* as editor early in the new century, not only reviving it but giving it a new life altogether.

Founding the *Forward*

After breaking completely with the De Leon faction, Cahan and a few cohorts met early in 1897 and established the *Forward* with Cahan as editor. As explained in chapter 1, whereas a number of his colleagues had wanted the new daily to be used as a weapon against their old De Leonist foes in the Arbeter Tsaytung Publishing Association and the daily *Ovent blat,* Cahan insisted on doing away with such polemics. He wanted to interest readers in socialism by employing their own vernacular and representing their world to them as they knew it. Cahan was interested not in analyzing socialist doctrine or proselytizing among the intellectuals but in both illustrating East Side life and offering practical advice on how to improve it. He also wanted to include entertaining features that would simultaneously amuse his readers and provide them with a brief escape from their problems. By the time the inaugural issue was published on 22 April 1897, Cahan was more secure in his views than ever before. He was no longer a novice journalist; he had gained fluency in English; he had become acquainted with William Dean Howells, the leading American novelist and critic of the day; he had published a novel in his adopted tongue; and his short stories were in demand among the popular monthly magazines. He was self-assured and had no desire to fight a constant battle with his staff over the direction in which the *Forward* was to move. When the tension became too trying in the summer of that year, he resigned.

Anna, his wife now for more than twelve years, was pleased, despite the reduction of their income, because she had wanted Cahan to give more time to his fiction, a vocation she felt was more appropriate for a Russian intellectual than writing and editing for newspapers. This was Cahan's feeling as well. The Yiddish press was enormously time-consuming and stressful. Four years earlier, in the summer of 1893, when Cahan had gone to Zurich as a delegate to the Third Congress of the Second International, his traveling companion was James K. Paulding, grandson of Washington Irving's collaborator on the short-lived periodical *Salmagundi* (1807–1808) and author of *Westward Ho!* (1833), among other works. Aware of Cahan's literary aspirations, Paulding tried to persuade him to write fiction based on his experiences. Surely, Cahan had been a sympathetic listener. Sanders points out, too, that even in his earliest contributions to the English newspapers, "incipient literary elements" existed in Cahan's descriptions of East Side life (Sanders, 192, 181). Moreover, under the epithet of "The Hester Street Reporter," he had written a series of sketches called "From a Word a Quart" for the *Arbeter tsaytung* that reflected ordinary existence on the East Side; in these short essays—with such titles as "An Ice-Box," "Misfit," and "Cats"—Cahan developed literary thoughts inspired by the commonplace (Chametzky 1977, 36). Here was evidence of Cahan's proclivity toward literary realism and his desire to incorporate it into his work, imaginative and expository alike.

When Cahan stepped away from the *Forward* in August 1897, he strongly desired to leave Yiddish journalism behind him altogether and devote his auctorial attention to writing fiction in English and publishing in the regular American press. Confronting him, however, was the need for financial support, a problem that became especially crucial when he learned that he was not to be offered a new teaching contract for the coming academic year. He turned to the major New York dailies. Cahan began to contribute a weekly article to the *Sun* and an occasional one to the *Evening Post,* for which Lincoln Steffens was then the city editor. Steffens, who knew his work, also had recommended him to the *Commercial Advertiser,* and Cahan successfully submitted his articles there as well.

That his scruples nearly undermined his opportunity with the *Advertiser,* however, is evident from an anecdote related by Sanders in *The Downtown Jews.* When given his first assignment by the editor, Henry J. Wright, to cover a Republican political rally, Cahan answered in distress that he could not do it because he was a socialist. But Wright insisted and told Cahan to write an objective report. Evidently, he could not do it, and the critical article he submitted was not published. Although Wright attempted to convince Cahan that a reporter need not be favorable toward his subject, Cahan admitted that he could not be objective in political articles, so he refused to write them. Typically, despite his vulnerability in this instance, Cahan prevailed, and he was assigned other topics to cover instead (Sanders, 210–11). Wright found his writing satisfactory, and consequently, as Moses Rischin notes, in the fall of 1897 Cahan was freelancing for three prominent city newspapers, though he still lacked a full-time position with a steady salary. This problem was remedied in November of that year when Steffens took over as city editor of the *Advertiser* and immediately hired Cahan as a regular reporter on the staff (Rischin 1953, 11–13).

On the Staff of the *Commercial Advertiser*

What the name *Commercial Advertiser* suggests to today's reader is no true indication of the daily's content or quality. While Cahan was on its payroll, it had been in print since 1793, when it was founded as the *American Minerva*.[3] Its readers were generally intelligent and often well-to-do businesspeople, so its influence at the end of the century was greater than its limited circulation of about 2,500 would suggest (Rischin 1953, 12; Pollock, 232).

The *Advertiser*'s aim, under Steffens, was reflective, moral, and literary. He wanted to present "everyday experience simply, honestly, and directly" (Rischin 1985, xxi). As city editor, Steffens replaced conventional reporters with well-educated writers oriented toward literature, so the *Advertiser* provided an exceptionally favorable working environment for Cahan. Steffens himself quoted Howells as saying that "no writer or artist could afford not to read the *Commercial Advertiser*" during his tenure.[4] Unlike Jacob Riis, the newspaperman and social critic, Steffens intended not to promote reform on the Lower East Side but to expose the different manner of existence there to polite society and thereby undermine its Victorian assumptions about American life (Rischin 1985, xxi–xxii). For Steffens, echoing the views of Theodore Parker and Margaret Fuller half a century earlier, the newspaper was the most effective vehicle of true realism, the authentic representation of local life (Sanders, 213). When Henry J. Wright left the *Post* to become editor of the *Advertiser,* Steffens had accompanied him, as did another *Post* reporter, Norman Hapgood, whom Steffens immediately assigned to cover the theater (Steffens, 311). Norman's younger brother, Hutchins, was also added to the staff; he and Norman alike had become very fond of the Yiddish theater, and their knowledge of German gave them access to enough of the language on stage for them to understand and enjoy the plays.[5]

Like Steffens, Hutchins Hapgood had come to the daily as a well-educated, well-traveled Yankee. The "more casual and Bohemian of the two" brothers, he loved roaming the East Side streets and cafés (Sanders, 218). Hutchins became closely associated with Cahan, who brought him more directly into East Side life and gave him an idea of what to seek there: not conventionality and stereotype but the kind of vital truth that Cahan himself attempted to grasp in his writing. As a result, Hapgood wrote a series of brilliant and original sketches on the Jewish district that were published in a number of first-rate newspapers and magazines, including the *Advertiser.* In 1902, they were collected and published as *The Spirit of the Ghetto,* beautifully illustrated with drawings by Jacob Epstein, which Rischin calls "the *Commercial Advertiser*'s most lasting contribution to literature, and the product of Hutchins Hapgood's unique friendship with Abraham Cahan."[6] Like Cahan as an author of fiction, Hapgood's aim was not reform but representation.

Steffens recalled becoming sympathetic to the Jews of the East Side while still working for the *Post*—so sympathetic that for a while he "was almost a Jew" himself, he said, and mounted a mezuzah on his office door (Steffens, 244). He attended synagogue on the High Holidays and said that Gentile readers were interested in the strange mixture of tones and moods they sensed in Jewish holiday ceremonies, a blend of comedy, tragedy, orthodoxy, and revelation. Consequently, Cahan wrote a series of descriptive, explanatory holiday sketches for the *Advertiser* during his first two years with that paper, each appearing in print as the particular holiday approached, beginning even before he had joined its full-time staff. Steffens also noted the difference between the well-established uptown (mostly German) Jews and those on the Lower East Side (mostly recent Eastern European immigrants). In his *Autobiography* he mentions that an uptown lady who asked resentfully why he gave such extensive, sympathetic treatment to the East Side Jews in the *Post* rather than to her "socially prominent" class, and Steffens responded that more "beauty, significance, and character" were evident downtown, which enraged her (Steffens, 243).

He advised Cahan to discover the motivations behind a story rather than simply describing what he saw and heard as a conventional reporter would do. While working as a reporter for the *Post,* Steffens had learned that "reporters know and don't report . . . news . . . from the sociologists' and the novelists'" point of view, which covers little beyond the surface of events (Steffens, 223). Cahan gained much by following his advice to dig below that surface, and he became "a highly effective" reporter (Epstein, 80).

A quarter-century later he looked back on his experience as a new full-time reporter with an English newspaper and recalled that in the 1880s there were no journalism schools; instead, "The basic course for a budding journalist was life itself" (*Education,* 357). When he began working for the *Advertiser,* he often met and walked with Steffens, who was then interested chiefly in literary views, whereas Cahan himself was concerned principally with socialism. By the time they both left that newspaper a few years later, their priorities had ironically reversed: whereas Steffens wished to discuss socialism, Cahan wanted to talk about literature (Epstein, 81).

Cahan's initial assignment on the *Advertiser* was the police beat, and one of the first reporters he met at the station house was Jacob Riis, then on the staff of the *New York Sun.* Riis was the author of two books that had shocked readers with their depiction of the poverty that ravaged the Lower East Side: *How the Other Half Lives: Studies among the Tenements of New York* (1890) and *The Children of the Poor* (1892). Cahan said that they did not care much for each other, but it is clear that Riis was "very helpful to him" (Epstein, 80). As a devout Christian, Riis did not like Cahan's socialism, nor did he appreciate Cahan's dismissal of currently popular British authors—especially Thackeray, Dickens, and Kipling. Cahan, for his part, regarded Riis as anachronistic, and he praised Turgenev and Tolstoy among the masters of contemporary Russian realism. Despite their differences, on Steffens's request, Riis helped acquaint Cahan with American journalism. He told Cahan about the specifics of a reporter's job with the English-language press and introduced him to people around police headquarters who could and would prove useful for him to know (Rischin 1953, 14, 20).

Cahan was not restricted to the police beat and the Jewish district, though the bulk of his contributions dealt with the people of the Lower East Side. Like the other reporters for the *Advertiser,* he had no by-line, so it is often difficult to identify a given article or story as his, especially when he shifted away from his usual subject matter, as he did, for example, when writing of the war in progress down in Cuba, or of the standing-room-only audience at the Metropolitan Opera, or of Andrew Carnegie. Generally, however, the subject of his sketch and his approach to it are sufficient to characterize the work as Cahan's.[7]

Hutchins Hapgood observed that Cahan's writing about the East Side is chiefly didactic, and not only with respect to socialism. Because Cahan aimed to provide a general modern education in science and culture through his journalism, he sought a broad readership by writing "in the popular 'jargon.'" Even in his humorous sketches, Hapgood notes, he intended "always to point [out] a moral or convey some needed information" (233). But for modern readers, the beauty in Cahan's contributions to the *Advertiser* generally resides less in the information or moral lesson than in the details of his portraits of ordinary people in commonplace circumstances. Each character is individualized, often through dialogue, be he or she a fish-monger competing for sales, a landlady after her rent, a young woman in love with a striking laborer, or a newly arrived immigrant waiting for someone to meet and escort her from the immigration office to a new home. More than anything else, his intention was to convey an authentic glimpse of immigrant life with each anecdote and sketch.

Typically, the characters are treated sympathetically, often sentimentally, with a slightly ironic tone that evokes a subtle, poignant humor. For instance, Cahan concludes a sketch about a successful fifteen-year-old strike leader and sweatshop worker by describing his facial expression as bearing "that stamp of melancholy which is characteristic of much older representatives of his race."[8] In "Ghetto Letter Writing," an embarrassed young woman seeks someone to write a Yiddish letter for her, and the *melamed*—here called a "rabbi" by his young Hebrew pupil—who writes one, proud of his work, complains to Cahan that the Anglicized Yiddish he reads for people even in letters from the Old Country has absorbed English words, whereas he writes "pure Yiddish" (*CA*, 23 July 1898, 11; *Grandma*, 305).

This anecdote clearly illustrates the transformative impact of the New World culture on the Old in terms of its effect on the traditional language of East European Jewry. Often Cahan emphasized the polyglot nature of the Lower East Side, sometimes evident within a single family. For instance, in "On the Second Floor," he describes the problem of Mr. and Mrs. McAllister and their daughter: Mrs. McAllister speaks German but not English, though she understands it, and Mr. McAllister neither speaks nor understands German if anyone but his wife is addressing him, so their daughter, Lizzie, speaks to her mother in German and to her father in English (*CA*, 3 June 1899; *Grandma*, 262). Here the misunderstandings are gentle and amusing, but elsewhere they expose intolerance, as when several Jewish worshipers are stoned by anti-Semitic "Gentile rowdies" as they stand at the docks and symbolically cast their sins into the water on Rosh Hashana ("Drowned Their Sins," *CA*, 19 September 1898, 3; *Grandma*, 94).

A few days later, Cahan's article for the Sabbath preceding Yom Kippur describes a controversy between two women selling fish. Their Anglicized Yiddish dialogue conveys a marvelous sense of the pictorial vernacular, especially when the speakers are angry. One shouts: "She never meant to buy any of your rotten fish. I know this lady, and she always buys fish of me. May I sink five miles into the earth . . . if she does not." Her competitor responds: "She buy fish of you. . . . It's dirt, poison, cholera that you are selling, not fish. You are an old customer of mine, dear little missus, are you not? Spit at her." The account has a happy ending, however, when the two fiery saleswomen are persuaded to apologize to each other because the Day of Atonement is at hand ("For Feast and Fast," *CA*, 24 September 1898, 8; *Grandma*, 96).

Some of Cahan's short pieces are simply anecdotal, delightful miniatures that stimulate the reader's interest but do not always bring the matter to a resolution—as is often the case in real life. In one such piece, a woman named Rachael fears she will be returned to Europe. Her cousin in America was so eager to free her from the detention center that she told the officials she was Rachael's sister. Now they charge Rachael with being a liar and warn her that they are sending her back to Europe because liars are not allowed in America! ("Oi, Oi, No Liars Allowed Here," *CA*, 1 April 1899, 11).

As Hutchins Hapgood indicates in *Spirit of the Ghetto,* the genre of the East Side writers was "almost exclusively . . . the short sketch," and in Cahan's work, too, "the sketch element predominates" (231). But in addition to the profusion of sketches he also wrote several amusing vignettes for the *Advertiser.* The vignettes had been little known until Rischin recently returned to them and published them along with the other pieces of Cahan's writing in *Grandma Never Lived in America,* in 1985. Two of the more charming items may be taken as representative; both were published early in 1902, within a few months of Cahan's departure from the *Advertiser* late the previous year. In the first, "'God Is Everywhere,'" *CA*, 11 January 1902; title as cited in *Grandma,* 207–13), Annie learns the difference between infatuation and love through the wisdom of a "saint," a kind-hearted rabbi to whom she turns skeptically for help. She asks him to turn a young man's heart from another woman to herself. The "saint" insists that she not see the young man for six months, and all will be well. By the end of that time, she is no longer interested in the young man; she marries someone else instead and is perfectly happy. Is it the six months away from the man or the "saint" that has transformed her heart? It depends on one's faith in the "saint," a confidant replies.

In the second, equally comic little narrative, "The Bake Shop Count" (*CA,* 8 February 1902; title as cited in *Grandma,* 244–48), a German baker becomes so wealthy by baking a special type of Bohemian rye bread that is in great demand but unavailable elsewhere that he acquires the sobriquet "Count Long-or-Round" by his asking customers which shape they prefer. Still, wealthy or not, he cannot persuade a young woman to marry him, despite his providing the money for her to sail to America. When she becomes infatuated with a former officer in the German army, her suspicious uncle learns that her suitor is a fraud, and two years after recovering from the shock of his deceit, she finally agrees to wed the baker, though she does not love him. Of course, the tale has a happy ending. After a short time working in the bakery, she finds she loves both him and the business, and the two lovers live in wealthy, wedded bliss together. The tone of both stories is light, not at all characteristic of the literary tales for which Cahan came to be recognized as a realist, yet they are among the last examples of short fiction in English that he published.

For Cahan, that terminus was unexpected. After leaving the *Commercial Advertiser* in the wake of Steffens's departure to edit *McClure's,* he intended to use his uncommitted time for more freelancing, particularly for writing fiction in English. But circumstances tempted him to return to Yiddish journalism and the *Forward.*

In fact, however, he had not been truly away from Yiddish writing for more than a couple of years or so. Early in 1898, only a few months after signing onto the *Advertiser* staff, he wrote a satirical but informative sketch called "East Side Journalism" on the Yiddish dailies (*CA,* 12 February 1898, 9; *Grandma,* 287–90). The satire is on the order of an interview, the subject being an unnamed East Side poet who earns a poor living sewing buttonholes. The bulk of his remarks constitute a sympathetic complaint about the lack of ethics and morality among the Yiddish publishers. The poet acknowledges refusing to comply with the duplicity of his editors, who, for instance, ask him to write endorsements of two opposing political candidates for the same newspaper on the same day. The Yiddish dailies, says the poet, wait for the English newspapers to appear on the street, then translate the news quickly and publish it themselves; moreover, he admits that sometimes they print Saturday's news on Friday because they must have the paper prepared before the Sabbath. With all of the light-hearted jabbing, however,

Cahan included enough information to inform readers of the rapid development of the Yiddish press in America.

Two years later another humorous article on Yiddish journalism appeared in the *Advertiser,* which was probably written by Cahan, though Rischin did not include it in his collection. It is worth mentioning here because it relates directly to both the commercial interests of the *Advertiser* and the machinations of the Yiddish press. The title of the piece almost makes the point in itself: "A Great Yiddish Paper/No Readers, No News, but Many Advertisements" (*CA,* 20 January 1900, 2). The article describes a Yiddish weekly with outdated news and an English dateline that is distributed only to its advertisers, all of whom are Gentiles unable to read Yiddish. With its highly appropriate but ludicrous Hebrew title—*Roeh v'lo niroh* (Sees but Is Unseen)—the weekly is not sold at newsstands. Deluded Gentile merchants advertise in it wrongly assuming that it has many Jewish readers, but only the advertisers receive copies. The article concludes: "And the Gentiles are indeed easy."

It bears pointing out that the widely distributed English newspaper in which the article appeared was owned by a Yankee millionaire. Few Gentile American readers are likely to have been affected, much less offended, by it, but many would have recognized the representation of the stereotypically clever Jew gaining the capital of his unsuspecting Christian neighbors by deceiving them—a kind of harmless and good-natured rendering of Shylock. Nor would such a portrait necessarily have been foreign to Cahan's pen, if he did happen to be the author. As Sanders observes, Cahan's first story published in English, "A Providential Match" (1895), was accompanied by grotesque illustrations that seem to conform with certain anti-Semitic stereotypes, and descriptions in his Yiddish version of the tale "support the spirit of the illustrations." Sanders took this as evidence of Cahan's "own ambivalence about Jewishness," though he was already on his way toward resolving it (195).

True, there can be little question of Cahan's ambivalence in this and other respects, at least during the first sixty years or so of his life, and those are the years of concern here. He was secular, but he remained a Jew; he was Russian, but he was rapidly Americanized; he was a journalist, but he is now remembered chiefly for his fiction; his *mame-loshn* was Yiddish, his adoptive tongue was English, and he made a career of employing both to good advantage.

More than a trace of Cahan's own nostalgia for the Old Country is perceptible in an imaginative account he wrote in spring 1899 of a young Russian woman who longed for her homeland after having spent years in America. But what melancholy may have existed is qualified in that Cahan presents her as so disenchanted with what she finds on going home that she returns to New York. "Back to Dear Old Russia/The Disillusionment of Sonia Rogova" is a Jewish illustration in miniature of Thomas Wolfe's famous refrain in *You Can't Go Home Again* (1940). "I was a stranger there," Sonia laments to the bewildered friends around her. "Did you say I was Americanized?" she asks them. "Well, now that I am here I feel that this is not my home, either. But one thing is certain, Russia can never be to me what it once was. Perhaps, it is because we are Jews—a persecuted, wandering people without a home. When I walked in the streets of my native town every policeman and the meanest tramp in the gutter would make me feel that I was a mere *Zhidovka* [a contemptuous Russian term for a Jewish woman]—a hated, inferior being." Yet for all the grimness of disillusion, ultimately it brings an awareness of loosened bonds and freedom, for even amidst her sorrowful song a "tender . . . chord" repeats to her, "The thread is broken" (*CA*, 15 April 1899, 11; *Grandma*, 474–75).

So it surely was with Cahan himself at this time as a naturalized American in whose consciousness reverberations from the homeland were still occasionally resonant. Moreover, his ambivalence as a dedicated socialist and a Jew created internal conflict at times, as in Sanders's recognition of apparently anti-Semitic descriptions in an early short story, but usually it did not. If these dualities generated a tension that was almost constant, they also kept him open to several avenues of expression in Yiddish and English, in both journalism and fiction.

Return to the *Forward*

For well over a year before leaving the *Commercial Advertiser* Cahan had been socializing with several of his old colleagues on the staff of the *Forward* at Herrick's café, 141 Division Street. He occasionally contributed articles under a pseudonym to his old paper as well, drafting some of them in the *Forward* office (Pollock, 294–95). Moreover, he was beginning to feel comfortable writing Yiddish again, partly because, despite his reputation as a promising author of fiction in English, he was not turning out much new work apart from that published in the *Advertiser* (Sanders, 246–47). Although it had been more than four years since Cahan had resigned the editorship of the *Forward*, he had not lost interest in the paper, which, after all, he had helped to found. Through visiting with his former colleagues there, he knew that the daily was foundering and was in danger of going under with a decreasing circulation. After several discussions and meetings, with Cahan and among themselves, the *Forward* staff voted to offer him the editor's chair again.

He had already given the matter considerable thought because he was well aware of the pressures the new office would bring, and he did not wish to cut himself off completely from his writing of fiction in English. He had insisted, too, that certain conditions would have to be agreed on or he would not even consider an offer, no matter how much the staff was in favor of his return. When they accepted his conditions in making the offer, Cahan agreed, fully confident that he could save the daily if given the authority to run it as he wished. This—absolute authority as editor—was one of the conditions on which they had concurred before tending the offer. Another was a guarantee of free time for his own writing, and a third was increasing the size of the paper from six to eight pages (Epstein, 85).

In spite of their agreements, the first condition created problems immediately. As his former colleagues might have known, Cahan intended to popularize the daily and broaden its readership, whereas several members of the staff wished to emphasize socialist theory and polemics—the same controversy that had led to his resignation in 1897 (Epstein, 74–75). He had his ideas for the paper, and he wanted to carry them through. With the publication of the first issue under his control, in mid-March 1902, the direction in which he intended to take the *Forward* was already clear; it was a matter of less overt socialism and more Americanization. The edition was a resounding success with the public; the additional two pages allowed more space for features without undercutting the revenue from advertisements, which covered about half of the original paper.

The success of that edition set off a surge in circulation, exactly as Cahan had expected. Unfortunately, however, the income could not keep up with the printing costs of the larger paper, and within a short time the *Forward* once again seemed to be in for financial trouble. This distressed Cahan and those on the staff who supported him, but for others, who still favored a distinctly socialist daily, it was no calamity.

In midyear, funds were offered by Cahan's erstwhile opposition on the *Ovent blat,* the De Leonist Social Democrats; their daily was on its way under, and they sought to reunite with their fellow socialists on the *Forward.* Of course, they, like Cahan's opposition on his own staff, still favored the doctrinaire journalism of the conventional Yiddish press. Because their money was needed, ostensibly to save the paper, Cahan's

authority to continue driving the *Forward* toward further Americanization was challenged, with the result that he resigned once again in September. In his few months as editor, however, from March to September
1902, he had radically modified the daily from a dull, conventional
paper of six pages to a larger, more colorful, and far more popular organ,
an effective voice for the Yiddish-speaking Jewish immigrants of New
York. But he had also undertaken to personalize the daily, make it an
extension of himself, and in doing so, Sanders points out, concurring
now with such opposition figures as Leon Kobrin, Isaac Hourwich, and
Paul Novick, he had created "a realm of charismatic [personal] power"
on the order of Hearst (who then owned the *New York Journal*) and
Pulitzer (then owner of the *New York World*) rather than continuing in
the liberal tradition of his mentor in the English press, Lincoln Steffens
(Sanders, 262; Howe, 529n; Novick, 14–16).

Cahan left this time for nearly a year, most of which he spent outside
of New York. In the spring of 1903, he began drafting his second novel
in English, inspired by an outrage in the ongoing annals of Russian anti-
Semitism. Soon afterward a massacre of Jews occurred in Kishinev—
shocking new evidence of yet another pogrom tacitly endorsed by the
authorities. News of the pogrom—some fifty Jews slain, hundreds
wounded, and enormous destruction of property[9]—led him to write an
editorial for the *Forward,* and before the summer was over, he was drawn
back to the editor's chair. Once more, the circulation of the daily had
dropped; the staff was no longer so eager to publish the usual ideology
and polemics. Most of them wanted him back, and he returned with the
previous conditions still intact.

Like other immigrant newspapers printed in readers' native languages, the Yiddish press was of primary importance in interpreting the
American way of life for new arrivals to the country—in this case, Jews
from Eastern Europe (Chametzky 1977, 24). Cahan understood this
from the beginning of his career with the *Forward,* and he saw himself as
being in an ideal position to lead the daily toward meeting this need. He
was, to be sure, a man of both worlds; the great advantage he gained
from this duality is clear from Leon Stein's proposal that Cahan "seemingly saw all things double as in a stereopticon: one view was that of a
Russian Jew, the other that of a new American."[10]

Indeed, Moses Rischin states that the key to the success and integrity
of the *Forward* after Cahan's return as well as the source of its inspiration
was in his duality as a representative of both *Yidishkayt* and modern
America.[11] In his series as the "Hester Street Reporter," written during

his last years with the *Arbeter tsaytung* and the *Ovent blat,* he had provided an accurate description of East Side life. Now in the *Forward* he
wanted to go a step further by both reflecting the existence of the Jewish poor and giving readers some variety in their daily paper—not only
news and addresses on socialism but also broad knowledge, self-under-
standing, and entertainment (Sanders, 206). His success in this respect
is evident from a comment by Robert E. Park at a conference of social
workers in 1920; he said that more than any other American newspaper,
the *Forward* was "a form of literature and a transcript of life" (Stein, xv).

Cahan also held firmly to the principle that people are most effectively persuaded when one appeals to them in their own vernacular, a
language they readily understand without recourse to textbooks or dictionaries. In a special number of the *Forward,* issued in May 1992 to
mark its ninety-fifth anniversary, Gus Tyler, a weekly columnist for the
paper, explains with a breathtaking comparison Cahan's successful
approach to his readers through their *mame-loshn:* the *Forward* "made a
people out of many peoples and made a language out of what were
many dialects of a language. . . . [Cahan] did for Yiddish what Dante
did for Italian. He gathered the many variations on a linguistic theme
and recomposed them into a common tongue."[12] As a young immigrant,
Cahan had detested the mixing of English with Yiddish, but as time
passed he combined the two himself, recognizing that the result was,
after all, the language people spoke on the streets, like it or not (*Education,* 241–43; see also Pollock, 90–91). Purists complained bitterly
about such universalization. For example, shortly after Cahan's death
late in 1951, Paul Novick expressed strong resentment, calling Cahan
"a bourgeois assimilationist" who corrupted Yiddish by injecting
adapted English words into it and thus hastening its demise as a viable
language (Novick, 16).

But such diatribes were futile; the *Forward* commenced to thrive
when Cahan returned to it, and it reached such heights that many years
later an editor of the *New York Post* said it should stand not only as "the
model, the exemplar" for all Yiddish dailies but as "one of the greatest
models for any other newspaper."[13] Its readers were devoted to it
through much of the first half of the century. Alfred Kazin recalls: "My
father revered the Yiddish labor paper, the *Forward. . . .* When he exul-
tantly read from the *Forward* to me, with its news of the international
working class, he was not alone. He was full of pride in what he was
reading aloud, positively worshipping every item. . . . The *Forward's*
masthead carried the opening line in every Socialist Bible: 'Workers of

the World Unite!'" (Kazin, 72). Though neither doctrinaire nor polemical, the *Forward* remained unquestionably a socialist paper in those early years of labor exploitation and unionization. Within a year or two of Cahan's return, it became the major voice of the *Yidishe arbeter bund* (Jewish Workers' Federation), which had followed the model of New York and organized in Russia in 1897. Cahan, of course, supported the bund, but he criticized its members for their relative lack of communion with the persecuted Jewish masses, an attitude with which he was all too familiar, having reacted acidly to the blatant anti-Semitism he had seen at socialist meetings in Europe a decade earlier (Sanders, 330–34).

Cahan was committed to the workers, to be sure; they knew it and trusted him, though serious differences occasionally arose to disrupt that trust. One of the most serious of those occurred in March 1913 during the climax of a widespread controversial strike by the garment workers. The *Forward* initially supported the strike and later the compromise offered by the manufacturers, which most of the United Garment Workers also favored, but some of the tailors—who Cahan believed had made a confidential settlement of their own—opposed the compromise in public, charged Cahan with treachery to the workers, and broke windows in the new *Forward* building (Pollock, 361–62). This occurred precisely when he was writing the original serialized version of *The Rise of David Levinsky* and had to undergo emergency surgery for a painful ulcer. The surgery was a success, the series was finished, and he helped to settle the strike, which ended the controversy.

Beyond the unions and nominal socialists, Cahan extended the range of the *Forward* to include as many Yiddish-speaking readers as he could attract. After 1902, it became "the immigrant's friend and confidant— nay, more, it was a patient and omniscient father, wise in the ways of America" (Sanders, 263). In 1912 Joseph Gollomb already could describe Cahan as "editor, family adviser, lay preacher, comrade, critic, littérateur, teacher, and political leader all in one, to half a million East Siders who read the *Forwards* {*sic*} daily. Everything is grist to his editorial mill—socialism and corsets, divorce and radium, Arnold Bennett and athletics, free baths, . . . and even table manners and personal cleanliness."[14] Cahan also preached tolerance to the Jews, who often berated Gentiles—especially to their children—having suffered from Christian anti-Semitism for centuries. He insisted that the Jews not be guilty of the same prejudicial attitudes they condemned in others, urging that people be judged as individuals, not as part of a group (Pollock, 341). This American acculturation of the immigrant Jewish multitudes con-

stituted his ultimate aim with the *Forward,* and he pressed hard to realize it.

But Cahan was sharply criticized for his broadened appeal. When
opponents complained that he "lowers himself to the masses instead of
lifting them up," Cahan replied: "If you want to pick a child up from the
ground, you first have to bend down to him. If you don't, how will you
reach him?" (Sanders, 265). Occasionally, Cahan was charged with over-
simplifying matters in popularizing them as he tried to provide readers
with the rudiments of a general education. Irving Howe mentions one
Yiddish-speaking intellectual critic, Chaim Zhitlovsky, an immigrant
socialist with a European doctorate, who derided Cahan. Secularized and
committed to the Yiddish language, Zhitlovsky also advocated Jewish
nationalism but not as a Zionist. He complained at length over the inac-
curacies and errors in Cahan's popularizations of science and alleged that
the education offered in the *Forward* was more limited than its readers
knew. Although Howe did not deny the presence of mistakes and unsup-
ported assertions in the paper, he believes that Cahan's efforts at mass
education in the *Forward* effectively stimulated the curiosity of readers to
consider much that they would otherwise have disregarded (507, 531).[15]

In addition to its diversified articles and features, the *Forward* published drama reviews, poetry, critical essays, and a considerable amount
of fiction, including original work written in Yiddish and translations
mostly from English, Russian, and German. Cahan recommended fiction to his readers as a means of helping "to cope with a complex new
array of emotions" in America.[16] Many of the Yiddish dailies, regardless
of the social and political views of its staff, depended on sensationalism
to sell papers, and the *Forward* was no different in this respect—though
Melech Epstein points out that even the many popular novels among
the literary ones it published were "superior to those in the other
papers" (Epstein, 93). Oswald Garrison Villard said in 1922 that the
Forward was publishing "by far the best fiction and *belles lettres* of any
newspaper in America."[17] The first American publication of I. L. Peretz
appeared in the *Forward,* and among the many other important Yiddish
fiction writers published in Cahan's daily were Sholem Aleichem; I. J.
Singer and his brother, Isaac Bashevis; and Sholem Asch, with whom
Cahan had a bitter feud in the 1930s and 1940s over Asch's novels on
the life and times of Jesus (Chametzky 1977, 22; Sanders, 447).

Nevertheless, Ellen Kellman has categorized most of the fiction in
the *Forward* as formula romances called *shundromanen* (Yiddish for "pot-
boilers"), nearly two hundred of which were serialized in the daily

between 1897 and 1940. She credits Leon Gottlieb, who began with the *Forward* in 1901, with thirty-four novels over the twenty-two years he wrote for the paper; and she describes most of them as "down-to-earth," with mostly Jewish characters, an American setting, and a standard of morality so high it bordered on the didactic.[18] As may be expected of a socialist at this time, among Cahan's own translations for the daily was Upton Sinclair's *The Jungle.*[19]

In the early years, Cahan himself wrote most of the drama reviews in the *Forward.* He believed the paper should encourage Yiddish theater with the aim of improving it; indeed, the stage had long held a strong appeal for him. Encouragement for Cahan was by no means synonymous with indiscriminate praise, however; he was a knowledgeable viewer with a sharp eye and tongue alike. Although he supported his critiques with specifics from the plays and productions, as a good critic must for credibility, his remarks may sometimes have been unnecessarily harsh, and they led to bitter responses and personal hostilities, such as his ongoing battle with Jacob Gordin, an extremely popular dramatist in the 1890s and at the turn of the century. By the time he died in 1909, Gordin had been devastated by Cahan's attacks, and many of Cahan's associates resented them as well (Sanders, 301–26; 389–90). Nevertheless, by then he had established a reputation for the *Forward* as the voice of critical authority over the Yiddish stage to the extent that the success or failure of a play could be determined by his reception of it (Rich, 25). Indeed, his attraction to the stage was an enduring one. Nearly three decades after Gordin's death, Cahan collected a series of articles he had written for the *Forward* on Rachel, a popular French-Jewish actress of the early nineteenth century whom he called "a heroine of the Jews," and published them in 1938 in a volume bearing her name as the title.[20]

"Bintl briv": Advice by Request from the Esteemed Editor

Cahan knew that interest in the *Forward* would be intensified and the circulation increased if he could stimulate readers to participate in the making of the paper by sending in questions to the editor, submitting answers to queries posed by the staff, expressing their views on subjects of concern to them, requesting assistance over matters trivial or grave, and so forth. From early 1902 through late 1905 he attempted a variety of approaches that did not prove satisfactory. Then, at the end of 1905, he found readers responding heart and soul to the question, "Is

Morality Stricter with Men Than with Women?" This opened the way for the inception of the single most engaging feature of the *Forward*, the *"Bintl briv"* (Bundle of Letters), which commenced early the next year and continued for decades (Rischin 1992, 23). For staff members still dissatisfied with this putative vulgarization of a socialist paper, the Forward Press Association inaugurated a new daily called *Morgn tsaytung* (Morning Paper) in mid-January 1906; it was meant to compete with other morning papers and to provide a vehicle for the more ideologically oriented staff members to indulge in their polemics (Sanders, 355). But this was not for Cahan.

The *"Bintl briv"* needed no trial period. Upon first publication it began to draw letters, though it took a while before it became a daily feature. The substance of this correspondence is so rich that a selection of the letters and editorial responses, the latter long written only by Cahan himself, was collected by Isaac Metzker and brought out in 1971 under the title *A Bintel Brief: Sixty Years of Letters from the Lower East Side to the Jewish Daily Forward.* To a large extent, the feature is a Yiddish version of "Dorothea Dix Talks," an advice column that had begun a decade earlier in the *New Orleans Picayune.* In a sense, Cahan might have anticipated in his letter-writing sketches for the *Commercial Advertiser* (23 July 1898; 22 November 1901) this apparent need for the immigrants to express themselves—their hopes, fears, worries, and dreams—to a trusted and compassionate adviser, rebbe, wise man, elder, parent, or confidant, call that figure what one will, who could touch the heart or satisfy the curiosity of the writer without causing the embarrassment of direct personal contact. The immigrants wrote with their problems to the "esteemed editor," who replied in the *"Bintl briv,"* thus replacing the "pious rabbi" of the Proletarian Preacher's column in the *Arbeter tsaytung* during the 1890s. The "esteemed editor" was admired as a modern man with contemporary values, in contrast to an Old-Country *rebe* or sage (Epstein, 92).

As the column increased in popularity, Ronald Sanders perceptively suggests, Cahan realized that "life itself had become his novel," and he assumed the role of "life's editor" (Sanders, 365). The letters were written by "greenhorns" and old-timers alike in America, by bewildered men and deserted women of all ages. Joseph Gollomb quotes from an affecting letter and its response from before 1912: "'I am a hundred years old and am all alone,' wrote an old woman. 'If I could only see my lost son before I die!' From South Africa came an answer: 'I am coming, mother. Send me your address'" (Gollomb, 674). A successful manufacturer wrote in 1906 that his conscience was throbbing over his past exploitation of his workers; reading letters from the suffering workers in the *"Bintl briv"* had awakened his conscience, and he asked for advice on how to assuage it. Follow your conscience, Cahan replied; you will lose nothing and gain true happiness.[21]

In 1908 a girl who signed herself "The Lonesome Orphan" began her letter: "I am an unhappy lonely orphan, fifteen years of age, and I appeal to you in my helplessness." She then detailed a tragic story of death and loss, concluding with a plea for aid. The editor replied that after her letter was published, he received many responses, some offering money and others adoption. In 1909 a woman of twenty wrote that she had fallen in love with a youth who planned to become a doctor, and he professed love for her, but her friends advised her not to tie herself down for seven years to put through medical school a husband who might then leave her. Moreover, her family proposed a match with a relative, also in America; he was a businessman, and they liked each other from the photographs and letters they exchanged. She requested advice: "How shall I solve this problem? . . . Whatever you advise me, I will do" (*Bintel Brief,* 91). Cahan discreetly informed her that being aware of the possibilities, she had to decide for herself.

Irving Howe notes that the *"Bintl briv"* introduced and fostered romantic sentiments largely unfamiliar to Eastern European Jews. "Romantic love" was not a part of premarital male-female relationships in the Old Country (Howe, 537), where marriages were arranged with the aid of a *shatkhn* (matchmaker) and dowries were expected. Indeed, according to Jules Chametzky, "'Love' in the western sense was foreign to the *shtetl* ethos" altogether (Chametzky 1977, 64). Letters on the topic, especially those dealing with courtship and sexual matters, were instrumental in expanding the readership of the *Forward,* but as a result of them, the *"Bintl briv"* was targeted for satire. For almost twenty years a comic weekly called *Der groyser kundes* (The Big Prankster) ridiculed Cahan for "pandering to the erotic impulses" of his readers; Moses Rischin observes that the satire only promoted the feature's appeal (Rischin 1992, 23).

Those interested in this feature should find Isaac Metzker's admirable collection, *A Bintel Brief,* and read these emotion-laden letters. They convey much insight into the suffering, grief, and uncertainty of the immigrants' lives, and many are still touching. These letters constitute ample support for Abraham Cahan's intense desire to assist his people in finding a true home for themselves in America, the Golden Land, as they had hoped and expected to do from the time they started to make plans to leave the Old Country. It was probably in part the correspondence he read in the *"Bintl briv"* that led Cahan to reconsider the role of Judaism in his life. Judaism is as much a culture as a religion; traditionally, the Jews have been regarded not only as a people but as a race apart, even by the socialists whom many of the intellectuals, including Cahan himself, had joined and supported. Upon his first return to the *Forward* early in 1902, one of the methods he employed in attempting to increase circulation was to appeal to his Yiddish readers as Jews rather than chiefly as socialists or laborers, and he did so with a sense of Jewish unity in mind (Sanders, 258–67). This innovation struck his more doctrinaire colleagues as a complete and unacceptable turnabout, for as they had embraced the principles of socialism, so had they loosened their affiliation with their religious beliefs, traditions, and heritage. It has been said before that socialism became the religion for many of these intellectuals, including Cahan himself for a time. His attempt to promote socialist aims by presenting them in relation to Jewish virtues and values seemed to his opponents both self-contradictory and self-defeating, but Cahan now obviously disagreed.

Early in 1907, when the *Forward* was again so strapped financially that it had to declare bankruptcy, a new business manager for the paper, Benjamin Schlesinger, suggested that premiums be offered to new subscribers, and Cahan agreed. The first premium was a major Yiddish-English dictionary compiled by Alexander Harkavy, an accomplished lexicographer with whom Cahan had worked on the *Arbeter tsaytung*. The offer was so successful that Schlesinger suggested the next premium be a Yiddish history of America that Cahan himself should write. Again Cahan agreed, though he knew how much time he would have to commit to the undertaking, a projected eight-volume history (Sanders, 386; Gollomb, 672). By 1912, after three years of research, he had completed two volumes on the discovery of the Americas, collectively and, according to Pollock, inaccurately entitled *History of the United States, with Details Concerning the Discovery and Conquest of America* (*Historye fun di fareynikte shtatn mit eyntselhaytn vegn der entdekung un eroyberung fun amerike*)[22]; it totaled nearly 1,500 pages, and some 25,000 copies of each volume were sold at $1 apiece with twenty coupons from the *Forward* or at $2.50 each without them. Pollock calls this work more than a history of the United States; he says that it is a "Marxist interpretation of the development of civilization" (Epstein, 99; Gollomb, 672; Pollock, 343–45).

From the point at which the *Forward* regained its financial stability after 1907 until the passing generations made a Yiddish daily anachronistic near midcentury, the paper was immensely successful under Cahan's control. It maintained high ethical standards, refusing advertisements from nonunionized firms and from organized ones in which the workers were striking. As Melech Epstein points out, its ethical practices were costly, but they led to the sustained trust of its readers; Gus Tyler, in recently describing the *Forward* as more than a newspaper, says it "gave moral meaning" to the chaotic whirl of daily events (Epstein, 94; Tyler, 24).

Whereas it began as a storefront operation in the late nineteenth century, by 1911–12 the *Forward* was ready to move into its new ten-story building on East Broadway, then the tallest edifice on the Lower East Side. By that time its paid circulation had reached 130,000, which meant a least half a million readers (Gollomb, 673). Two years later it proved to be influential and powerful enough "to break Tammany's hold on the Lower East Side and send the first socialist, Meyer London, to Congress"; then it had reached "the height of its power" in the Jewish district (Hindus, 20; Sanders, 413). Unlike other socialist papers, the *Forward* clearly welcomed women readers, who liked the paper because it addressed their needs and interests (Rischin 1992, 23). In another decade, its circulation would nearly double to a quarter million, with local editions published in eleven major cities (Emery and Emery, 250).

Like other Yiddish papers during the early period of World War I, the *Forward* favored Germany, partly because of Russian anti-Semitic hostility and partly because Germany was the center of democratic socialism, but Cahan was pressed by the U.S. government to stop criticizing American support for the war or lose the daily's privileges for second-class postal rates (Sanders, 429; Howe, 539–40). Not long afterward, when the United States entered the war on the side of Russia against Germany, the *Forward* and its readers were fully supportive, with no further reluctance because by then the revolution seemed to hold promise for Jewish freedom in Russia at last. The promise did not endure long, however, and soon after the decade ended, Cahan had inklings of a dark future for Russia and the Jews under Lenin's new form of tyrannical communism. When he traveled to Russia in 1923 to see for himself the effects of the revolution, the transformation was complete; he perceived even less freedom under Lenin than there had been under the Czar (Sanders, 435–36; Howe, 541–42).

That trip locked the era of Cahan's radical socialism tightly behind him. He and the *Forward,* though it would still be printed in Yiddish for decades to come, were fully acculturated. He had only now to return to his past and describe it as he had recalled it for the tens of thousands of admirers who had followed him through the gates of Castle Garden or Ellis Island. Cahan did so in writing a five-volume autobiography published over a period of almost six years: *Bleter fun mayn lebn* (*Pages from My Life;* 1926–31). Unfortunately, to date, only the first two of these volumes have been translated and published, under the title *The Education of Abraham Cahan* (1969). In 1934 he edited *Hear the Other Side,* a collection of essays by his socialist colleagues defending democratic socialism and condemning Soviet totalitarian communism; the title essay is his own. Also in 1934, Cahan provided a two-page introduction to *Socialism, Fascism, Communism,* edited by Joseph Shaplen and David Shub; this volume, too, offers a defense of socialism in contrast to the apparent shortcomings of communism, and it foreshadows the evils already being introduced by the Fascists in Germany. Apart from his book *Rashel,* published in 1938 by the Forward Press, Cahan brought out little if anything more outside the pages of the *Forward,* and his career as a journalist, as well as the state of the Yiddish press itself, had already entered a long period of decline.

But perhaps even then he had an inkling of the resurgence that would occur in the *Forward* a couple of generations later, when an English version appeared weekly alongside the Yiddish original and an edition in Russian commenced in 1995 for recent immigrants from the former USSR. According to figures published by the *Forward* late in 1994, the circulation of the English edition then was about 25,000, and it had been increasing "at the rate of 20 percent a year"; in 1995, moreover, paid subscriptions "expanded by slightly more than 50 percent," and advertising income increased "nearly 40 percent."[23] And as for Yiddish itself, Motl Zelmanowicz, current director of the Forward Association, writes: "Yiddish is not dying. Nor will it die" because contemporary young people are increasingly attracted to it as they "are returning to their roots, to their beginnings" in their wish to revitalize the traditions that had almost been allowed to slip away.[24] Indeed, Cahan's legacy as both an assimilationist and a speaker and writer of Yiddish is still flourishing in the Jewish newspaper he cofounded and headed for half a century.

Chapter Three

Yekl, by a "New Star of Realism"

When Abraham Cahan immigrated to the United States in 1882, the realists had been gaining increasing prominence in American letters, both building on literary traditions and practices of the nation's past and moving in new directions, largely under the influence of European authors.[1] Before leaving Russia, of course, he was already familiar with the realistic fiction of Turgenev and Tolstoy, whose work he admired profoundly. While writing for the *New York Commercial Advertiser* he was among the earliest critics to bring the new Russian writers, including Gorky and Chekhov, to the attention of the American reading public (Rischin 1985, xxxix).

For Cahan, the great Russian realists brought fiction to life, and he wished to do the same, not by simply imitating but by emulating them and striving to reach their standards. In reviewing the works of Tolstoy in English for the *Advertiser* in 1901, Cahan explained that the reality of Tolstoy's fiction comes through his "depth of psychical penetration," which makes the stories so effective "as an educational agency." It takes a greater imagination to represent everyday experience than to devise and manipulate a fantastic plot, he points out, observing that in Tolstoy's fiction, every detail in a relationship among characters has an underlying significance.[2] As for Chekhov, Cahan describes him as "the Tolstoy of the Russian short story."

"In literary matters Cahan was first to last a Realist," Jules Chametzky writes (1977, 29). A year or so after his arrival, Cahan purchased a complete but shabbily printed set of Dickens and not long afterward a well-printed two-volume set of Hippolyte Taine's *History of English Literature* (*Education,* 270–71). Still new to English, he struggled nightly with Dickens, shifting between fiction and dictionary, until he gradually overcame his difficulty as the new language grew familiar. Taine's realistic philosophy of literature in relation to environment would prove important later to Cahan the novelist, as it had to Howells many years earlier. Indeed, aspects of *The Rise of David Levinsky* clearly reflect the influence of Taine's view that literature should provide a means by which humanity may be "observed, analyzed, and classified. Fiction should be the scientific laboratory of society . . . in which the complex components of our social system are mixed with each other, so that the race may watch the experiment, see the result, and be better able to make decisions affecting its life."[3]

Cahan himself theorized scientifically on realism near the end of the decade. On 6 April 1889, when writing regularly for the *Workmen's Advocate,* he contributed an article entitled "Realism" that was a printed version of a lecture he had delivered before the New York Labor Lyceum three weeks earlier, on 15 March. In that published lecture he attempted to provide a philosophical and quasi-psychological foundation for a realistic literature founded on natural sensations and responses to nature.

His Aristotelian opening sentence is: "Man is an inquiring, social, imitating creature." "Inquiry," he continues, leads man to seek "the sources of phenomena"; "sociability" is the instinctive desire to unite with others for self-preservation; and "imitation" is generated by the reflective nature of our sensations; that is, it attempts to translate sensation—"the mental counterpart of nature"—into impression. Because art satisfies a natural tendency to imitate, it stimulates the senses as would nature itself, Cahan professes; therefore, idealists who desire pleasure alone from art unattached to reality are seeking unnatural restriction and limitation. Such art cannot truly satisfy because it does not give access to "the sources [in nature] of the very pleasures for which [they are] hunting." On the combined bases of his current atheistic view and his socialist cause, Cahan also said that because realism shows nothing to revere beyond reason and natural law, acceptance of this truth will lead to "progress and happiness" through a society developed in accord with the instinct of "sociability."[4]

In his autobiography, nearly thirty-five years later, Cahan summarizes those points he had raised in the lecture, calling realism "a philosophic consideration of the nature of art." Having read Howells and James as well as Tolstoy by the time he wrote the lecture, he said that he had explored "the relationship between literature and social problems" and determined that "the power of realistic art arises from the pleasure we derive from recognizing the truth as it is mirrored by art." He held then that capitalists do not want the truth, however, because it would defeat their class-oriented roles; they favor, instead, representation of the ideal, which enables them to avoid confronting the darker aspects of the real world, with its problems and social responsibilities. From his altered perspective of the 1920s, Cahan concludes that much of his argument in

"Realism" was pure socialist propaganda he could no longer support (*Education*, 404–5).

Nevertheless, his views on realism in the late 1880s and afterward, at least through the years of writing *The Rise of David Levinsky*, corresponded with those of Howells and other contemporary realists. Their views contrasted sharply with the romantic and idealist critical dicta of Edmund Clarence Stedman and other spokesmen for the Genteel Tradition, who had no wish to deal with the commonplace or to expose the raw, physical aspects of life. In this respect, it should be noted that at the very time Cahan was lecturing and writing theoretically about realism, what Edwin H. Cady called a "Realism War" was in progress between those authors and critics who sided with Howells and James, and the neoromantics—Horace Scudder, Thomas Bailey Aldrich, Stedman, and others—whose ideas met with more popular favor during those years.[5] Ultimately, the realists never really won the battle, Cady says elsewhere, because romance remains as dominant in American literature as it has been since the revolution (Cady 1971, 12). In addition, throughout the period of critical conflict, the more "genteel" fiction writers and the neoromantics earned far more money from their publications than did their most prominent opponents.

Moreover, if the major American realists proved more influential on literary authors of the next century, they were still largely unknown and certainly unappreciated by most American readers. This became clear to Cahan in the mid-1880s, when he joined a "literary debating society" with about thirty members, and not one of them had even heard the names of W. D. Howells or Henry James, who were too avant-garde for them. He also found them to be utterly naive on sociopolitical issues, which for Cahan at the time was even worse, and he was so sickened later when two of the members joked about the Haymarket executions that he left quietly and never returned to the group. This could not occur among young intellectuals of Russia, he said (*Education*, 349–51). It was evident to him that they neither knew nor cared anything about the matters of most concern to him.

Ten years later, when writing for the *Advertiser*, he interviewed Howells himself; the central issue was the trial of Zola over his support of Dreyfus, and Cahan noted that Howells and Zola had much in common, including their aesthetic views, their humanity and compassion, and their readiness to confront injustice. Howells said that as a novelist, Zola "is indecent . . . but not immoral. The truth presented as it is in his novels cannot be immoral" ("Howells on Zola," *CA*, 26 February 1898;

Rischin 1985, 511–12). Howells felt uncomfortable with Zola's fiction, but he had great respect for the vitality and art that brought it to life. By this time, Cahan's naturalistic realism was already going beyond Howells's moralistic realism, but their shared ideas on the relation between literature and life are still unmistakable. Perhaps the clearest distinction between them in this regard is that whereas Howells's realism was largely guided by his idealism, for Cahan the reverse was true: his "idealism was always guided by his sense of the real," as stated many years later in a eulogy of Cahan by Alexander Kahn, then general manager of the *Forward.*[6]

This bond between literature and life also reflects Cahan's taste in the visual arts, which leaned heavily toward a photographic mode of reproduction on canvas. One of the painters he found most admirable in this respect was Vasili Vasilievich Vereshchagin (1842–1904), who exhibited in New York in 1888 a series of paintings on the Russo-Turkish War of 1877 that Cahan and his wife went twice to see, though they had almost no money at the time and had to depend on the tea and pastries served at the gallery for sustenance. The paintings exposed the suffering and brutality of the war in graphically realistic terms. The wounded and dying soldiers were portrayed not as heroes but as wretched human creatures, and they generated a powerful sympathetic impression in the viewers.

In Cahan's view, Vereshchagin's paintings are not simply well rendered imitations created only for the sake of stimulating pleasure. Because they cause the viewer to empathize with the suffering soldiers, they offer a powerful lesson on the value of avoiding the horrors of war. They are lifelike, to be sure, but they surpass the level of interest and appeal that imitation alone can provide by evoking an emotionally charged repugnance to nationalized violence and death (*Education,* 407).

Cahan himself drew a persuasive association in 1902, including not only Vereshchagin and Tolstoy but also Tchaikovsky: "The overwhelming seriousness and melancholy of Tolstoy is [*sic*] paralleled in the canvases of Vereshchagin and in the symphonies of Tchaikovsky" ("Mantle of Tolstoy," *Grandma,* 535). These are the qualities evident in Cahan's English fiction, especially that written through the first year or two of the new century. Afterward, his social, journalistic, and literary experience in America seems to have deepened and individualized his creative impulses, because the *Forward* virtually blossomed under his guidance and the two novels in English that he produced after the turn of the century are considerably richer and more substantial than the limited format of his shorter fiction, including *Yekl,* would allow.

Heeding Lincoln Steffens's advice that to be a first-class reporter he must probe below surfaces served Cahan well in the later novels, particularly in his psychological analysis of Levinsky. For example, Steffens sent Cahan out to write a report on a man's bloody murder of his wife, telling him to disregard the violence of the murder in favor of the story behind it. If the man loved her enough to marry her at one point, what led him to hate her enough "to cut her all to pieces"? Steffens advised Cahan on the way out, "If you can find out just what happened between that wedding and this murder, you will have a novel for yourself and a short story for me. Go on now, take your time, and get this tragedy, as a tragedy" (Steffens, 317).

With Steffens's aid, then, Cahan's attempt to promote Russian realism in America had a direct effect on the nature and quality of his fiction, at least the English stories after *Yekl,* for which he always showed more concern and took more care. As Jules Chametzky says, Cahan had a "more casual attitude towards writing in Yiddish than in English"; more tendentious in its advocacy of socialism, the Yiddish fiction shows less consideration for structure and the subtleties of characterization. These limitations, he said, confirm "the somewhat lower status he afforded Yiddish as a literary vehicle—at least in his own work" (Chametzky 1977, 107, 109–10, 112–13). Of course, heavy-handed propagandizing through fiction would necessarily undermine any attempt to achieve true realism, because everything is subordinate to the idea that gives the work its raison d'etre.

In his English fiction, however, Cahan's passion for realism was as strong as it was for socialism in the 1880s and 1890s, and, according to Hutchins Hapgood, he was not alone in this respect among the intellectuals on the East Side. To a stranger in the Jewish district, Hapgood wrote, "Love of truth . . . seems . . . the great virtue of that section of the city," however pleasant or unpleasant it may be; intellectuals there hold to the "principle that literature should be a transcript from life . . . [and] Cahan represents this feeling in its purest aspect" (Hapgood, 235).

Near the end of the century, Cahan contrasted the goal of a realist like himself with that of a "romanticist"—that is, the popular romancer's aim for escapism and sentimentality—and in doing so, he advocated the kind of literary "truth" for which both Emerson and Howells had called:

> Would that the public could gain a deeper insight into these [sweatshop] struggles than is afforded by [scornful] newspaper reports! Hidden under

an uncouth surface would be found a great deal of what constitutes the true poetry of modern life,—tragedy more heart-rending, examples of a heroism more touching, more noble, and more thrilling, than anything that the richest imagination of the romanticist can invent. While to the outside observer the struggles may appear a fruitless repetition of meaningless conflicts, they are, like the great labor movement of which they are a part, ever marching onward, ever advancing. ("Russian Jew," 135)

Cahan also noted the essential role of Judaism in the lives of the Eastern European immigrants, especially the older generation for whom the *Yidishkayt* of the shtetl had provided a pattern of cultural existence that guided their daily behavior. In America, many of them retained of it what they could; even under vastly different circumstances, Cahan observed, the strong ties of their Hebraic traditions helped them sustain their faith. He emphasized the relation of historical piety to the daily pressures of East Side poverty, writing that "their religion is to many of them the only thing which makes life worth living. In the fervor of prayer or the abandon of religious study they forget the grinding poverty of their homes" ("Russian Jew," 138).

A little more than a decade later, the novelist Ernest Poole represented Cahan in the title of an *Outlook* article as a journalist and socialist rather than a novelist. He concludes, however, with one of Cahan's sharpest statements as the outspoken critical realist he was. Cahan sarcastically complains that most American novels of his day "smell of rouge and powder. . . . they're a literature of stunts and phrasemongery," and although American businessmen are

the shrewdest men on earth, with a deep, keen understanding of human nature *as it is* . . . [they] delight in plays and novels whose authors apparently have not the slightest idea of human nature. They give you cant and cheap sentimentality, burlesque and the most ridiculous plots. This is not fiction: it is mere fake! . . . Is it not a time for sincerity here? Will it not be well for this Nation if strong, new, American writers arise who will dare to give us life—*real life,* with its comedy and its tragedy mingled—giving us what in my Russian day we called the *thrill of truth?*[27]

This conjunction of poetry and fiction in Cahan's statements, and of romanticism and realism, may appear anomalous—they seem too glaringly different to represent the same literature and the same mode of life. Different they may be, but they are not necessarily conflicting. It is more helpful—and accurate—to see these terms in the present context

as contrasting rather than contrary, more complementary than opposi-
tional. Indeed, at times late in the nineteenth century their meanings
even appear to be reversed. An attempt to explain this semantic ambiguity occurs in a theater review in the *Century* by Emma Lazarus, the
first major Jewish-American poet; published within days of Cahan's
scornful anti-Romanov article in the *New York World* (28 May 1883), it
includes one of her most pertinent comments on realism. Of special
interest is her seemingly paradoxical association of *realistic* with *romantic,*
though immediately after juxtaposing the two words, she explains her
usage with reference to Ludwig Barnay's art:

> [It] belongs to the romantic, realistic school, as opposed to the classic
> and antique. I use, advisedly, the apparently contradictory terms
> "romantic" and "realistic," for the great romantic revival initiated in lit-
> erature by Rousseau and his followers, and developed by Goethe, Byron,
> Scott, and all the poets of the eighteenth [nineteenth?] century, was but
> the protest of truth, nature, and realism, against cant in morals and the
> artificial in art. By the singular effect of a violent reaction, romanticism
> to-day in its turn has come to signify the very antithesis of truth and real-
> ity. But this interpretation is only a passing accident resulting from the
> extreme point to which the movement was carried, and does not alter the
> fact that the best art may be at the same time very romantic and very
> real.[8]

For this reason, it is not ill-advised to consider the romance that often
glimmers both in the optimistic, idealistic core and on the sentimental
surface of realistic fiction, especially by Cahan and his contemporary
Jewish-American authors, even while focusing on the dark, hard details
of the commonplace in a world of pushcarts and tenements. In fact,
application of the distinguishing terms themselves—*romance* and
realism—is often not at all clear. Not only ambiguous, they are inter-
changeable at times according to individual usage.

To this point Cahan has been presented as if he existed in the United
States largely within a literary vacuum, surrounded by socialist intellectuals and journalists, theorizing on realism with little support or reac-
tion from other American authors. Of course, nothing could be further
from the truth. In both Yiddish and English he commented on authors
of literature in all genres, Gentiles and Jews alike, though his sharpest
criticism was addressed to fellow immigrants on the East Side. For those
whose work corresponded with his views, however, he was gentle and
accommodating.

While with the *Advertiser,* for example, he reported on a gathering early in 1899 at the Nineteenth Century Club, where Hamlin Garland and Israel Zangwill discussed the novel. Zangwill "spoke as an unqualified realist," pointing out that the novel takes all into its sphere and injects it with life. Cahan then quotes Garland at length in explaining that while a novel must have a specific setting, it need also be in spirit national or international. Moreover, it must be based on life, and the artist must be "true to his own angle of vision. . . . Life is the model, truth the master, and the heart of the artist the motive for work" ("Novelists on the Novel," *CA,* 24 February 1899, 7; *Grandma,* 513, 516). Heavily Emersonian in both thought and language, Garland nevertheless here professes part of the gospel of American literary realism in full accord with Howells and Cahan himself. In a *Forum* review from the same month, Cahan praises Zangwill's *Children of the Ghetto* for its "pulsating bits of life." Showing the old Talmudic Jewish world disintegrating under modernity, "[i]t is a breathing throbbing picture of a social phenomenon instinct with historical as well as dramatic interest" (Rischin 1953, 27).

Cahan's attraction to "dramatic interest" not only in fiction but no less powerfully in the theater extended back to his student days in Vilna. He had "a passion for the theater" there, but even then he liked only those few actors who delivered their lines naturally. At one point he complained to his friends that a popular actor declaimed instead of speaking from life, but his friends disagreed with his criterion of quality and said that one should not expect actors to speak as people do on the street (*Education,* 138, 277). Cahan was to find that the popular views regarding American theater corresponded more closely with that of his friends than his own. Nevertheless, he held that the plays themselves should be equally realistic to provide a viable vehicle for actors to speak and move naturally on stage.

With this in mind, one must seek beyond the issue of realism to apprehend the source of his hostility to Jacob Gordin, one of the principal dramatists of the New York Yiddish theater in the 1890s and early 1900s. During that period Cahan's criticism of his plays was increasingly biting and personal. Gordin did not write his first play until after he had emigrated from Russia in 1891, and he was altogether unfamiliar with the usual features of the Yiddish theater in New York. Whereas the Yiddish stage at this time was traditionally supported with music and given to ad-libbing, Gordin's first play had little music, used straightforward dialogue extensively, and had no provision for spontaneity. Consequently, the audience at first was bored and disappointed, though the play was ultimately a success. Cahan recognized genuine merit in this work and responded favorably at first but with qualifications, and he remained uncertain of Gordin's quality as a playwright through the 1890s (Sanders, 306–8).

Yet Gordin's aesthetic values were similar to Cahan's: he advocated realism and found a virtue in didacticism. As "The greatest educational institution in the world, . . . the theatre socializes great ideas," says Gordin. "The *realism* of a literary work," he emphasizes—clearly paralleling Taine's theory—analyzes social types and characters. For him, "realism" meant that the play was to "deal with the lives and problems of 'ordinary Jews,'" be those problems familial, economic, cultural, or whatever (Howe, 469n, 474).

In 1915 A. H. Fromenson praised Gordin for "produc[ing] living, breathing entities," but he also complained that the playwright's "main faults are his stubbornly mistaken conception of 'realism' and his persistent exposures of phases of life which are better left unrevealed."[9] This, of course, is the criticism that the American naturalists faced early in the century from the initially aborted publication in 1900 of Dreiser's *Sister Carrie* on, and Cahan had already addressed such critiques in an article called "The Yiddish Theater and American Novels," which had been published in the *Arbeter tsaytung* several years earlier. He complains there about the "rectitude" and "false modesty" pervading American literature, professing that if literature is to be true to life, "the dark parts" must accompany "the light," including the sex and class warfare that he observed in contemporary French writing (Chametzky 1977, 39–40).

Acknowledging that the issue of realism was not the major source of alienation between Cahan and Gordin, Sanders plausibly suggests that the antipathy between them was apparently more personal than professional. Moreover, both were sensitive and stubborn enough to antagonize each other rather than truly attempt to come to terms. Cahan's vehement critical attacks and well-supported charges of plagiarism made the playwright's last year of life a miserable one by exacerbating the suffering and weakness brought on by the cancer that finally killed him early in 1909 (Sanders, 301–26, 387–90).

Cahan's role as a writer and spokesman for the American Jews, especially the Eastern European immigrants who accompanied him in the last two decades of the nineteenth century and the first two of the twentieth, suggests that his perspective on American life and literature differed significantly from that of such contemporary native realists as

Howells, Twain, James, and the local colorists. Inevitably, his immersion in the culture of the Lower East Side as a Yiddish-speaking socialist, journalist, drama critic, and fiction writer gave him access to attitudes and materials that were generally inaccessible to Gentile American authors. For this reason, it may be helpful to distinguish Cahan and other Jewish-American authors of the period from the mainstream of American literary realism and consider them more specifically as a sub-group within it, under the heading of Jewish-American realism.[10]

But one must not overemphasize the differences either, because the correspondences between Cahan and the American-born realists were more crucial. Howells noted them immediately and predicted that this Russian Jew with imagination, literary interests, and polyglot skills could herald the addition of a vital new component to American realism; still more important, he did what he could to support Cahan's English fiction. It was only with Howells's help that Cahan published, after considerable frustration and effort, his first English novel, *Yekl, A Tale of the New York Ghetto,* in the middle of 1896. By then he had already brought out his first Yiddish novel, *Rafael naritsokh Became a Socialist.* A long didactic work about a simple immigrant carpenter who learns about socialism and becomes a proselyte, it was published separately in 1894 after being serialized in the *Arbeter tsaytung* earlier that year, Cahan's last one there as editor. Jules Chametzky notes that the carpenter's "nickname 'Naarizokh' comes from the name of a portion of the Sabbath service that he continually hums and sings while engrossed in his work" (Chametzky 1977, 44), but his initial simplicity is also phonically implied by the first syllable, because in Yiddish a *nar* is a foolish person. Eventually, as the title suggests, the light of socialism shines through his density, and he awakens into a new life.

According to Chametzky, Cahan's aim with this tendentious work was not chiefly to tell a story but to promote socialism to his readers; it was, after all, first published in a socialist newspaper. Though Cahan's intention was didactic, the novel met with wide favor, partly because he used the common Yiddish vernacular peppered with the Americanizations his readers themselves often employed in conversation. After serialization, the novel was brought out in book form with the subtitle *A Carpenter Who Came to His Senses;* it went through six revised editions, the last appearing in 1917. Cahan said that the Russian version gave Jewish socialists overseas the clearest picture of American life (Chametzky 1977, 44; 150n1ch3). In the broad context of Cahan's career, the principal importance of *Rafael naritsokh* is that through writing it and seeing it widely accepted, he confirmed his ability to compose an extended work of fiction and gained the confidence he needed to execute the same task in English.

Yekl, Cahan's First Novel in English

The nature of Cahan's topic in *Yekl*—the problematic Americanization of Russian-Jewish immigrants amid the pressures of the Lower East Side—actually made it less of a struggle for him to write the novel in English than to publish it. Why? Publishers did not believe that most of their readers would be interested in fiction dealing only with East Side Jews, the sordid ghetto environment, and unhappy endings. For example, after his manuscript was rejected by *McClure's Magazine,* one of the most popular contemporary serials of the day, Cahan confronted the editor directly and asked why. He was told that the novel was only about Jews, and nothing beautiful was in it. Cahan asked if literary truth and nobility of soul inhered only in "beautiful things," but the editor, knowing his reading audience, held firm (Sanders, 201–2; Kirk, 35–37).

Cahan had not expected that problem, though Howells had cautioned him about it; consequently, he found the situation so difficult to face that late in 1895 he elected paradoxically to translate the work into Yiddish and serialize it in the *tsaytung* rather than sustain the search for an American publisher. Howells, however, equally distressed over the dilemma, continued pressing for publication in English and finally succeeded with D. Appleton and Company, the firm that brought out Stephen Crane's *The Red Badge of Courage* only two weeks before *Yekl* began appearing in the *tsaytung* on 18 October under Cahan's pseudonym "Sotsyus" and the title *Yankel the Yankee.* It ran through 31 January and was "a resounding success" (Pollock, 206–7). Howells said the Yiddish printing would not affect production of the book in English.

Published in July 1896 as *Yekl, A Tale of the New York Ghetto,* the English version has become recognized as "the first novel . . . *by* an immigrant wholly about the immigrant experience" (Chametzky 1977, 57). In contrast to *Rafael naritsokh,* socialism is barely evident in *Yekl,* which is driven by a combination of character development and personality conflict as individuals struggle for their freedom in America between the imposing environmental forces of the East Side and the suppressed voices of their European past. This novel, which Howells lauded for its realism,[11] offers a graphic illustration of the gains to be enjoyed and the losses to be suffered through the rapid process of Americanization. As the central figure learns, the price of assimilation can be high.

A Free Spirit in the New World

After immigrating to America from Povodye, a shtetl in northwestern Russia, Yekl Podkovnik changes his name to Jake and takes a job in a sweatshop; he rapidly becomes secularized and detached from his homeland and family, though he sends a monthly "allowance" to his wife and child. By the end of his third year in the New World, everything and everyone in Russia seem nothing more to him than parts of "a charming tale, which he [is] neither willing to banish from his memory nor able to reconcile with the actualities of his American present."[12] But when he learns of his father's death, a reconciliation must be attempted. His wife, Gitl, comes to America with their three-and-a-half-year-old son in her arms, and Jake sees immediately that he no longer has anything in common with the typically disheveled, unsophisticated "greenhorn" who has just stepped off the ship. Compatibility with her is impossible, and Jake, in his arrogance and pride, longing for the uninhibited bachelor's life he had been enjoying, continues to sink into a well of despair until he begins to wish for her death. Finally he turns for divorce money to Mamie Fein, a voluptuous Polish Jew he had met in the dance hall they frequented, and she elicits from him a promise to marry her in exchange for the necessary cash. He realizes too late that he has made a bad bargain.

Meanwhile, although Gitl tries gamely to become a "Yankee" like her husband, her first efforts are futile. Bewildered and panicked, she turns for help to a childless, middle-aged neighbor, Mrs. Kavarsky, a sympathetic, sharp-tongued woman who assumes responsibility for reconciling the alienated young couple. It is more than she can accomplish. As Jake's anger and hostility increase, however, the passing time has benign effects on Gitl, for the subtle process of Americanization commences. Moreover, Jake's lost affection is supplanted by that of his scholarly coworker, Bernstein, who has been boarding with them. By the time Jake buys his divorce, Gitl is nearly as much an independent American as he, though she has not been secularized, and her future with Bernstein is far more promising than his. Jake, on the other hand, is locked into a stultifying relationship with Mamie, whose domineering personality will give her full control over him and their marriage. For good and for bad, American acculturation has done its work by enabling the immigrants to draw on their strengths or succumb to their frailties. In the case of Gitl and Jake, ultimately she proves to be quieter but stronger, whereas her brash, egocentric husband is victimized by his own shortsightedness.

The Realism of *Yekl*

One can readily see why Howells was immediately attracted to the manuscript of *Yekl,* which emphasizes realistic character development and representation of circumstance, including the East Side setting. The novel opens with a description of a cloakmaker's sweatshop; the contractor-owner is out, and the workers are lounging, waiting for bundles of cloth to be brought in and distributed among them. Each of the workers is briefly portrayed before Yekl—now Jake the Yankee—is introduced. A Jewish immigrant of twenty-five, he passed the first two of his three years as a "Yankee" in Boston. Having become adept as a tailor making men's pants, he has moved to a cloakmaker's shop in New York, where he can earn better money because cloaks are more remunerative, and he is already a fast worker on his Singer. Young, strong, attractive to the unmarried women in the shop and neighborhood, and cocksure of himself, Jake is a purported Mike Fink[13] of the sweatshops, flexing his biceps, taunting his competitors, boasting of his abilities, and showing off his two daunting American acquisitions—a quasi-familiarity with professional athletics and a command of heavily accented English.

As a professed "Yankee," he assertively reiterates, *"Dot'sh a' kin' a man I am!,"* an American, in a country where "a Jew is as good as a Gentile" (*Y&IB,* 5). Although his attitude may strike readers as arrogant, Edward Shapiro observes that it was far from uncommon. "From the beginning," he says, "Jews sought to demonstrate that they were 100-percent Americans, and that, at least as far as they were concerned, the travail of the wandering homeless Jew was over."[14] But Jake's inflated ego is at work here, not his Jewish sensibility. Time and again he offers "to bet" with opponents to make his point. In the shop his audacity and braggadocio nearly engender violence with a coworker, but the contractor returns with bundles of cloth ready to be tailored into cloaks, and the quick knowledge that in the sweatshop time wasted is money lost cools the tempers. Jake takes one of the largest bundles and sits down at his Singer.

He operates the machine almost unconsciously, and with its rhythmic stitching sounds, his mind drifts from the work at hand to his family in Povodye: his grieving parents, his sweet wife, and his infant son. None of Jake's acquaintances in New York know that he is a married man with a child in the Old Country, and he persistently swears to himself that he will send for Gitl and little Yosselé as soon as he can save enough money for tickets, but no sooner does he leave the shop than he wanders as if against his will to "Professor" Joe Peltner's dancing academy on Suffolk Street in the heart of the East Side Jewish district. A center of attention there among the ladies and gentlemen alike, Jake dominates the floor; his dancing partners are envied, and his instructions are heeded as if he himself were the owner. The Wednesday evening on which the novel opens is no different from others. He tells his coworker Fanny Scutelsky, a talkative "milk-faced blonde" obviously infatuated with him, that he will not go to the academy, but he rationalizes and soon finds himself amid "the waltzing swarm" (*Y&IB,* 4, 15).

The intensity of Cahan's realistic description is nowhere more apparent in *Yekl* than in his exposure of the neighborhood squalor as Jake works his way through the filthy, crowded streets of the East Side on his way to the dance hall:

> He had to pick and nudge his way through dense swarms of bedraggled half-naked humanity; past garbage barrels rearing their overflowing contents in sickening piles, and lining the streets in malicious suggestion of rows of trees; underneath tiers and tiers of fire escapes, barricaded and festooned with mattresses, pillows, and featherbeds not yet gathered in for the night. The pent-in sultry atmosphere was laden with nausea and pierced with a discordant and, as it were, plaintive buzz. Supper had been despatched in a hurry, and the teeming populations of the cyclopic tenement houses were out in full force "for fresh air," as even these people will say in mental quotation marks. (*Y&IB,* 13)

He describes Suffolk Street itself as situated "in the very thick of the battle for breath. . . . It is one of the most densely populated spots on the face of the earth—a seething human sea fed by streams, streamlets, and rills of immigration flowing from all the Yiddish-speaking centers of Europe" (*Y&IB,* 13–14).

Mamie Fein is one of Jake's constant partners among the "damp-haired, dishevelled, reeking crowd" (*Y&IB,* 15) at the dancing academy—and elsewhere. She has been in America longer than Jake; her English is better, her greater sophistication and cleverness evident. She contrasts sharply with Fanny in appearance and behavior, yet they are equally attracted to Jake, and the narrative implies that he has had intimacies with both. Neither, of course, knows that he is a family man, each one seeing him less as an ordinary suitor than a potential husband, a strong, clever worker likely to bring in a comfortable income.

Most unmarried young women on the East Side were eager to find capable, willing, and reliable spouses, husbands similarly interested in beginning a family and rearing children. Of course, they were free to work as necessary to earn their own living and assist in providing for their parents and siblings, but marriage and a family of their own were solid indications of respectability as well as a means of vital economic, social, and psychological support under the most trying circumstances on the East Side. Therefore, when Jake turns to Mamie, it is easy to understand Fanny's bitterness; and when Mamie herself learns of his wife and child soon after their arrival, her quiet outrage over being deceived is equally comprehensible.

Jake is obliged to send for Gitl and Yosselé when informed of his father's death by the scribe who reads and writes his correspondence. Like his father, a blacksmith, Jake can neither read nor write Yiddish, a liability that Gitl shares. As a youth in Russia he had religious leanings and attended a *kheyder;* when he wed and Gitl bore a son, the small family was elated, anticipating a life of favor ahead. But the restrictions and anti-Semitic hostility of the czarist government made it impossible for the old smithy to sustain them all, so Jake emigrated for the Golden Land, expecting to send soon for his wife and child. Three years later, under the shadow of his father's death, Jake briefly reverts to prayer, but the words are no longer familiar to him; moreover, he cannot weep because he remains preoccupied with his present affairs. His three years in America have made him a new man in conformity with his new name, but neither a better nor a happier one now that his days of irresponsible pleasures have ended.

Gitl and Yosselé arrive at Ellis Island in one of the most dramatic scenes of the novel, a climactic one, though it occurs as early as chapter 4. During the past three years, Jake has allowed his imagination to flower with romantic pictures of an idealized Gitl. Consciously, he is well aware of her minor physical imperfections—her wide mouth, prominent gums, and little black eyes—but he dismisses them from his thoughts, preferring to believe they are negligible in contrast to the "individual sweetness of her rustic face" (*Y&IB,* 31). On his way to Ellis Island, dressed stylishly and looking even younger than his twenty-five years, Jake is "in a flurry of joyous anticipation" over seeing again "his dear wife and child" (*Y&IB,* 33).

He is nearly overcome with disgust, however, when he first glimpses her within the fenced-in immigrant pen. He turns away, delaying their actual meeting until he no longer has a choice. Disheveled from her long trip in steerage across the Atlantic, and wearing a conspicuous black wig because of the traditional Jewish restriction against a married woman's showing her hair in public, Gitl is far from the materialization of his fancy. Not only does Jake find her repulsive in appearance, but when he finally embraces and kisses her he is offended "by the strong steerage odors which were emitted by Gitl's person" (*Y&IB*, 35), as the narrator gently phrases it. The difference between this stout, bewigged immigrant and her handsome, modish young escort is so glaring to the amused immigration officer that he cannot be certain the couple are really man and wife, so he insists on interrogating Jake before releasing Gitl. Jake immediately upbraids the bewildered woman for her unfashionable appearance and ignorance of American ways, whereupon little Yosselé in her arms reacts angrily to the father he has never known. Finally, Jake's "illusion took wing and here he was, Jake the Yankee, with this bonnetless, wigged, dowdyish little greenhorn by his side!" (*Y&IB*, 36). The scene has its comic aspects, to be sure, but on the whole it is a dreadful confrontation of hard realities with anticipated dreams.

Transformations

From that turning point on, Jake loses control of his life and future. He cannot reconcile himself to Gitl, who in her lingering but diminishing Old World naivete becomes more distasteful and oppressive to him with each passing day. He is an intolerant, uncompassionate egotist who considers himself a free American insusceptible to Old Country restraints, including Gitl, though he remains ambivalent to the end over his son, whose name he Anglicizes to Joey and whom he finally loses. Meanwhile, as he continues to see Mamie, Fanny Scutelsky, feeling jealous and betrayed, visits Gitl to inform her of Jake's infidelity. Stunned, Gitl turns again to Mrs. Kavarsky for help, but her well-meaning neighbor's efforts are fruitless.

By the time Jake is actually preparing to seek a divorce, Gitl's "rustic, 'greenhornlike' expression was completely gone from her face and manner, and . . . there was noticeable about her a suggestion of that peculiar air of self-confidence with which a few months' life in America is sure to stamp the looks and bearing of every immigrant" (*Y&IB*, 83). All along, Gitl has hated and feared to be rebuked by her overbearing husband as an ignorant "greenhorn": "Better she had never known this 'black year' of a country . . . [where] everybody says she is green" (*Y&IB*, 42). "Really, a curse upon Columbus!" she cries to Mrs. Kavarsky, earnestly echoing what Cahan says was "a current joke of the Ghetto" (*Y&IB*, 66).

Yet, however despicable she seems to Jake, she radiates a subtle appeal to her scholarly boarder, Bernstein. On one occasion she inadvertently interrupts his reading, and when he raises his head "his eyes [are] on Gitl's plumpish cheek, bathed in the roseate light" (Y&IB, 53). The compression of this novel is strikingly evident when one realizes that only a single chapter separates this suggestive scene from the traumatic one of her meeting Jake at Ellis Island.

Bernstein is one of several secondary figures in Yekl who appear partly as foils but also in their own light. Despite the compactness of the novel, Cahan has given each of these characters a modicum of individuality, though each may also be taken as representative of a type. Yet because they have distinctive features, Yekl has more depth than might be expected of a short work that highlights a limited group of immigrants in a highly specific locale. Were this not true, Yekl could simply be categorized as an urban local-color novel, but it is, in fact, considerably more than that by virtue of individualized if not fully developed characters as well as an expansive theme.

Like Gitl, Bernstein is also victimized by her husband's taunting, though his education commands Jake's respect, and the sarcasm is never carried too far. Scholarly and meditative, Bernstein is a lonely man who longs for a compatible wife but is not attracted to the raucous, coarse working women around him. He is sensitive to Jake's abuse of Gitl, but though her sweet domesticity appeals to him, he does not acknowledge it; instead, he attempts to ease her pain by rationalizing that her husband remains in love with her but, under the pressures of work and change, behaves badly at times. How could Jake not love her, Bernstein asks, obviously smitten himself: "Why, are you not a pretty young woman?" (Y&IB, 54). Gitl, of course, a traditional and provincial young Jewish wife, is discreet about receiving such personal compliments from a man other than her husband, but his kind remarks about her attractiveness should make a reader question Jake's harsh observations from the time he first sees her at Ellis Island. She apparently is a "pretty young woman" once her clothes are changed and the effects of her many days in steerage have been slept and washed away.

Moreover, Gitl wishes to believe Bernstein about her husband's true feelings toward her, but Jake's outrageous verbal attacks often threaten violence, and despite her efforts to appease him by succumbing completely to his will, his irrational responses leave her weeping and defenseless. Finally, when Jake insists on a divorce, Gitl sees little choice; no longer a naive greenhorn by then, she shrewdly demands from Jake all the money that Mamie, his new "predestined match" (*Y&IB*, 82), will give him to purchase his freedom, and Bernstein quietly awaits her return with little Joey, when his own dream of a loving family will be realized.

Mamie's Complexity

Mamie, too, is more than an aggressive, sexually alluring Jewish woman, though these qualities are certainly hers. Affecting a hypermasculine disposition in her presence on the dance floor, Jake is nonetheless intimidated by her. After she unwittingly lends him $25 for furnishings to accommodate his wife and child when they arrive, Mamie gains complete control over him. When she appears at his front door in outlandish queenly garb—"resplendent in a waist of blazing red, gaudily trimmed, and with puff sleeves, . . . surmounted with a whole forest of ostrich feathers, which adorned her head" (*Y&IB*, 49)—Jake is no less stunned than Gitl is bewildered. To Gitl she looks like a noblewoman, and Jake knows well that she has come to twist him, wring him tightly, and humiliate him before his uncomprehending wife in the process of regaining the money she has lent him. Jake pleads with her, begs her to speak in Yiddish rather than English so that Gitl will understand them and not assume they are plotting behind her back. Mamie has total control over Jake from that time forward, though his increasing subservience to her leads to his commensurately hostile treatment of his terrified wife.

But Cahan does not portray Mamie as simply a domineering shrew, either. The cash she lends Jake has been taken from her savings of more than $350, money that has been put away from years of tailoring in a shirtwaist shop, and as a woman her pay was probably no more than half of the $12 Jake was earning weekly. Although her color and audacity make her appear hard-featured, at times her portrait suggests domesticity. For example, after finishing work on the day after her dramatic visit to his flat, Jake goes to Mamie's apartment instead of his own and "found her with her landlady in the kitchen. She looked careworn and was in a white blouse which lent her face a convalescent, touching effect" (*Y&IB*, 59). This is the picture of Mamie that often returns to him as his distress over Gitl increases.

This "touching" whiteness contrasts sharply with the ominous white sheets wafting around them later, during their tryst on the roof of her tenement. As she and Jake plan their future together, she seals their illicit bond with a passionate kiss, telling him that he can no longer back out of his commitment to her, though she is well aware of her role in destroying his little family: "'Am I to blame?' she continued with ghastly vehemence, sobs ringing in her voice. 'Who asked you to come? Did I lure you from her, then? I should sooner have thrown myself into the river than taken away somebody else's husband. You say yourself that you would not live with her, *anyvay*. But now it is all gone. Just try to leave me now!' And giving vent to her tears, she added, 'Do you think my heart is no heart?'" (*Y&IB*, 78).

With these remarks and her portrait in the kitchen suggesting convalescence, Mamie surely gains the reader's sympathy as a deeply troubled woman. She has lost her youth, she has worked hard for the money she has saved, she has fallen for Jake ignorant of his marriage and child, and the presence of her active conscience is unmistakable. Nevertheless, the dark side of her ambiguous character is emphasized, for Cahan's earlier depiction of her in the same scene lingers, and there she more resembles a contemporary manifestation of Lilith than a clever, sensual working woman. When Jake swears that he has always cared for her, "A flood of wan light struck Mamie full in her swarthy face, suffusing it with ivory effulgence, out of which her deep dark eyes gleamed with a kind of unearthly luster" (*Y&IB*, 76). Here the portrait is almost demonic, a presentation in keeping with the setting itself.

Their passionate meeting occurs at night, and the tenement roof is festooned with drying sheets and pillowcases that flutter around them with the breeze. A memory of the distant past seems to have been revitalized in Cahan's imagination; as a child he had ridden with his mother from their shtetl to Vilna, and as he drafted these passages of *Yekl*, he must have recalled the many gallows he had seen against the horizon as they rode past, the bodies wrapped in sheets and moving with the wind (*Education*, 4). The eerie surrealistic effect complements the dreadful situation in which the two characters find themselves, inexorably driven by passion toward the destruction of one sanctified bond and the execution of another.

Here the situation recalls several of Nathaniel Hawthorne's most dramatic scenes in which the dark heroine—Hester (*The Scarlet Letter*), Zenobia (*The Blithedale Romance*), Miriam (*The Marble Faun*)—is engaged with an impassioned hero, and destruction follows. Theodore Marvin Pollock notes that during the early 1890s, when Cahan was editing the *Arbeter tsaytung,* he was reading Hawthorne as well as Howells, James, and others (194). Moreover, having discussed literature at length with

Howells before the composition of *Yekl,* Cahan was probably familiar with these romances as well as much of Hawthorne's other fiction because Howells considered his predecessor a master, and Cahan surely knew it.

Language and Style

To a large extent, Cahan's assimilation of stylistic contrasts in the narrative is complemented by his manipulation of the Yiddish vernacular and "Yinglish," Leo Rosten's popular term for the adaptation of American English into Yiddish. (Later the process would be reversed, and Yiddish adapted into English—as with bagel, schlemiel, nosh, and chutzpa, for a few examples.) He well knew that the acquisition of language was a primary stage in the acculturation of a people, and to foster the process of Jewish assimilation, he did all that he could to promote the learning of English by the recent immigrants from Eastern Europe.

According to Elsa Nettels, in *Yekl* "language is as important to [defining] the characters as in any work of fiction Howells reviewed."[15] Some heavily accented English is usual in *Yekl,* but for the most part the dialogue throughout the novel occurs in Yiddish—the only language in general use among Jews on the Lower East Side—though Cahan rendered it as a combination of Yiddish and English. Jules Chametzky describes the "fractured English" of the characters as "comic when it is not grotesque" (Chametzky 1977, 63), which it often is, particularly as spoken by Mrs. Kavarsky, with her rich store of pictorial curses. Bernstein's rabbinical studiousness, in contrast, calls for no such pidgin terms as those expressed by most of the other characters; instead, his articulate Yiddish, presented in English, reflects his intelligence and thoughtfulness.

Cahan's method in *Yekl* recalls that of James Russell Lowell in *The Biglow Papers* and of T. B. Thorpe, A. B. Longstreet, and other story writers of the early Southwest, including Howells's good friend Mark Twain, all of whom gave their accounts in highly polished and sophisticated English while the local characters they "quoted" spoke in the regional vernacular. Thus the sharp contrast between narrators and participants is immediately evident and the source of comic irony—once the reader has penetrated the difficult orthography necessary to transcribe the peculiar variants—strikingly effective.

Jake's English is coarse and vulgar, and Gitl's is nonexistent until he repeats the first few words to her soon after leaving Ellis Island. Mamie's English, like that of most of the women among the dancers, is more fluent than Jake's and that of his male coworkers; her pretentious Yiddish, too, reflects a broader background. That Cahan had an acute ear for language has already been stated, and in *Yekl* this facility is quite clear when he describes Mamie's vernacular: "She spoke with an overdone American accent in the dialect of the Polish Jews, affectedly Germanized and profusely interspersed with English, so that Gitl, whose mother tongue was Lithuanian Yiddish, could scarcely catch the meaning of one half of her flood of garrulity" (*Y&IB,* 49–50). Cahan distinguishes between her speech and Jake's "Boston Yiddish," which is "more copiously spiced with mutilated English than is the language of the [New York] Ghetto" (*Y&IB,* 2). The sensitivity to language that Cahan acquired largely from his father, together with his determined attention to pronunciation as he struggled first to acquire perfect fluency in Russian, then in English, left their clear traces in the linguistic distinctions detailed in *Yekl,* where they add not simply to the local-color interest of the novel but also to the definition of character and the assimilationist theme.

The Americanization Theme

Read chiefly as a fictional account of the struggle between the two central characters, most of *Yekl* describes Jake's frustration over living with Gitl and his longing to regain his freedom. Because his internal tension is high, his pattern of behavior comprises an erratic series of suppressions and releases of emotion that keeps him psychologically off balance and ultimately brings him to resignation and despair. Gitl's pattern, on the other hand, is more complex, because even as her despondency increases over Jake's brutal treatment from his first sight of her in the immigration hall, she rapidly becomes Americanized and commensurately independent. From the confrontational meeting at Ellis Island, she appears increasingly destined for failure and grief, but in reality her promise of success and happiness is continually gaining strength. Consequently, at the end of the novel, Jake foresees a bleak future beneath the eye of an overpowering spouse, whereas Gitl anticipates a life of fulfillment with the soft-spoken scholar who loves her.

Both are the subjects and products of Americanization in that America gives them the opportunity to live and develop according to their individual inclinations. Ronald Sanders proposes that the "corrupting force" seems to be "not specifically the dollar . . . [but] . . . nothing less than America itself, or at any rate some vision of America that captures the souls of immigrants like Jake and Mamie" (Sanders, 200). Similarly,

David M. Fine suggests that by rejecting traditional Judaism, Jake has "sold his birthright for a distorted version of Americanization" (54).

Of course, a good deal of difference exists between America itself and one person's vision or version of it, for the first is external to the viewer and the latter is an individualized conception. Jake has been corrupted by his own perverted leanings in a country that permits him the freedom to follow them. Mamie works, saves, and acquires what she wishes by virtue of her own initiative, which American freedom allows her to follow—something impossible for her as a Jew in her native Poland—and her coming between Jake and his family occurs not intentionally on her part but as a consequence of his deception. As for Gitl, she and Bernstein seem to be on their way to happiness and probably prosperity by virtue of realizing the American Dream as many immigrants before them had conceived it.

But to consider the novel by focusing chiefly on the two principals is to reduce it to little more than an amusing turn-of-the-century situation comedy about Jewish immigrants on the East Side. Instead, its joint theme of alienation and assimilation in America predominates over both character and setting, despite the graphic detail with which these are presented. Cahan's novel corresponds with the best of Howells's in this respect, for in the latter's fiction, too, the moral issue predominates. In the work of both authors, the novels are memorable chiefly because of the characters and the circumstances they confront, but the universal relevance of the fiction inheres in the developing theme. In Howells, for example, it may be the moral rise of Silas Lapham or the belated compassion of Jacob Dryfoos (*A Hazard of New Fortunes*), both of which illustrate the author's fundamentally benign view of life. In *Yekl*, Cahan offers no suggestion of transcendent morality, but he does convey a strong sense of the intrinsic promise that Americanization can fulfill, which he expresses through the developing self-reliance of Gitl and the germination of her new association with the caring, responsible Bernstein—two new Americans in the Golden Land.

Critical Reception

The critical reception of *Yekl* was far from uniform, for the "Realism War" was much in evidence among the reviewers. Howells, instrumental in its publication, praised the novel enthusiastically in a full-page joint review with Stephen Crane's *George's Mother* in the *New York World* (26 July 1896), giving most of his attention to *Yekl*. Probably even more exciting to Cahan than the laudatory remarks about the novel was Howells's decision to distinguish him in a special acclamation printed between the byline and the text as "a New Star of Realism," adding that "He and Stephen Crane Have Drawn the Truest Pictures of East Side Life." Coming from Howells especially, this was a magnificent tribute to the immigrant novelist, and his comments in that important review warrant close attention.

In comparing *Yekl* with *George's Mother,* Howells says that Cahan's "picturesque, outlandish material . . . makes a stronger appeal to the reader's fancy" than Crane's, and Cahan "has more humor than the American, too." Howells makes a striking distinction in this statement between Cahan as the Russian immigrant and Crane as "the American," though Cahan had by then been living in the United States for fourteen years. Elsa Nettels finds this implicit process of differentiation to be characteristic of Howells's writing, however, rather than unique in his treatment of Cahan. She points out that although Howells often wrote of the common spirit that unites all Americans despite their ethnic and regional differences, he also emphasized such distinctions in his writing, implying that they alienated Americans of other backgrounds from those of British heritage (Nettels, 100–102).

Howells himself was continually on the alert for the "picturesque" when wandering through unfamiliar neighborhoods, especially those of the lower classes, because he perceived dramatic possibilities there. Born in Ohio, with Welsh blood from his father and strains of Irish and Pennsylvania Dutch from his mother, he was an honest, compassionate man who experienced his due share of personal suffering, yet one rarely feels a true sense of empathy between him as author and those sympathetic, ethnically different, characters he often portrays among the picturesque. Cahan here constitutes an excellent case in point, for Howells introduces him as "a writer of foreign birth [hence not a real American like Crane] who will do honor to American letters. . . . He is already thoroughly naturalized to our point of view; he sees things with American eyes, and he brings in aid of his vision the far and rich perceptions of his Hebraic race, while he is strictly of the great and true Russian principle in literary art." Moreover, directing attention to Cahan's English, Howells says: "In its simplicity and its purity, as the English of a man born to write Russian, it is simply marvelous." In this portrait Cahan himself stands as a living symbol of acculturation and assimilation, whether a true American or not in Howells's eyes.

An anonymous reviewer for the *New York Times* was no less enthusiastic than Howells over Cahan's representation of reality and character on the Lower East Side, which he says should unveil a way of life that is virtually unknown among people who do not live there, not even those in neighboring communities. The "charm, the verity, the literary value of the book depend upon its study of character, its 'local color,' its revelation to Americans of a social state at their very doors of which they have known nothing." In contrast, the reviewer continues, "The author . . . knows the Ghetto by heart, and he pictures it truthfully, without seeking for sensational effects or writing as one who is pleading a cause,"[16] implicitly comparing Cahan with the tendentious Jacob Riis.

Other contemporaries found *Yekl* equally impressive. Looking back on it in *The Spirit of the Ghetto,* for example, Hutchins Hapgood judges it as "alive from beginning to end," and he praises Cahan's writing generally for always containing the "universal element of art," that is, "the touch of common human nature" (Hapgood, 245, 237).

But the caustic realism of *Yekl* was too intense for universal admiration near the turn of the century. One of the most notorious critiques came from Nancy Huston Banks, writing for the *Bookman* in October. She complains that the characters and situations in *Yekl* are too lifelike to be appealing, the major figures too flawed to be truly representative Jews. It is evident that Banks was speaking for the large body of readers who preferred sentimentality and idealism to distasteful reality, the readers who made it so difficult for Cahan to find an English publisher for the novel that he resorted in frustration to translating it into Yiddish. Like Howells, Banks acknowledges the fluency of Cahan's English, but she criticizes it, too, for showing excessive "journalistic familiarity and too little literary reserve."[17]

Despite the occasional hostility, however, Howells's remarkable praise led to the temporary lionizing of Cahan. Soon after the Howells review was published, the Lanthorn literary club held a reception for Cahan, Crane, and Hamlin Garland. Forty to fifty people attended, and Cahan was immensely flattered. Uncharacteristically for him, he found himself at a loss for words and said almost nothing, but those present attributed his reticence to humility, and it gained him all the more favorable attention (Epstein, 79). Garland briefly describes this reception in *Roadside Meetings,* one of his four volumes of memoirs, but he does not mention Cahan.

Unfortunately, the limelight did not shine on Cahan for long at that time, nor did it lead to dramatic sales for *Yekl*. According to his autobiography, "Its effect on the book stores wore off after three weeks" (quoted in Epstein, 79). Still, an edition was published the next year by W. Heinemann in England, and a translation was published in Russia a few years later (Pollock, 291), confirming that Cahan was already gaining at least some international attention.[18]

Chapter Four

The Imported Bridegroom
and Other Short Fiction

Over his career as an author in English through 1901, Abraham Cahan had published only a short novel, a novelette, and ten stories apart from the dozens of anecdotes, sketches, and vignettes he wrote for the *New York Commercial Advertiser* during the little over four years he was with the paper. All twelve of these works came out over a period of seven years, from February 1895 to August 1901. In April 1898 his first (and then only) four short stories were collected with his most recent piece, a novelette from which the small volume received its title, *The Imported Bridegroom and Other Stories of the New York Ghetto;* it was brought out by the Boston firm of Houghton Mifflin and Company, then publisher of the *Atlantic Monthly.* This time Cahan was invited by the editor to submit a collection; no longer was it necessary for him to hunt down a publisher willing to risk bringing out fiction that dealt only or predominantly with the East Side Jews. Unlike the two stories he had published in 1895, both of which first appeared in the relatively obscure *Short Stories,* the two written after *Yekl*'s warm reception in 1896 came out in *Cosmopolitan* and the *Atlantic.* Cahan's English fiction had become marketable.

Although his stories vary considerably in situation, plot, and tone, the predominant theme in all of them is alienation, a sense of isolation from a loved one, a community, a lost way of life. With respect to the major theme, then, the stories are similar, but because the variables among them differ so distinctly, they are not repetitious. In fact, the difference is more often than not a matter of reversals. The problem of poverty in "Circumstances" leads to a disintegrating marriage, whereas the same problem in "A Ghetto Wedding" bonds a young couple as they prepare to struggle against a hostile environment. In "A Sweat-Shop Romance" a young man loses his sweetheart through timidity, whereas in "Tzinchadzi of the Catskills" the sweetheart is lost through the ardent suitor's arrogance. In "A Marriage by Proxy" a young immigrant who marries by proxy before sailing to America is alienated from her new husband as soon as she sees him in the flesh; and in "A Predestined Match," the betrothed young woman is successfully courted aboard ship as she sails to meet her "predestined" husband. In "The Apostate of Chego-Chegg" a Jewish woman converts to Christianity to wed her Polish Catholic suitor, thus alienating herself from family and community; and in "Dumitru and Sigrid" two young immigrants of different nationalities are permanently separated soon after beginning to fall for each other at Castle Garden. In "Rabbi Eliezer's Christmas," an elderly Jewish artist leaves his Old Country way of life for an impoverished existence in the ghetto; in "The Imported Bridegroom," a brilliant young Talmudist from Poland joyfully relinquishes his faith to acquire Gentile learning and a secularized American wife (a variation of the situation developed in *Yekl*); and in "The Daughter of Reb Avrom Leib" the cantor's daughter accepts an unloved older suitor after the death of her father as a sacrifice to his memory. The stories differ markedly, and each has its own virtues, but the theme of alienation predominates in all.

The Imported Bridegroom and Other Stories of the New York Ghetto

"A Providential Match"

The first of Cahan's stories in English, "A Providential Match," was the one brought to Howells's attention by his wife, Elinor, early in 1895 after she had noticed it in the February issue of *Short Stories* at a newsstand. Howells was so favorably impressed by it that he invited Cahan to visit, an occasion that quickly led to their becoming reacquainted (Sanders, 197). The version that Howells read, however, was not Cahan's first. In 1891 he had published it in Yiddish as "Mottke Arbel and His Romance" in five consecutive midyear issues of the *Arbeter tsaytung,* of which he had been editor. Between its initial publication and its appearance as "A Providential Match" some three and a half years later, a friend had introduced Cahan to Chekhov's short fiction, and, strongly affected by the Russian author's conversion of mundane reality into genuine literary art, he had become an immediate admirer of this new realist's work (Sanders, 189–90). Although the life and circumstances from which Chekhov drew for his stories were not enhanced in the fiction, his unpretentious manner of representing the ordinary in clear, simple language greatly appealed to Cahan. Rightly or wrongly, from that point on, Cahan's estimate of Chekhov's art steadily rose as his appreciation for Turgenev's fiction declined commensurately.

Despite this admiration, however, Cahan translated "Mottke Arbel" into English with minimal revision and no apparent Chekhovian influence. After comparing the two versions, Ronald Sanders found that Cahan had done only a little "tidying" up on the rather crude Yiddish original. He also observed that accompanying the English version in *Short Stories* was "a set of illustrations that pushed heavy-handed irony into the realm of anti-Semitic caricature, full of greasy, aquiline, viciously acquisitive faces." These suggested to Sanders the author's ambivalence toward Judaism; he believes the text of Cahan's story provides enough detail to support the distasteful rendering, a conclusion that not all readers have reached (Sanders, 194–95). Unfortunately, Sanders does not indicate whether Cahan had control over the publication of the illustrations or if he even knew about them before publication. He probably did not. Because this was his first story in English, he undoubtedly felt gratified that it was accepted for publication at all and gave no consideration to the possibility that stereotyped illustrations suggestive of anti-Semitism might appear alongside his text.

The principal figure in "A Providential Match" is Rouvke Arbel, who emigrated from Kropovetz, a Russian shtetl, four years earlier at twenty-one or twenty-two, roughly the same age as Cahan when he first arrived in Philadelphia. Illiterate and uncouth when he settled in New York and became a peddler, Rouvke (an informal version of Reuben) acquired the nickname "Arbel," Yiddish for "sleeve," because he regularly employed his coat sleeve in place of a handkerchief. This allusion already suggests a comic tone, and Washington Irving's prose may well have served as Cahan's model for the humorous narrative style. One early paragraph, for example, describes Rouvke's bouts with Leike, the servant-maid, when he was employed by Hanele's father in Kropovetz: Rouvke "would bestow an occasional pinch" on her cheek, and she "would so amply repay him with the ladle, that there would ensue a series of the most complex and the most ingenious oaths, attended by hair-tearing and by squeaking, till the mistress would come" (*Y&IB*, 165). Such prose, clearly echoing Irving's tongue-in-cheek manner, seems out of place in Cahan's stories of alienation, and if suggestions of its influence occasionally appear in his fiction, he rarely allows it to dominate the tone as it does in the opening pages of his first English story.

It should be noted that Irving's reputation as a classic author endured well past the early nineteenth century in both Europe and America, and his work was readily available in several European languages, including Russian. If Cahan "was fond of Cooper's and Mayne Reid's stories," as he indicated in "How a Young Russian Pictured It," a personal sketch published in the *Commercial Advertiser* (6 August 1898, 9; also in *Grandma* as "Imagined America," 147), one must reasonably assume that he was also familiar with Irving's. It is equally likely that as a developing writer in English himself, Cahan returned to Irving's work so as to read the stories in their original language as opposed to the Russian, in which he possibly first became acquainted with them. Passages such as the one above suggest that Irving was likely a stylistic influence on Cahan.

In tracing Rouvke's success, Cahan comically but authentically defines the stages through which an immigrant passed on the way to becoming a "custom peddler." First, he carried his wares in a large kerchief, then progressed to using a basket; from there, he began climbing tenement stairs to sell from door to door, and finally he graduated to the position of "custom peddler," which enabled him to distribute business cards advertising a cornucopia of goods. On the cards that Rouvke distributes is not his Hebrew name but the Americanized "Robert Friedman."

Rouvke successfully acquires capital, but he is lonely and fearful as well as illiterate; he is also self-conscious about his pock-marked face, which reflects Cahan's own uneasiness over his crossed-eyes as a young man—a problem corrected by surgery only a few months after this story was published. In Kropovetz Rouvke had worked for a wealthy distiller with a lovely daughter, Hanele, whom he had adored, but because his love was unrequited he left for America. Because his longing for her has not altogether disappeared, he eagerly seeks information about Hanele on meeting recent immigrants from the shtetl. Now twenty-five, "his heart was 'stretching' and 'stretching'" (*Y&IB,* 169) for someone to share his portion, but he flees in fear from the semi-Americanized women around him. In the core of his heart reigns the image of Hanele.

He meets Feive, a *melamed* recently arrived from Kropovetz, and asks the elderly man about the shtetl, about Hanele's family, and finally about Hanele herself. To earn a little extra money, the poor *melamed* also serves as a *shatkhn.* He reveals that Hanele is as attractive as ever, but at twenty-five she is no longer being courted; seeking only the best possible match and rejecting all others, she and her father seem to have waited too long. After learning that the distillery has been closed by anti-Semitic government decree, Rouvke wonders if Hanele is now accessible to him. Feive promises to investigate, calculating his profits with dancing fingers as he explains his plans to Rouvke.

Meanwhile the dreamy Hanele finds actuality difficult to face. She is "really a 'true daughter of Israel,'" meaning that she is altogether provincial and limited in her reading to a Yiddish version of the Pentateuch; "her greatest pleasure was to be knitting fancy tablecloths and brooding over daydreams." Hanele, meanwhile, after her initial shock over the possibility of marrying Rouvke, romanticizes the match and dreams of being in "an unknown far-off land, where she [sees] herself glittering with gold and pearls and nestling up to a masculine figure in sumptuous attire" (*Y&IB*, 181–82). The beautiful dream is slightly marred by the vague image of Rouvke, hovering somewhere in drab workman's clothes. At last, after much negotiating with Feive, Hanele and her father agree to her marriage with Rouvke. He pays for her trans-Atlantic ticket and awaits her with Feive at Castle Garden.

In the scene immediately preceding their meeting, romance and reality confront each other directly in Cahan's imagery. First, Rouvke has hired a pair of highly polished carriages to carry them from Castle Garden to the East Side; he is stylishly dressed with a huge rose pinned to his lapel. But the next paragraph begins with a naturalistic description of the immigrant station: "The atmosphere of the barn-like garden was laden with nauseating odors of steerage and of carbolic acid, and reeking with human wretchedness." To compound the repulsiveness of the setting, the same paragraph ends by identifying the cacophonous noises that "made the scene as painful to the ear as it was to the eye and nostrils, and completed the impression of misery and desolation" (*Y&IB*, 184). The reader is prepared for Rouvke's shock as he sees Hanele on the arm of a young Russian intellectual, wearing glasses and vaguely reminiscent of Cahan's own likely image as a new immigrant. To the stunned Rouvke and Feive, she introduces her escort as Levinsky, thus anticipating by nearly twenty years the initial appearance in 1913 of Cahan's millionaire industrialist in the pages of *McClure's*. Outraged, brokenhearted, and threatened with violence by a teamster ready to carry the young couple into the city, Rouvke can do no more than shout for a policeman to help him regain the money he has lost by providing Hanele with a ticket, money that Levinsky promises to pay him back.

Although this story lacks the subtlety of his better ones to come, "A Providential Match" anticipates many characteristics of Cahan's later English fiction: the pathetic schlemiel as hero, the comic irony, the "stretching heart," the overpowering sense of loss, the lack of pretentious diction, and the realistic, at times naturalistic, description of the local setting, especially evident near the conclusion. His manipulation of the vernacular in this story, too, constitutes a fair sample of what is to come in the later work. Cahan employs an articulate third-person narrator knowledgeable about the culture being described, and the characters speak variously in the immigrants' broken English, low-life English, and Yiddish translated by the author (Chametzky 1977, 49, 51). This rendering of common speech combined with realistic descriptions of the immigrant milieu are the elements of Cahan's fiction that led Sanders to call him "the first 'local colorist' of the New York Jewish quarter" (Sanders, 195).

"A Sweat-Shop Romance"

The editor of *Short Stories* was pleased enough with "A Providential Match" that he requested additional submissions from Cahan, who agreed to write one on the recent phenomenon of the sweatshop. "A Sweat-Shop Romance" was written almost immediately and published as the lead story in the June 1895 issue. Three years later, he included it in *The Imported Bridegroom* collection. It is another tale of love and loss.

Heyman, Beile, and David are coworkers in an East Side sweatshop. Shy and somewhat effeminate, Heyman has been openly courting Beile, who wishes to believe that she loves him but in truth feels little emotional attraction, and he is too reticent to press his affection. Consequently, three months pass, and the relationship appears to have grown stagnant. David, also quietly fond of her, says nothing so as not to interfere. When Lipman, their employer, comes to the shop one day with his wife, Zlate, and two visitors from the Old Country, Zlate, eager to impress their guests with her authority, orders Beile to bring them soda from the store. David, urging her not to go, whispers it is not her job to do such things, and she nervously refuses the order. Lipman is reluctant to press the issue, but his dominating wife insists, and when Beile continues to hold her ground, he fires her, and David quits. Heyman mutters resentfully to the wall but says nothing aloud. The jobless pair leave and go their separate ways. After work Heyman is too ashamed of his inaction to visit Beile, and for two weeks, gnawed by fear and remorse, he delays going to her flat as she quietly awaits him. When he finally works up the courage to go, he arrives in time to see her with David a few minutes after their wedding. While she waited for Heyman, David had courted her himself, and Beile realized at last that it was him she had loved all along.

In "A Sweat-Shop Romance" Cahan combines his interests as a socialist with his emotional sensitivity as a writer. As David M. Fine suggests, the difference between America as a dream and as a reality is perfectly realized in the sweatshop, a "symbol for modern urban labor" (145). The story opens with a short, informative description of a "cockroach" sweatshop, defined as "a very small shop . . . [with] a single team" of employees: a machine operator, Heyman; a baster, David; a finisher, Beile; and a presser, Meyer (*Y&IB*, 188–89). The contractor receives business from a Broadway firm for which the designer is his wife's second cousin. Here Cahan illustrates the type of networking that enabled merchants and other entrepreneurs to take advantage of extended family relations; of course, this was a major economic advantage where competition was fierce, especially during the slack season in the garment manufactory when any work that could be found was at a premium.

As for the workplace itself, "[t]he shop was one of a suite of three rooms on the third floor of a rickety old tenement house on Essex Street, and did the additional duty of the family's kitchen and dining room. It faced a dingy little courtyard," and the parlor overlooked "the very heart of the Jewish markets" (*Y&IB*, 189), with their bustle and noise. Although Chametzky considers this story as "obviously slight," he praises its realistic description, paradoxically, the very aspect of Cahan's work that Hutchins Hapgood minimizes in terms of fictive value (Chametzky 1977, 52). Cahan emphasizes the stuffiness and chaotic nature of the crowded tenement flat, appropriately called a sweatshop not only because of the work entailed but also because of "the overpowering temperature" generated by a "red-hot kitchen stove and a blazing grate full of glowing flatirons combined" (*Y&IB*, 188). One can readily see from such language why Stephen Crane was so impressed with Cahan's writing and eager to meet the author, which, with Howells' help, he did soon after the publication of *Yekl*. Indeed, this is the kind of forceful, potent imagery that Crane himself had employed in *Maggie* (1893) and *The Red Badge of Courage* (1895) and the kind he would rely on again for its dynamic effects in such later stories as "The Blue Hotel" (1898) and "The Monster" (1899).

The exploitation of labor by the bosses, even in such small operations as this "cockroach" shop, is evident in Zlate's ordering Beile to "fetch"—Cahan's choice of diction—sodas for his guests. Working on the "task" system, Beile would be taking money from her own pocket to carry out a menial chore on time that she would otherwise be putting into finishing another garment. Cahan emphasizes Beile's inherent

nobility as a worker by comparing her with Zlate, as one of the contractor's own guests observes the two women. Dressed to leave in a new
coat and trimmed hat after being fired, Beile "looked like a lady, with
Zlate for her servant, rather than the reverse" (Y&IB, 199). Moreover,
she and David have no difficulty finding better jobs. These two details
suggest the high value Cahan placed on well-motivated, self-reliant
workers.

It is not a socialist message that drives "A Sweat-Shop Romance,"
however, but the psychological and emotional pressures put on the characters in an oppressive setting. Sanders suggests that this story manifests the weakening of Cahan's didactic inclination and shows that he
was already succumbing to a stronger representation of his "mournful
inner self" (Sanders, 197), but the same may be said of "A Providential
Match." His creative impulse in English led him to write a kind of fiction different from the tendentious, socialist-motivated work he turned
out for the Yiddish press. Each of the active characters in "A Sweat-Shop
Romance" is developed sufficiently for individualization, not merely as
immigrant and Jew, which they all are, but as a member of a conflictive,
competitive community in which behavior is governed by one's own
personal advantages or liabilities. Cahan was a verbal illustrator of
actual conditions in this story, not a social or psychological analyst but a
naturalist through whose few portraits one can gain insight into the
internal and external forces that determine the behavior of his characters. Long afterward, Cahan regretted the ending of his story, which he
then considered as contrived for the sake of an overwrought socialist
message, but Sanders believes that the conclusion is "thoroughly pertinent and not at all contrived," for it reveals the shift then occurring in
the author's creative impulse from didacticism to what Cahan later
called "the thrill of truth" (Sanders, 197; Cahan quoted in Poole, 478).

"Circumstances"

Nearly two years later, during which time Yekl was published, Cahan
came out with his next story in English, "Circumstances"; it appeared in
the April 1897 issue of Cosmopolitan. Despite its division into seven sections, "Circumstances" is a more constricted story than the others. All
but the final section are set in the same small tenement flat, and apart
from a few lines sung by someone else near the end, the dialogue is confined to three characters: Boris Lurie; his wife, Tanya (Tatyana
Markova); and their boarder, Dalsky, a medical student. Chametzky

considers "Circumstances" to be "the best-realized work in the book" (Chametzky 1977, 78). Although no evidence exists to confirm that Cahan had a genre other than short fiction in mind when he composed this story, the limited setting and few characters connote its suitability for staging in the form of a one-act drama. Moreover, Cahan had recently become acquainted with Chekhov's writing, possibly his plays of the late 1880s as well as his short fiction, which also implies that he may well have had Chekhovian realistic dialogue in mind as his story took shape. Certainly, the very qualities he most admired in Chekhov's work are more evident in "Circumstances" than in any of his previous writing.

Boris and Tanya are recent Russian-Jewish immigrants who have been forced by poverty to live on the top floor of an aging East Side tenement. Both are well educated, Tanya having graduated from an excellent Russian gymnasium and Boris from a university with a degree in law. They had anticipated a comfortable life in Russia, but when Boris tried to take his bar examination, he was thwarted by one impediment after another, and on questioning government officials he was told that he would have a better chance of scheduling the examination if he converted to Christianity. The young couple fled in outrage to New York, where Boris can find no other work than in a button factory and Tanya remains at home. His salary of $6 weekly is subject to seasonal demand, and although Tanya is willing to work in a factory, he refuses to allow it, and she, a young sophisticate from a middle-class family, lacks the enthusiasm to debate the question. When Boris returns from work, she wishes to discuss questions raised as she read the Russian literary magazine to which they subscribe in spite of their poverty, but Boris is too tired and frustrated from their grim situation to debate intellectual issues. Envisioning a bleak future unless he can learn English and acquire an American college education, he suggests that to save money toward that end they take in a boarder. When she weeps over the loss of privacy that would mean, Boris angrily responds: "'Cry to our circumstances, not to me. Circumstances, circumstances, Tanya!' he repeated, with pleading vehemence" (*Y&IB*, 210).

Initially, he relents to her refusal, but when he is laid off at the factory, they see no alternative, so Boris brings Dalsky to the apartment. He is a good-humored young fellow, an English teacher as well as a medical student, and he quickly endears himself to the couple as if he were one of the family. Dalsky tries to help Boris learn English, but when the button factory calls him back, he is too tired to study. As time passes, Boris is increasingly morose, unkempt, and irritable, while Tanya finds herself falling for Dalsky, to whom she consistently turns for intellectual companionship as well as his positive outlook on life. After three months with the Luries, Dalsky realizes how their relations with each other have changed, and, without explanation, he moves out of the apartment to preclude being tempted by Tanya. Having lost Dalsky and no longer in love with her embittered husband, she leaves him, going to work in a factory. The story ends with the couple's loneliness, despair, and mutual alienation: in the sweatshop where Tanya now works, a "cruel anguish choked her," and in the "dead emptiness" of the apartment they had shared, Boris "burst into tears" (*Y&IB*, 222–23).

Theodore Marvin Pollock says the editor of *Cosmopolitan* generally liked the story, but not the unhappy ending, and requested a sequel from Cahan, expecting the reconciliation of Boris and Tanya. But the sequel was nearly as grim, for although Boris and Tanya are reconciled, their marriage lacks its original happiness, and the manuscript was rejected (Pollock, 228–29). The couple's Russian background and problematic marriage suggests, according to Sanders, that "Circumstances" is the most autobiographical of Cahan's stories thus far, though he believes that the personal parallels diminish as the story develops. The marriage of Boris and Tanya collapses while they are still young, for example, whereas Cahan's marriage to Anna remained intact for more than sixty years. Certain physical features are also shared by Boris and his creator. For instance, although Boris is taller than Cahan, he is equally authoritative, well read, and compatible in student circles; moreover, he has a defacing scar over his left eye, suggestive of Cahan's crossed eyes when he immigrated. A partial resemblance is also evident between Tanya and Cahan's wife, Anna, in that both are well-educated young women from Kiev; for Chametzky, Tanya, is "a pure intellectual," as was Anna, though the latter was surely more profound and emotionally mature than Tanya, even in the early phase of her marriage to Cahan (Sanders, 227; Chametzky 1977, 114).

The chief strengths of "Circumstances" lie in its tightness and realism. Indeed, oppressive "circumstances" undoubtedly do determine the existence of the two central figures, and Cahan well knew that they were identical to those faced by countless immigrants whose lives were broken by poverty. Usually it was the husband who deserted rather than the wife, but desertion among the Jewish immigrants was all too common. For a while, after perceiving the success of the *"Bintl briv"* feature in the *Forward,* Cahan initiated a weekly column called the "Gallery of Vanished Husbands," for which wives submitted pictures of their missing spouses to the editor, but it did not fare as well or continue as long as the established "Bundle of Letters" (Epstein, 93). Unlike most actual desertions, the fictive one described in "Circumstances" leads not to the freedom of either spouse but to mutual distress. Cahan's story realistically suggests that without strength of will and character, the force of circumstances can be crushing.

"A Ghetto Wedding"

Neither willpower nor strength of character but faith in love gives Nathan and Goldy the courage they need to face a threatening future at the end of the final story in the *Imported Bridegroom*. "A Ghetto Wedding" first appeared in the February 1898 *Atlantic Monthly,* only two months before the collection was published. Despite the increasingly somber tone and sense of disillusionment toward the end, it is a charming tale that concludes on a hopeful note.

Essentially, "A Ghetto Wedding" describes the ambiguous effect of a foolish gamble based on unreasonable hope. Nathan and Goldy are garment workers in love during a slack season when money is tight, and Nathan believes that with their savings of $120, they still have enough to marry without further delay. Goldy, however, insists on a "respectable wedding," meaning a grand ceremony and celebration, though she understands it will be expensive, so they must work and save until they can cover the costs. But as months pass, the times become harder; not only can the young couple no longer save, but they must draw from their cash in order to live, however frugally.

With only about $75 remaining, Goldy proposes that they spend it all on a splendid wedding. They will invite many guests who will be so impressed over the planned celebration that they will send expensive gifts in abundance and thus provide most of the furnishings that a newly married couple is likely to need. Doubtfully, Nathan agrees to the plan because he has none better to offer. The room is rented, the food ordered, and the desired personnel—including musicians—hired.

But if times are hard for Nathan and Goldy, they are the same for their invited guests, many of whom do not come because they cannot afford to send a gift; moreover, the sparse presents received are far smaller than expected. With few diners, most of the food remains uneaten, and the musicians cannot help but play somber tunes. When the beer is served, however, the mood lightens, and amid higher spirits and welcome gaiety, Nathan and Goldy are united. To save money when the celebration ends, they walk back to their tenement flat, but on the way, as if to undermine whatever joy they might have gleaned from the modestly attended festivities, they are harassed by Gentile rowdies on the dark pavement. Goldy urges Nathan not to return their hostility, but to leave them alone, which he does, and the story closes with a sense of enchantment hovering about the unharmed newlyweds.

What can one make of "A Ghetto Wedding"? What reasonably intelligent couple would seriously propose spending all of their hard-earned savings on a frivolous wedding ceremony with no reliable source of income? How can anyone but a *luftmentsh* (impractical dreamer) expect to furnish an apartment from wedding gifts alone when the times are so bad that no one can afford to give them? Is this reasonable? Is this *realism*? Of course, the expectations and actions are both unreasonable and unrealistic—but the motivations behind them are not. In "A Ghetto Wedding," Cahan brilliantly combines the essence of the romantic influences that have touched him and the realistic impulses that govern his creative drive. In *Criticism and Fiction* (1891), Howells writes that he could not judge work of the imagination without first answering the question: "Is it true?—true to the motives, the impulses, the principles that shape the life of actual men and women?"[1] In reviewing *The Imported Bridegroom*, he wrote nothing about a lack of realism in this or any other story in the collection, but, on the contrary, praised Cahan for his earthy characters, who "have often a noble aspiration, to which he does justice with no straining or vaunting."[2]

With splendid insight, Jules Chametzky perceives in the conclusion of "A Ghetto Wedding" "a note that is beautiful—the sweetness and wonder of Chagall, an anticipation of Malamud" (81). Again I suggest as I did earlier in discussing *Yekl* that a good part of the marvelous effect of this story comes from Cahan's familiarity with Hawthorne's fiction. The almost whimsical wistfulness of the two simple, innocent characters in love, naively believing that the Lord above will provide for them what they wish for themselves, is familiar enough to readers of Hawthorne's tales, as are the imagery and the ambiguous phrasing. Cahan seems to have learned from Hawthorne without imitating him, and he put the lessons to good effect in "A Ghetto Wedding." Indeed, to this point, Cahan had written nothing finer.

"The Imported Bridegroom"

Jules Chametzky points out that Cahan introduced through his stories "a Yiddish sensibility" into American literature. Although he wished to

address a Gentile American readership even more than a Jewish one
with this English fiction, he could not evade in this writing his immersion in the culture of *Yidishkayt*. His stories conveyed to his East Side
readers truths of which his broader American audience was unaware, yet
they recognized his work as that of the realist he was (Chametzky 1977,
77). According to the traditions of *Yidishkayt* in America, one of these
"truths," as Irving Howe observes, is that "[i]n principle, the *shul*
claimed the whole of its members' attention" as in the Old Country, but
in practice its influence was considerably diminished (Howe, 191).
Nowhere in Cahan's collection is this idea more pertinent than in "The
Imported Bridegroom" itself, where it becomes the motivating factor
behind the sudden transformation of the flustered hero, Asriel Stroon,
from religious apathy to renewed faith and piety. In this story, the shul is
the synergetic center of *Yidishkayt* for an aging Jewish community, but it
is an anachronism and an impediment to rapid Americanization for
most others, especially the younger people.

"The Imported Bridegroom," which opens the collection, is the last
piece written and the longest of the five works included; it is the only
one that had not been published previously. This novelette largely anticipates the major conflicts of Cahan's later fiction, including the central
one in *The Rise of David Levinsky*. In "The Imported Bridegroom," the
traditional past of the Polish shtetl is brought in touch with the Americanized present of the younger generation on the Lower East Side
through the whimsical aspirations of Asriel, the "boor." A widower of
fifty-eight, he is a retired man of property and leisure struggling to
restore his attenuated faith and yearning nostalgically to see his old
home in Pravly: the longing "is pulling me by the heart," he tells his
widowed cook, Tamara (*Y&IB,* 97). Asriel travels to the unchanged
shtetl and pretentiously flashes his wealth in the shul; by offering an
immense dowry, he literally purchases Shaya, a Talmudic genius, as the
providential groom for his attractive daughter, Flora. Shaya will be the
son he now lacks to say kaddish (prayer over the dead) for him when he
is gone.

After a soul-wracking visit to the graves of his parents in the cemetery at Pravly, Asriel returns to New York with a curious if dutiful
Shaya. Flora is furious when she learns what her father has done. Insist-
ing on marrying a doctor, she adamantly refuses to wed this old-fashioned, unsophisticated, ultra-pious prodigy regardless of Asriel's fear of
an unhallowed afterlife. At length, however, Shaya's fervent piety
diminishes, then disappears altogether, for as the handsome youth learns

English, he also commences to study the "Gentile books" with which
Flora secretly provides him as her attraction to him increases. The two
fall in love as Shaya, too, is rapidly secularized. Although they keep his
transformation a secret from Asriel, the foolish "boor" eventually learns
that his "predestined" son has become an atheist; to Tamara he laments,
"America has robbed me of my glory," and to Flora, "America has done it
all" (Y&IB, 154, 156).

But Asriel himself is at fault, not America. Shaya has changed, as did
Asriel himself after immigrating thirty-five years earlier. Suddenly, after
a sermon of a new young rabbi awakens him to the danger of a rueful
afterlife if he does not make amends for his exploitative career, Asriel
decides to restore his faith. For years he has sat half asleep in his shul,
but now reminded at fifty-eight of death's certain arrival, he constantly
reads from the Scriptures and when intoning the Psalms makes "every
line melt like sugar in [his] mouth" (Y&IB, 99). That his imagery constantly refers to food and eating suggests his compulsion to ingest what
is missing from his life.

Furthermore, it is Flora, the daughter he has reared with little or no
concern for religion, who instigates Shaya's rapid acculturation in the
New World. She indoctrinates her brilliant fiancé so quickly that he is
soon far beyond her in the "Gentile" knowledge of mathematics and
natural philosophy to which she has introduced him. The novelette ends
as Flora sits in a garret on her wedding night, ignored and despondent,
vaguely hearing the animated discussion of a group of Bohemian intellectuals—Jews and Gentiles together—among whom is her new husband. "A nightmare of desolation and jealousy choked her,—jealousy of
the . . . whole excited crowd, and of Shaya's entire future, from which
she seemed excluded" (Y&IB, 162). To compound her alienation, her
widowed father marries Tamara, and they prepare to spend the remainder of their lives together in the Holy Land. Here again is the dominant
note of loneliness and estrangement, of despair and anguish, that characterizes all of Cahan's fiction in English.

As in the earlier stories, so in "The Imported Bridegroom" one can
recognize the harmonious conjunction of the romantic and the realistic.
Repeating continually that he is only "a boor," Asriel makes no effort to
correct his vulgarity but only to compensate for it. He loves Flora, but
he assumes that what is best for himself is also best for her, and she, having been reared and educated in his middle-class home as a secularized,
independent personality—"a Yankee," as Yekl would put it—insists on
making her own choices, though she is no less devoted to him as a

daughter than he to her as her father. Baring his soul in the cemetery at Pravly after bidding successfully for Shaya, Asriel prays to his father's spirit that "no ill wind blow [Flora] away from me, that no evil eye injure my treasure" (*Y&IB,* 116), but the melancholy conclusion reveals that his prayers remain unanswered.

Cahan suggests as much with what proves to be an ominous reading of Asriel's consciousness as the "boor" and Shaya sail home from Europe: "The nearer Asriel, with the prodigy in tow, came to New York, the deeper did Pravly sink into the golden mist of romance, and the more real did the great American city grow in his mind" (*Y&IB,* 119). The literary contrast implied by his allusion to "romance" and "real" testifies to Cahan's purposeful use of these terms in creating an ambiguous moral situation for the aging businessman of restored faith and for the new American couple he has brought together but unwittingly set free to go their own way—for better or worse.[3]

Howells's Qualified Response to *The Imported Bridegroom*

As he had done some two years earlier in reviewing *Yekl,* Howells praised *The Imported Bridegroom* warmly in his review for *Literature* issued on the last day of 1898: "No American fiction of the year merits recognition more than this Russian's stories of Yiddish life, which are so entirely of our time and place, and so foreign to our race and civilization. Being a Russian, Mr. Cahan's art is of course naturalistic, and, being a Hebrew, his knowledge of his material is perfect." Howells went on to commend Cahan's subtle combination of humor and earthy authenticity, admiring the "noble aspiration" often seen in his characters, lifelike as they are, which, of course, corresponded with the Dean's own views on morality and American possibilities (Howells 1898, 629).

But Howells also posits an important qualification that may well have been the chief stimulus behind Cahan's attempts to extend his range beyond the Jewish characters who had populated his fiction thus far. "It will be interesting to see," Howells muses, "whether Mr. Cahan will pass beyond his present environment out into the larger American world, or will master our life as he has mastered our language." But then, as if to underscore his confidence in this "New Star of Realism"— as he had called Cahan in his review of *Yekl*—he concludes, "But of a Jew, who is also a Russian, what artistic triumph may not we expect?" (Howells 1898, 629). With all of the laudatory rhetoric, which he surely welcomed, Cahan was still identified as a Russian and a Jew rather than an American, yet Howells was clearly encouraging him to enlarge his social scope as an American author. In a few of Cahan's later stories, he seems to have tried, and in his next novel, *The White Terror and the Red,* he moved into a different sphere altogether.

Unifying Threads in a Realistic Pattern

Cahan wisely chose to open *The Imported Bridegroom* with his most recently completed work. As a longer and more complex piece than the other stories in the collection, it introduces the theme of alienation that predominates in all of them. Yet regardless how isolated many of the central characters feel in the circumstances that entrap them, the general subject in all four stories and the novelette, ironically enough, is marriage—initiating it, sustaining it, dissolving it. With this in mind, one cannot help but ponder over the nature of relations between Abraham and Anna Cahan during their first ten or twelve years together, but there is little evidence to go on beside hearsay and speculation over the stories, though we do know that their marriage endured for over six decades. In contrast, Rouvke Arbel's "predestined match" does not materialize, Boris and Tanya separate into mutual despair, and Flora seems to anticipate an alienated existence amidst Shaya's new intellectual friends; as for the two remaining couples—David and Beile, Nathan and Goldy—it is still too early to judge their marriages as successful, but Cahan's imagery and the prevailing mood bode well for them.

Although all the fiction in *The Imported Bridegroom* focuses exclusively on Jews living in New York's East Side ghetto, none but the novelette gives specific attention to Judaism itself, that is, to the religion and its practices. Only Asriel Stroon, the "boor," reverts to his faith, but even he does so less from genuine devotion than from fear of divine judgment in his afterlife. Yet in *From the Ghetto,* Jules Chametzky is surely correct in pointing to the importance of a Yiddish sensibility that suffuses all of the fiction, a consequence of Cahan's own immersion in the culture of *Yidishkayt* from the time he arrived in New York—not to mention his upbringing as a child in Podberezy and Vilna. Yiddish is the language spoken by nearly all of his characters, Yiddish and the variations of it that evolved through its absorption of English words and phrases. This use of the vernacular gives a special flavor to the fiction that ties it directly to the millions of Jews among the first and second generations of the immigrant culture who brought it with them from Eastern Europe, however secularized and Americanized they became later. This

quality of language and the authenticity it brings to the fiction constitute much of the power inherent in Cahan's art, which often seems as
much oral as written, the intimate and traditional art of the storyteller.

Especially worth noting, too, in all of this early fiction, including *Yekl,*
is the manner in which Cahan has intertwined elements of romanticism
and realism so as to create an aura of ambiguity in developing alternatives within the moral situations that emerge among lovers, spouses,
and family members. He seems to have employed Hawthorne's work
and to a lesser extent Irving's as models for his prose style and imagery;
Pollock has confirmed his direct familiarity with Hawthorne's writing
(194), and the similarities are unmistakable, particularly in "A Ghetto
Wedding" as well as *Yekl,* discussed in the previous chapter. Unlike
Hawthorne, however, Cahan does not vacillate between fact and fancy,
sunlight and shadow, in order to cast uncertainty over what actually
does or does not exist. Instead, he uses the suggestive imagery of
romance to create a special tone, or mood, or attitude that either complements what it was meant to color or contrasts with it—but it was not
intended to throw the reader into uncertainty over what is and what
merely seems to be. Thoroughly dedicated to what Howells calls "the
truthful treatment of material" (Howells 1891, 93), Cahan was too
much the realist to sidestep for even a moment into the land of shad-
ows—though in "A Ghetto Wedding" he did come close.

Sketches for the *Commercial Advertiser*

Moreover, echoes of Hawthorne's style also appear occasionally in his
early writings for the *Commercial Advertiser*; the correspondences are
clear, for example, in his first contribution to it, printed before Steffens
had hired him onto the full-time staff. The article describes a part of the
synagogue service for the holiday of Simchas Torah, which celebrates joy
in the Torah with the finishing of one year's cycle of weekly readings and
the commencement of another. This is a festive holiday in which all in
the congregation participate. Cahan describes the occasion as if he has
just put down a volume of Hawthorne's Puritan tales. Note his phrasing: a child's face was "as rapt as some of the venerable countenances
preceding him"; "he obeyed his mother with grave mien"; "'Please, sir!'
a dark-eyed maiden besought a gray-bearded old man. 'May I ask you to
pause a little and allow me to kiss your Purity scrolls, for I fear that I
have missed it'"; "the women's gallery was crowded . . . with dark-haired
maidens and wigged old matrons"; and so forth ("Rejoicing of the Law,"

CA, 19 October 1897, 4; *Grandma,* 77–78). As in parts of *Yekl* and "A Ghetto Wedding," this diction is much too close to Hawthorne's to be mere coincidence.

But from a chronological point of view, such parallels might be expected, for by the time *The Imported Bridegroom* was published in the spring of 1898, Cahan had been enjoying full-time employment as a reporter with the *Commercial Advertiser* since November of the previous year, a position that provided him with enough spare time to write fiction. Moreover, the *Advertiser* itself called on him to do more than cover the police beat (initially his primary job), interview important people visiting in New York, and write news articles dealing with the Lower East Side. From his first months with the *Advertiser* he was contributing a variety of pieces, from short anecdotal items to longer fictionalized sketches and vignettes, many of which deal with his observations among the immigrants in a sympathetic, lightly comic mode uncharacteristic of his previous writing in English.

Even the more substantial of Cahan's *Advertiser* narratives are not equal in length to the stories he published two and three years later in the popular magazines, but they are nonetheless long enough to introduce and develop an engaging, usually amusing situation with credible voices for characters and a neat ironic twist at the end that leaves a reader smiling. That, of course, was what he intended with these features, which are generally meant to entertain rather than teach, though one need not probe very far to find a useful moral lesson in many of them.

Two examples of these early pieces will suffice to convey Cahan's appeal to a broad American readership. As may be noted from their dates of publication—December 1897 for both—they were printed several months before *The Imported Bridegroom* and approximately a year prior to Howells's review of that collection, in which he wondered if the author would try to widen his scope from the narrow confines of the Jewish immigrant culture of the Lower East Side. Neither of these pieces includes notably Jewish characters.

In the first, "The Story of a Chance Meeting in the Big City," a distinguished-looking Russian artist in his fifties daily meets an attractive Polish piano-teacher in her thirties in a pleasant French restaurant in New York. They encounter each other there regularly before a chance remark in Russian by the artist discloses to the teacher that he must be conversant in that language, as is she, having received part of her education in Russia. Her awareness leads them to converse, and eventually he falls in love with her. Though favorably impressed with him, she sadly rejects his offer of marriage, but his willingness to remain on good terms leads to another meeting, during which he reveals his background. As he speaks, she is stunned to perceive that he had been an intimate friend of her father when they were in the Russian military together; he tells her that soon after her father was executed for supporting the rebellious Poles, he himself resigned from the service. She then recognizes him immediately as the gentleman she played with many years earlier in childhood when her father had brought him home as a guest, and she tells him of a faded picture in her album, a photograph of him with her father. Then he, too, is enlightened, not realizing that he has been speaking with the daughter of his old friend. After learning who he is and loving the memory of him for decades past, she accepts his proposal (*CA,* 4 December 1897, 9; *Grandma,* 151–56).

The scintillating effect of the piece comes through the unexpected revelation near the end, an ironic twist that leads to the happy ending the popular press would want to please its readers. Once the initial circumstances are established, the sketch is presented chiefly through dialogue, so what one reads is little more than a dramatic situation that eventuates in a surprising climax and fully satisfying resolution. Cahan presents no ambiguities and leaves no loose ends; he was after entertainment with this piece, and that is precisely what he provides.

The second example, too, is developed through conversation, more monologue than dialogue, however, until shortly before the end, and again the conclusion is a happy crowd pleaser. In "Result of a Friendship Begun in a Reading Room," a forty-year-old Dane becomes acquainted with an older, stern-faced Englishman in a reading room and tells him the sad result of a foolish mistake he made years before. He says that he came to America seeking a Swedish woman who had loved him in Denmark; despite his affection for her, he did not propose because he had aspirations to be a poet that he did not believe he could fulfill if encumbered with a wife and children. After she immigrated to America, he realized his folly and followed her, but his unsystematic search has been futile, and he is nearly without hope—though once they had crossed paths on elevated trains going in opposite directions. Since then, he has not seen her. Touched by this story, the Englishman secretly commences a systematic search of his own. Because the Dane mentioned that the woman teaches French and embroidery, he places notices in many local papers advertising for someone with these talents, and, eventually, she responds. After making the necessary arrangements and maintaining strict confidentiality, he surprises the two isolated lovers by reuniting

them at his home as a Christmas gift. They marry and return to Copen-
hagen, where they now live in perfect happiness (*CA,* 11 December
1897, 11; *Grandma,* 156–61).

Are these two narratives from the same hand that wrote *Yekl* and the
oft-depressing stories in *The Imported Bridegroom?* Yes. But, of course,
these and many others on the same level were intended to reach a different audience or at least to serve a different purpose. As features in a
daily newspaper, especially one that emphasized commercial interests
among an educated readership, they provided a few minutes of entertainment amid the columns of news for which most readers purchased
the paper. Cahan's short features of this kind gave them something to
smile about, but these items are not to be confused with the literary fiction he would publish several years later in the most prominent American monthly magazines of the day, including *Cosmopolitan, Scribner's,
Century,* and the *Atlantic.* When he began publishing in these highly
respected periodicals, Abraham Cahan had arrived as an esteemed
author of short stories.

The Uncollected Periodical Fiction

The six uncollected stories he brought out during a little over four years
with the *Commercial Advertiser* were both similar to and different from
those he had written only a little while before, during the mid-1890s. As
suggested earlier, they do share a common central theme of alienation.
Three of the stories deal with Jewish characters, and the other three with
Gentile immigrants of various nationalities. Of the six, only one—"A
Marriage by Proxy"—is a basically comic piece, though an element of
poignant humor occurs in at least three of the others: "Rabbi Eliezer's
Christmas," "Dumitru and Sigrid," and "Tzinchadzi of the Catskills."
The third story of the six, "The Daughter of Reb Avrom Leib," reveals
sparks of ironic humor throughout, but for the most part it is dark
humor, like the grin on a skull. In contrast to the others, "The Apostate
of Chego-Chegg," the first story brought out after *The Imported Bridegroom,* is one of almost unrelieved bleakness; it approaches the naturalism
of Stephen Crane and Hamlin Garland more closely than does any other
example of his short fiction. One might compare it in this respect with
Yekl, except that it lacks the redeeming qualities represented by Gitl,
Bernstein, and Mrs. Kavarsky. "The Apostate of Chego-Chegg," in the
November 1899 *Century,* is Cahan's starkest and perhaps most powerful
fiction before the publication of *The Rise of David Levinsky.*

"The Apostate of Chego-Chegg"

In "The Imported Bridegroom," Asriel Stroon flies into a rage because Shaya, his "predestined" son (that is, son-in-law) becomes an atheist in America, but at least time brings him the tolerance to see the youth married under a ritual canopy to his daughter according to the Hebrew tradition. In contrast, Michalina's father, in "The Apostate of Chego-Chegg," eliminates her from his life; for him, she is dead because, even worse than an atheist, she is a *meshumedeste,* a female religious convert—"an apostate, a renegade, a traitoress, something beyond the vituperative resources of Gentile speech"[4]—having committed probably the most unforgivable sin possible as seen by her Old Country Jewish father, who adheres steadfastly to the faith, its laws and traditions.

The playfulness of Cahan's title is deceptive. As the narrator explains early in the text, "A local politician had humorously dubbed the settlement Chego-Chegg (this was his phonetic summary of the Polish language), and the name clung" ("Apostate," 96). It is a farm village on Long Island inhabited chiefly by Poles, an apt spot for Michalina to have settled with her Polish-Catholic husband, Wincas, on immigrating to America. Vilified by Jews for her conversion and scorned by Gentiles for her Jewishness, she is virtually isolated from both communities. Moreover, although she longs to return to her Hebrew faith, she loves her Catholic husband and does not know where to turn. When the itinerant young Rabbi Nehemiah passes her on his way to a nearby Jewish village, she follows him in desperation, only to be harassed by the villagers as a *meshumedeste.* Despite their hostility, she longs to associate with them. When she returns home, an enraged Wincas demands to know where she has been so long, but she satisfies him with an evasive answer, and together they lament the poverty they face on what appears to be an accursed farm.

The next time she meets Nehemiah, his earlocks and beard are gone. "I am Rabbi Nehemiah no longer," he quietly tells her. "They call me Nehemiah the Atheist now. . . . Religion is all humbug. There are no Jews and no Gentiles, missus. This is America. All are noblemen here, and all are brothers—children of one mother—Nature" ("Apostate," 100). But he fails to convince her. Michalina still yearns to return to Europe and to Judaism, but she loves her husband too much to leave him. So she must live under her father's dreadful curse and suffer the hunger of unsatisfied spiritual desire always within her: "Nobody will give me anything but misery—nobody, nobody, nobody!" she laments ("Apostate," 102).

Tempted by Nehemiah to leave Wincas and marry him for a happier life, Michalina almost succumbs to his arguments, but finally she returns to her husband to resume a life of alienation from all but him, for no community welcomes her, and she sees neither happiness nor fulfillment in her future.

"The Apostate of Chego-Chegg" is a brilliant story of moral ambivalence for which no satisfactory resolution seems to exist. Not only Michalina but Wincas and Nehemiah as well all long for help, though her suffering is the most severe because she yearns deeply for her faith while loving her Catholic husband, and she knows that she cannot have both: "Curse me; I deserve it," she cries on refusing to reject Wincas. "I know I am doomed to have no rest either in this world or in the other, but I cannot leave him—I cannot. Forgive me. . . . What shall I do? Oh, what shall I do?" ("Apostate," 104). With no other avenues open to her, she has no answer, and Cahan has none to propose.

"Rabbi Eliezer's Christmas"

Only a month later, *Scribner's Monthly* included his next story, "Rabbi Eliezer's Christmas," in the December issue; it was illustrated by William Glackens, noted realist of the Ashcan school. Although alienation remains central, the theme is treated with levity, as would be appropriate for a story about a rabbi's Christmas published during the Yuletide season.

"Rabbi" is an honorific title given Eliezer only because of his piety and noble beard. He is observed by two Christian ladies at his magazine-and-tobacco stand in the ghetto, situated near the College Settlement, a charitable social institution where one of them, Miss Colton, is the head worker. Having learned Yiddish through her knowledge of German, she interprets for her philanthropic friend, Miss Bemis, "a frail, sharp-featured little Gentile woman with grayish hair," who has "recently become infatuated with a literary family and ha[s] been hunting after types ever since."[5] Cahan's exaggerated language and piling up of aesthetic clichés make it clear that he is satirizing here the many Gentile writers who had been venturing to the East Side seeking picturesque literary material. Could he have had Howells in mind as he wrote this story? He possibly did because Howells had initially sought Cahan in the ghetto for a similar reason about seven years earlier. " 'Look at that man!' [Miss Bemis] said, with a little gasp of ecstasy. . . . 'Don't you think there is a lion effect in his face? Only he is so pathetic

. . . . A more exquisite head I never saw. Why, it's classic, it's a perfect—tragedy. . . . Why, [his eyes] are full of martyrdom. Just look at . . . that sea of white hair and beard. . . . He looks like a lion in distress" ("Rabbi," 661).

Ironically, they learn on speaking with him that in Russia Eliezer had been a scribe, and a lion was one of the illustrations he used to adorn passages from scripture that he printed in minuscule Hebrew letters by hand. Encouraged in Europe to emigrate and become wealthy selling examples of his art, he came to America but soon learned that no one here was interested in his handcrafted work; it was too expensive and less perfect than machine-printed scripture with pictures. Now, he complains, he is "all alone in the world," struggling for pennies at his stand to eke out a living in "America, the land of machines and of 'hurry-up!'" ("Rabbi," 663, 664).

Moved by his story, Miss Bemis gives Eliezer $20 (a substantial sum in those days when most workers earned less than $10 a week) to restock his stand. As soon as she leaves, the market people who saw them talking flock around him and ask how much the women gave him as a Christmas gift. Stunned over this possibility, he inquires at the settlement house if he was given the money for Christmas, but despite their denial, he returns it after being assured that it would be handed back to him after the holiday season. The story ends with his ambivalence—satisfied with his piety over returning the money and the assurance of its being given back but somewhat regretful over no longer having the bill in his possession and sensing in the background of his consciousness the question: "Will the Gentile lady pay him the twenty dollars?" ("Rabbi," 668). Meanwhile, fish peddlers nearby hawk their stock with yells taken directly from one of Cahan's sketches of the previous year in the *Commercial Advertiser,* "For Feast and Fast/Jewish Fishwives and Housewives Make Ready" (*CA,* 24 September 1898, 8; *Grandma,* 95–96).

"Rabbi Eliezer's Christmas" is one of Cahan's more lighthearted short stories, though he would surely acknowledge his gentle satire of the littérateurs walking the tenement streets for authentic examples of the picturesque. Moreover, although the caricature of Eliezer may be exaggerated, the old man's complaint has undeniable merit, for with rapid American industrialization the quality of good handwork was nearly always sacrificed for the sake of efficiency and low cost. That is to say, democratization had its price in "the land of machines and of 'hurry up'"—and it still does.

"The Daughter of Reb Avrom Leib"

"The Daughter of Reb Avrom Leib" is not only the longest and most complex of Cahan's short stories, but it is also the last to deal specifically with the Jewish community. It was published by *Cosmopolitan* in May 1900. Chametzky assesses it as "something of a tour-de-force [that] . . . unfolds within a carefully structured framework based on the Jewish religious calendar and the most traditional aspects of its culture" (Chametzky 1977, 97).

The story is divided into eight numbered sections, all but one dealing specifically with an important Hebrew holiday or festival, as seven of the eight titles suggest. The first two sections are set on Friday evenings, Sabbath Eves, and the third occurs on *erev yom kipur,* the eve of the Day of Atonement. The fourth section is set on the eve of Simchas Torah, the completion of one and beginning of another annual cycle of reading from the Torah in the synagogue during the Sabbath service; part of Cahan's depiction of this celebration was drawn from a description of the holiday in his first sketch for the *Advertiser* back in October 1897, though little remains of the Hawthornesque phrasing that controlled the mood of the earlier piece. The fifth section takes place on the first evening of Chanukah. The sixth is set on an unspecified date in July rather than a holiday, but Tisha b'Av, the ninth of Av, falls during that month, commemorating the destruction of the two Temples in Jerusalem (though Cahan refers only to the Romans' destruction of the Second Temple). In this section Reb Avrom Leib is dying as he prepares a final cantorial song for the days between Rosh Hashana and Yom Kippur that gives the seventh section its title, "Days of Awe." The concluding section returns to the "Rejoicing of the Law" on Simchas Torah.

Each of the eight parts marks the progress or regression of Aaron Zalkin's pursuit of Sophie, the daughter of Reb Avrom Leib, who is not actually a rabbi but a cantor; "Reb" is honorific. Zalkin, a successful businessman living in a hotel outside the Jewish area, is badgered by "a great feeling of loneliness"[6] that makes him yearn for his old life and home in the ghetto. To assuage this sense of isolation, he returns to the East Side to attend a Sabbath service and welcome "the Sabbath Bride,"[7] the first time since leaving the Old Country fifteen years earlier that he has been in a synagogue. There he becomes attracted to Sophie, whom he sees in the women's gallery (in the Orthodox shul men and women are seated separately); enchanted by both the service and the cantor's daughter, he returns the following week and sends a *shatkhn* to Reb Leib soon afterward.

Invited to visit, Zalkin is disappointed when he sees Sophie outside of the synagogue and under "the light of common day." In shul, under the romantic influence of prayer and music, Sophie is captivating as she leans forward to hear her father's song; at home, however, she is merely " 'domestically' pretty—just what he was looking for—but she seemed quite another girl" ("Daughter," 54). Nevertheless, a brief exchange with her father on Talmudic passages endears the aging cantor to Zalkin; soon he decides to overlook Sophie's imperfections—she plays the piano only by ear and not very well, she talks too much—in favor of her virtues and his need for someone to love, so he continues to court her.

This story is one of Cahan's most intriguing because the development of the relationship between Zalkin and Sophie, who worships her father, progresses and regresses in a continuing analysis of ambivalence— Zalkin's toward her and Sophie's toward him. Both characters suffer from internal conflicts between romantic visions and realistic observations. As indicated below, only her father's death near the end of the story forces them to come to terms with their ambivalence by virtue of a sheer act of will. Before their betrothal, Zalkin perceives something peculiar and ominous about the young woman: "She was forever bubbling over with the solemn consciousness of being on the eve of the greatest event in her life, but she was haunted by a dim impression that there was an annoying tang to her otherwise complete happiness" ("Daughter," 56).

The problem she faces is that no man can supplant her father in her life. When she ponders marriage to Zalkin, she does not think of him but fears leaving her father alone. When Zalkin takes her hand, "her whole being revolted" ("Daughter," 57). Yet when she confesses on *erev yom kipur* that she has had negative thoughts toward him and begs his forgiveness, an appropriate act of remorse on that solemn holiday, Zalkin's "heart turned to ice" ("Daughter," 58), and on the Day of Atonement itself, he breaks their relation. But on Simchas Torah, a day of rejoicing, he realizes that he "cannot live without her," and their engagement is restored. Before the year is out, however, Reb Avrom Leib becomes ill, Sophie gives him all of her attention, and Zalkin broods over her indifference toward him. Again they separate.

After Reb Leib's death, Sophie devotes herself to promoting her father's music in other synagogues, but the narrator alleges that because

cantors are vain and competitive, they will sing only their own composi-
tions ("Daughter," 62–63). Ironically, the only person who consistently
praises the music of Reb Avrom Leib is her distraught suitor, and when
he returns after the cantor's death to plead for her hand in her father's
name, she assents, swearing by her father that she will marry Zalkin to
ensure her commitment against possible doubts in the morning
("Daughter," 64). "The Daughter of Reb Avrom Leib" is suffused with
the consciousness of *Yidishkayt*. Never before in his fiction and not again
until *The Rise of David Levinsky* would Cahan so effectively integrate the
traditions of Judaism with psychological insight, form with content, and
reality with romance.

"A Marriage by Proxy"

Cahan's next two stories are closer in kind to his vignettes in the *Adver-*
tiser than to those in *The Imported Bridegroom* or the three uncollected stories just discussed. The first, "A Marriage by Proxy," appeared in *Every-*
body's Magazine December 1900. It opens with the portrait of a
particularly attractive young Italian woman whom the narrator calls
Philomena; he sees her among the new immigrants at the Barge Office,
near Castle Garden, waiting for their sponsors to escort them from the
station. Philomena has married by proxy in the church an Italian barber
named Roberto, while she was in Italy and he in America; the proxy was
Roberto's handsome younger brother, Antonio. According to the narrator, such "vicarious marriages . . . are not an uncommon occurrence in
Italy."[8] Until she meets Roberto at the immigrant station she has seen
him only in a photograph and assumed that he would resemble Antonio
more closely than he does. Soon after her arrival in New York, she
acknowledges her disappointment over her husband and refuses to be
his wife, despite the pleas of Antonio and Roberto, who not only pays
her expenses so that she can live in comfort but also regularly sends her
candy and flowers.

    When months pass with no change in her attitude, Roberto consults
a "wine-woman" with the reputation of a superb fortune-teller; she
advises him to stop pleading with Philomena and sending her gifts.
Meanwhile, Philomena desperately tries to annul the marriage, but her
mother forbids it, reminding her that she has made a vow before the
altar ("Marriage," 574). Before long, because of her constant weeping,
her landlady advises Philomena to see the wine-lady. When she does so,
the shrewd fortune-teller informs her that Roberto has also come for

help—to find a new bride—and she has given him a potion to change his love from Philomena to a banker's daughter. Philomena leaves appalled, and after receiving no further attention from Roberto, she pleads with the wine-woman to send him back to her. Suddenly the marriage is a happy one, and when the narrator next sees Philomena, she is collecting "cash" from the barber's customers in his shop.

Like the vignettes, "A Marriage by Proxy" has its charm as pure entertainment, but it lacks the verisimilitude for which Cahan had become noted by the turn of the century. The story is not driven by an authentic sense of motivation but by trickery in the plot. Moreover, the narrator is also simply a device. Cahan speaks in his own voice as a reporter covering the immigrant station; he knows the officials there, one of whom conveys information to him, which is thereby passed on to the reader. After receiving from Philomena herself an account of her proxy marriage, he learns the rest of the story from Antonio once the problems have been resolved. Later the narrator tries to interview the wine-woman, but she is always unavailable, probably because she prefers to avoid "'the American who writes for the papers,' as [Philomena's] brother suggested" ("Marriage," 572). His self-identification as "the American" seems to be an implicit but assertive response to Howells's allusion to him in his reviews as a Russian writer, not an American one, like Crane, a distinction that may have stung after his living in the United States for over fifteen years. One thing that Cahan does not explain, however, is how he (or the narrator who seems to be him) can speak directly with Philomena straight off the boat from Italy. He gives no indication that he speaks Italian or that she speaks English, much less Russian or Yiddish! This anomaly, too, distracts from auctorial credibility and further undermines the realism of Cahan's amusing narrative.

"Dumitru and Sigrid"

"Dumitru and Sigrid" followed Cahan's Italianate story by only three months; it appeared in the March 1901 issue of *Cosmopolitan*. As Cahan notes in his autobiography, he based it on his experience aboard the *British Queen* when sailing as an immigrant to the United States before he learned English (*Education,* 214). Using an English-Russian/Russian-English dictionary he had purchased, he served as the interlocutor between the steerage passengers and members of the crew. The story is a clever fictionalization of this episode, reduced to the experience of two immigrants of different nationalities who become tenuously acquainted at the Barge Office, a temporary immigration center in use near the end of the nineteenth century while Ellis Island was being renovated after a terrible fire in 1897. It offers a sentimental account of their learning to communicate in English with the aid of two bilingual dictionaries, but it also includes the more serious undertones characteristic of Cahan's realistic fiction as the developing theme of alienation becomes apparent.

A sketch on this identical topic, published in the *Advertiser* about a year and a half earlier as "Smiles, All Smiles/And Nobody Knows Where They Will End," appears to be Cahan's though Rischin did not include it in *Grandma*. In the sketch, a young Dutch fellow is attracted to a pretty Hungarian girl in the immigration waiting center, but they cannot communicate; he brings her breakfast each day and sits beside her so that before long, smiling at each other, they "become close friends." "Where will it all end?," the reporter asks the "Barge Mother." "But she only smiled, too" (*CA*, 11 October 1899, 7).

In "Dumitru and Sigrid" Cahan transforms the sketch into a charming story that suggests such meetings are doomed to end in disillusion. Dumitru is an educated, French-speaking Romanian immigrant who becomes attracted to the Swedish Sigrid as she sits alone in the Barge Office. He has been attempting to teach himself English with the aid of a bilingual dictionary, but he finds it difficult because he cannot "take these queer words seriously, as parts of real human speech, and as he grappled with their unmanageable sounds, his sense of desolation grew and grew upon him" ("D&S," 494). Here in a sentence is an obvious representation of Cahan's own initial frustration over the difficulty of acquiring even a rudimentary knowledge of spoken English and an illustration of the despondency that besets so many of the isolated characters in his fiction who cannot overcome their loneliness. On seeing Sigrid, Dumitru attempts to communicate in French, but she responds in Swedish, her native language being the only one she knows. Cahan immediately suggests with this contrast the existence of a class distinction between Dumitru and Sigrid that would be difficult to bridge, and a careful reader may already begin to perceive that a true and lasting relationship between them is unlikely.

Eventually, they learn to communicate in a beguiling manner as they find words to express themselves. "You have sweetheart?" he writes, and she slaps his hand; when he insists on an answer, she touches her heart and shakes her head negatively. "Sad! Sad! Sad!," Dumitru then writes, and Sigrid begins to weep. He tells her that she is "good angel," and she replies, "And you bad man"; then she giggles. The poignancy of their situation is touchingly humorous as Dumitru writes, "I not joke, Sigrid. . . . Know not where I be and where thou be, but I eternal remember thou."

Sigrid responds, "I also never forget thou. . . . Never, never" ("D&S," 498). The inevitable happens when Sigrid is called away, and he romanticizes her in his fancy to the point that all touch with reality is gone. Although he establishes himself in New York, he remains alone, always keeping Sigrid in mind and watching for her, checking in every way he knows to see where she might have gone. Once he misses her in an elevated car, as the Russian immigrant misses his lost Swedish sweetheart in a sketch for the *Commercial Advertiser* over five years earlier ("Result of a Friendship," *CA*, 11 December 1897, 11).

About four years after their immigration, Dumitru is still dreaming of finding his idealized Sigrid when she calls to him as he happens to pass her seated with her baby on the steps of her tenement. Although she has matured and become a mother, she remains pretty, but Dumitru is embarrassed and "keenly ill at ease" as he listens to her Swedish-inflected English: "Her speech made another woman of her" with "the flabby consonants of her Swedish enunciation" ("D&S," 501). "Dis is de gentleman vat mashed me in Castle Garden," she tells her husband as she introduces him to Dumitru, who feels extremely uncomfortable as she speaks—it was "like one listening to the scratching of a window-pane." Completely disillusioned, he leaves the small family as quickly as possible and drives all three of them from his mind as "equally uninteresting and incomprehensible to him."

"Dumitru and Sigrid" is an entertaining story, to be sure, but it also shows how Cahan could select details from his own experiences as he struggled to learn English and adapt them to fiction. Initially, the dialogue between the two main characters is amusing and a little sentimental, but the conclusion of the story reveals that Cahan understood language—even conversation—to be considerably more than simply a means of communication. The way that language is used conveys much about the speakers, including class, education, sophistication, and the degree of interest they have. Clearly, Dumitru is less disillusioned over Sigrid's altered appearance and status as a mature married woman with a baby than over her vulgar English speech, for more than anything else, that is the factor that punctures his foolish dream and obliterates it, instantaneously transforming the romance that has bewitched him into the reality he is ready to face.

"Tzinchadzi of the Catskills"

The last piece of short fiction in English that Cahan published outside the pages of the *Commercial Advertiser* was "Tzinchadzi of the Catskills," which appeared in the *Atlantic Monthly* August 1901. Because it is highly suggestive, it is perhaps his most enigmatic story, yet the essential questions remain unresolved. For this reason, it should be of particular interest to readers of *The Rise of David Levinsky* because although the circumstances of the two works are altogether different, the problems voiced by Tzinchadzi and Levinsky are strikingly similar, and both are left without answers. One might say with this in mind that this story satisfies Chekhov's aesthetic aim as closely as anything else from Cahan's pen because for Chekhov the principal concern of an artist should be to present a problem of life correctly without necessarily proposing a solution.[9]

On the face of it, "Tzinchadzi of the Catskills" is an outlandish tale, so far-fetched that thinking of it in terms of literary realism seems absurd. As in "A Marriage by Proxy," Cahan again employs a first-person narrator who does little more than portray Tzinchadzi in the Catskills setting and report his story as the Circassian horseman has related it to him. The narrator establishes the basic modal contrast in the opening sentence when he acknowledges that while gazing at the distant mountain slopes, he cannot "decide whether they were extremely picturesque or extremely commonplace."[10] Here a division is already suggested between the romantic and realistic elements of his narrative, for if one thing is clear by the end of the story, the two modes are constantly intertwined but never synthesized.

After seeing the astonishing Tzinchadzi on horseback and in the full regalia he had worn in his homeland, the narrator hears an account of his past. Tzinchadzi and another suitor named Azdeck loved the same young woman, who was fond of them both. To determine which would gain her hand, she requested a show of horsemanship, and to assure his victory in the race, Tzinchadzi went through a long period of rigorous practice, perfecting tricks of all kinds on the horse that seemed made for him, and when the day of competition came, he proved far superior to Azdeck. Therefore, Zelaya selected him, but when the villagers taunted Azdeck over his loss and Tzinchadzi, governed by vanity and arrogance, did nothing to stop them, she reversed herself in sympathy and chose Azdeck instead. In despair, Tzinchadzi left his homeland; he rode until he was seen by an American consul and brought to the World's Fair as a master rider. Since then, Tzinchadzi has been alienated from his homeland and all who know him there.

"You mustn't forget," he tells the narrator sadly, after displaying his brilliant horsemanship to no applause, "that these mountains are not mine, and the beast [I now ride] does n't know me" ("Tzin," 224). After the Fair, he purchased a stock of Circassian goods and on the advice of a Jew, commenced selling them at resorts in the Catskills—Jewish resorts, of course. Although he has earned a lot of money, he says, it cannot replace Zelaya in his life, and it cannot "turn the Catskills into the Caucasus" ("Tzin," 226). Throughout this part of his account, Tzinchadzi emphasizes his horse and sword, both of which are prominent symbols of masculine sexuality.

Six years later, the narrator again sees Tzinchadzi, but his beard is gone, as are the steed and sword; also, his name has been changed to Jones, and he wears a blue serge suit; now "fat and ruddy," he glistens "with prosperity and prose" ("Tzin," 226). Moreover, his "heart is cured of Zelaya," who lives happily married to Azdeck. Yet, although "America is a fine place," and he has all the wealth he needs, he is unhappy. Why? He has concluded that "a man's heart cannot be happy unless it has somebody or something to yearn for. . . . My heart ached, but its pain was pleasure, whereas now—alas! The pain is gone, and with it my happiness. I have nothing, nothing! . . . Sweet twinges, where are you? . . . I have plenty of money; but if you want to think of a happy man, think of Tzinchadzi of the Catskills, not of Jones of New York."

In a trenchant analysis of this story, Sanders relates the dichotomy between the romantic Old World Circassia of horsemanship and maidens and the realistic contemporary America of democracy and capitalism to Cahan's own ambivalence, suggesting that the author was drawn to past and present, unable to overcome the strong attraction of either side. Sanders identifies the gap between them with the title of a novel that Cahan had been planning to write and had probably begun while working for the *Advertiser;* it was to have been called "The Chasm," but it was never published, and no trace of the manuscript has been found, which may well represent his continuing irresolution over the duality (Sanders, 237–45). Sanders also perceives the strong Jewish component that exists in the nature of Tzinchadzi's movement from romantic Russia into the reality of peddling in America and gaining economic success through investment and sales, though the story deals nominally only with Gentiles. For Chametzky, too, the title of "The Chasm" symbolizes "the cleft between Cahan's various worlds—Old and New, Talmudic and modern, Jewish and American." To him, Tzinchadzi, the narrator, and "all of Cahan's characters" learn that adaptation to the American social and material life does not satisfy "the pressing needs of the human soul" (Chametzky 1977, 75, 105). If Sanders and Chametzky are correct in their assessments, and I believe that they are, readers cannot help but wonder if Abraham Cahan was truly the atheist that he professed himself to be.

What both commentators might have added to their readings is that with no horse to ride, no sword to wear, and no Zelaya in his dreams, Jones has been symbolically emasculated. He longs, indeed, for what he can never regain and consequently finds himself discontentedly yearning for nothing at all. Three years earlier Cahan had written an article for the *Advertiser* on his youthful vision of the United States; in this sketch he recalled that his idea of America was a lush "many-colored meadow, with swarms of tall," young, beardless men in gray topcoats running about, but he could not account for the fact that "the scene contained not a single woman" ("How a Young Russian Pictured It," *CA*, 6 August 1898: 9; as "Imagined America" in *Grandma*, 147).

He did not mention his age at the time this vision came to him, but a correlation may well exist between it, the unresolved ambivalence either expressed or implied in his novels and stories, and the helpless situation in which men and women alike often find themselves trapped by the end of nearly all his serious fiction in English, from *Yekl* to *Levinsky*, including "Tzinchadzi of the Catskills."

Chapter Five
The White Terror and the Red

In the fall of 1902, after his second resignation from the *Forward*, Cahan and Anna decided to live apart for a time, partly to save money by moving from their expensive apartment into smaller independent quarters and partly because they, and possibly their marriage, were under a strain over the problems he had been facing with the *Forward*. Also, Cahan had been looking for an opportunity to write about a Jewish agricultural community in Woodbine, New Jersey. Whereas Anna remained in a furnished room in New York, he settled temporarily in Woodbine, where he had plenty to do. He freelanced for the *Forward*, wrote by arrangement with the *Commercial Advertiser* a series of articles about the community, enjoyed walking the countryside observing birds, and attempted to progress on his manuscript of "The Chasm" (Sanders, 272).

This long unpublished novel in English on which Cahan had been working for the past few years was probably complete or nearly so, when he put it aside. Citing contemporary sources, Pollock describes it as based mainly on "the chasm" between the liberalized "uptown" German Jews, who had come to America and prospered, and the Orthodox "downtown" Jews from Eastern Europe, who were flocking to the East Side, where their traditional Jewish past remained vital though no longer prevalent. Nor was this controversial issue among American Jews limited to New York. The forthcoming novel was publicized in *Bookman* as early as January 1900, but Cahan may not have returned to the manuscript after beginning to write *The White Terror and the Red: A Novel of Revolutionary Russia* during the summer of 1903 (Pollock, 273, 310–13).

He had remained in Woodbine until early April that year, when he moved to New Milford, Connecticut, planning to continue the leisurely program he had begun in New Jersey. But his plans were interrupted at the end of the month when he learned of the pogrom that had occurred during the recent Easter season in Kishinev (Pollock, 307; Sanders, 273–74). Forty-five or fifty Jews were massacred there (the exact number varies with the source), and hundreds were wounded; during the violence, more than fifteen hundred Jewish shops and homes were also ravaged (Sachar, 320–21; Sanders, 274). Horrified, Cahan quickly returned to New York to discuss this new episode of Russian barbarism with his former colleagues on the *Forward* staff, submitted essays on the massacre for the English press, and wrote Yiddish editorials for the daily, with which he had maintained cordial relations. After a brief stay in New York, he traveled back to New Milford, where Anna joined him, and they remained in Connecticut until the fall; then they returned together and settled down once more in lower Manhattan. Although Cahan had rejected several invitations to serve as editor of the *Forward* again, he was unanimously elected to the position without having agreed to be a candidate, and he could not turn down an offer to head the daily once more with full control.

While still in New Milford during the spring and summer, however, Cahan had continued with his writing. Apparently, "The Chasm" had not been advancing well over the past year; in any case it no longer held his primary attention. Instead, he had been inspired by the pogrom in Kishinev to begin a novel set in Russia and based on the revolutionary activity he had observed in Vilna nearly a quarter century earlier, ferment that had been steadily increasing both in magnitude and violence, with corresponding governmental reactions. Started in mid-1903, *The White Terror and the Red* was completed in the autumn of 1904 (Sanders, 336), taking Cahan only a little more than a year to write despite the pressures of his full-time editorial post with a newspaper still in financial jeopardy. Brought out by A. S. Barnes in February 1905, it was Cahan's most personal and longest publication in English to date.

Although the novel deals ostensibly with the period shortly before and after the assassination of Czar Alexander II in April 1881 rather than with contemporary events, Cahan's journalistic engagement with current revolutionary activity, especially his tracing of the recent Kishinev massacre, suggests that *The White Terror and the Red* should be read from a historically stereoscopic rather than strictly chronological perspective. In other words, Cahan seems to have conflated historical incidents in different regions by interpolating current events with those of a quarter century or so earlier, including those of his own background. The shocking scenes in chapter 39 ("The Riot"), for example, appear to have been modeled more directly on the recent Kishinev massacre than on Elisavetgrad or Kiev, though in his autobiography, as in the novel, Cahan does refer to an incident after the Kiev riot in which contrite assimilated Jews acknowledged their hypocrisy in the synagogue upon realizing that they, too, were vulnerable to the anti-Semitic rioters (*Education,* 182).[1] Cahan was well aware of the series of pogroms terrorizing the Jews of the empire even as he wrote, from the horrors of Kishinev through the depredations of the Black Hundreds, armed bands of thugs ransacking cities and villages with the tacit approval of the government, two years later. In his *History of the Jews,* Abram Leon Sachar notes that during the summer and fall of 1905, the very year that *The White Terror and the Red* was published, the Black Hundreds slaughtered and wounded thousands of Jews in more than fifty different locations (Sachar, 321).[2]

Consequent to this massacre, in an essay written for the *North American Review,* Cahan asserted, "a cry of horror went up from the civilized world, and the [anti-Semitic] crusade had to be stopped" ("Jewish Massacres," 60). As Sachar reveals, however, this observation was no more than the wishful thinking of a romantic socialist. If it appears anomalous to describe Cahan's expectations here as romantic, one may note that he concluded his essay with a quotation from Emerson, the seminal figure of American romanticism: "Of no use are the men who study to do exactly as was done before, who can never understand that to-day is a new day" ("Jewish Massacres," 62).[3] Further, he still believed that where the revolutionary movement was strong, anti-Semitic riots would not occur, because the radicals practiced that freedom among themselves which they advocated for all and did not discriminate according to race or religion. Therefore, he alleged, when such riots threatened, the revolutionaries prevented them; because the movement had not been strong in Kishinev, the Jews there were vulnerable. In an earlier essay, which had appeared in the *Commercial Advertiser,* Cahan had predicted that the "civilized world" would raise its voice and squelch this outrageous anti-Semitic rampage (*Grandma,* 46–47), having apparently forgotten the bitter disillusionment he had suffered in the company of his fellow travelers at the Second International in Brussels twelve years earlier, when they refused to condemn anti-Semitism within the socialist movement. Moreover, his expectations of ultimate rapport among the socialists, the Jews, and "the people" remained alive for nearly two more decades until he completely lost faith in the Bolshevik revolution and rejected the Communists absolutely in the early 1920s. But while writing *The White Terror and the Red* in 1903 and 1904, he still held faith in the cause that had once inspired him toward radicalism and massive social reform in his native Lithuania.

The White Terror and the Red—The Radicals in Fiction

Cahan's second novel is set in Miroslav, a city partially resembling Vilna; at the time, roughly a third of the population in both places was Jewish (Sanders, 338). With the exception of a slight piece editorially designated beneath the title as "A Story," but in fact little more than a fragment, published a few years earlier as "The Share of Count Brantsev,"[4] *The White Terror and the Red* is Cahan's only work of fiction in English set outside of New York (though "The Apostate of Chego-Chegg" and "Tzinchadzi of the Catskills" are set outside of Manhattan).

Prince Pavel Boulatoff: An Unlikely Revolutionary

Also uncharacteristic is Cahan's use of a Gentile hero, Prince Pavel Alexeyevich Boulatoff, the son of a countess by her previous marriage. Pavel lives with his wealthy mother, Anna Nicolayevna Varova, in the only colonnaded house in Miroslav. He is eighteen when the novel opens in 1874 in an unnamed German spa that Pollock identifies as Baden-Baden (Pollock, 313). Pavel is a sensitive youth, but his values have developed according to those of the Russian nobility and other conservatives among the friends and associates of his mother. Consequently, he has adhered to the traditions and mores under which he was reared, knowing no better and affecting a snobbery with which he is increasingly uncomfortable because of an innate benignity that stings him with remorse when he has consciously hurt or offended someone undeserving of such treatment.

Basically, with regard to the hero, *The White Terror and the Red* is a bildungsroman, though it covers only a relatively short period of Pavel's life. It traces the course of his development from a complacent, socialistically naive youth to an active revolutionary married to a young Jewish woman even more radical than himself, and simultaneously from the splendid residence of a countess to a fortress dungeon, from which he is not likely to emerge alive unless he is exiled to Siberia. This rapid transformation in circumstances occurs by virtue of Pavel's awakening to the exploitative tyranny of the czarist government.

His burgeoning awareness motivates him to join an underground group, while his mother believes he is attending the university in St. Petersburg; sympathizing with the nihilists, he becomes a participant in their clandestine activities. Recognizing that he is no longer the docile bon vivant, the countess gradually becomes suspicious of her son and his secretive behavior, though ultimately she is less concerned about his radicalism than his safety because she shares his uneasiness about the obvious injustices in their country. She cannot reconcile, for example, the Czar's cruelties and the implacable "iron-clad" church with the benign qualities she observes in both. But instead of attempting to resolve her ambivalence, she simply "accept[s] it all as part of that panorama of things which whispered the magic word, 'Russia'" (*WT&R,* 9), until she, too, is awakened through discussions with her radicalized son and the forbidden publications he gives her to read.

Here Cahan's ambivalence becomes apparent, as it had a few years earlier in Sonia Rogova's yearning to return to "Dear Old Russia" (*CA,* 15 April 1899, 11) and Tzinchadzi's longing for the Old World amid the capitalist advantages he enjoys in the New. The "magic word, 'Russia,'" suggests the glowing aim toward which the idealists strive, an imagined society of camaraderie, equality, and social justice, if only the despots can be forced out or at least persuaded to loosen control and govern with genuine benevolence toward all.

A clue to this attitude in Cahan himself appeared in his article on recent Jewish massacres in Russia (discussed above), where he states that the radicals who harassed Alexander II in the late 1870s and early 1880s "had started out as peaceful propagandists. They had begun as innocent dreamers and apostles of a new era, which was to evolve from the survivals of primitive communism retained by the Russian village commune," but the government sent them to Siberia and tortured them. That was when the nihilists became terrorists, he said, to defend themselves and demoralize the czarist regime ("Jewish Massacres," 55–56).

Written even as he was drafting *The White Terror and the Red,* these comments clearly expose the relationship between Cahan's romantic idealism respecting the inspiration behind the underground activities in Russia and the aims that continued to motivate them. It is brought out expressly in his portrayal of Makar, one of Pavel's fellow nihilists, who is specifically called a "romanticist" by another of the group for his "rich fancy" and anticipation of "new plans, of new sacrifices" after the arrest of four associates (*WT&R,* 277). This inclination toward romanticizing may have been reinforced by two revolutionary novels from which Cahan drew in composing *The White Terror and the Red*—Nikolai Gavrilovich Chernishevsky's *What Is to Be Done?* and Sergius Stepniak's *The Career of a Nihilist.* In the words of Ronald Sanders, both are "characterized by an inordinately stilted romantic tone" (336).

Pavel himself is no less romantic than Makar, and as he voices his complaints against governmental exploitation and suppression of the people, readers familiar with Cahan's views on the revolutionary movement will recognize the correspondence between the author and his protagonist. Although Pavel's rapid transformation from aristocratic snob to radical nihilist may seem unrealistic, quick changes of heart are possible in intelligent, sensitive, and essentially benevolent young people when they become aware of social realities from which they have been isolated by an overprotective network of family, class, and tradition. Under these circumstances, Pavel reveres the czar as more divine than human; nor does he question the rigid social hierarchy or the injustices it breeds. As if to highlight his own arrogance, he upbraids his mother for associating with a Polish woman who refuses to bow to Alexander, and he tells his servant, Onufri, a retired hussar: "There ought be some difference between noble people and common" in Russia as exists elsewhere, such as in the caste system of India and (anachronistically) slavery in America (*WT&R*, 10–11). But after speaking patronizingly and mockingly to old Onufri, whose mother was whipped to death while Pavel's grandfather, her master, stood by, the young prince is kept awake much of the night by sharp pangs of remorse over his harshness and insensitivity, which leads him to write the countess an effusive note of apology.

During their visit to the spa, Pavel and his mother are accompanied by Alexandre Alexandrovich Pievakin, one of his teachers at the gymnasium, whom they have employed as a private tutor. Not long after they return to Miroslav, Pievakin suffers an injustice that provokes Pavel's sympathy and quick radicalization. Pievakin is called to account by the director of the school for defining and explaining the word "parliament," which is used in the text but not defined there. Because it is forbidden to go beyond the text, he is reprimanded, reported to higher authorities, and soon dismissed; initially ordered only to leave the community, ultimately he is exiled. Pavel is bewildered and angry over this outrage, but he can do nothing about it, though it awakens his social conscience and changes the direction of his life. Shortly after Pievakin's dismissal, he sees a young ensign tormenting a sergeant in front of the soldier's wife or girlfriend. Angered, Pavel challenges the ensign, exposes his arrogance, and embarrasses him; of course, the officer cannot respond because he recognizes the nobility of Prince Boulatoff. After pondering over the implications of these incidents, Pavel returns to his elegant home and tells the countess: "The world is divided into tormentors and victims" (*WT&R*, 38).

By the time he graduates from the gymnasium and leaves for the university in St. Petersburg, Pavel is ready to work toward correcting this injustice. His return to that city after several years reflects Cahan's first visit as Pavel is moved by its diversity and beauty, enthralled over the Neva River, the pinkish buildings, and the prevailing tone of excitement. Whereas Cahan toured the city with his uncle and shopped at the open book stalls, however, Pavel indulges in a six-week binge before he begins to consider seriously why he is there. When that occurs, he notes that like the underground itself, the best unforbidden literature glorifies the peasant, whom it depicts as "a creature of flesh-and-blood reality, but shed over him [is] the golden halo of idealism" (*WT&R*, 43). He perceives that this "peasant worship," a combination of realism and ideality, symbolizes the anticipated future for Russia as the most important authors and the revolutionaries alike envision it: a communistic political economy will evolve without having to pass through capitalism; this would bring freedom and equality to the "semi-barbaric," innocent peasant, long martyred, who embodies the moral and material glory of Russia's future (*WT&R*, 43).

Eagerly seeking access to underground circles in St. Petersburg, Pavel is quickly indoctrinated, and by 1879, some five years after his visit to the spa, he has become an "important revolutionist" (*WT&R*, 57–58). In December of that year he conspires with Feivish Parmet (whose aliases are "Bismark" and "Makar") to help an imprisoned collaborator escape; the other nihilists with whom he associates are known chiefly by aliases such as "The Janitor" and "Purring Cat" to avoid both implicating their families and being identified through family connections. In St. Petersburg, Pavel becomes reacquainted with Elkin, a thin Jewish youth who had been his classmate at the gymnasium in Miroslav, though in those earlier days as Prince Boulatoff, he had studiously avoided associating with so lowly and alien a figure (*WT&R*, 35–36). Caustic and aloof in his own way, Elkin had recognized Pavel's aristocratic snobbishness in Miroslav, and he remains distant, knowing nothing yet of the prince's new social awareness.

Elkin seems to have been based on a young man named Belkin, "a pioneer of the pro-Palestinian movement," whom Cahan had met in Mohilev during his flight from Russia (*Education*, 185). Cahan himself wanted to go to Switzerland, acquire false papers, and return to Russia as an "illegal" to support the revolutionist cause, an intention expressed later in the novel by Pavel's bride. Belkin had asked Cahan why he would head for certain imprisonment and probable death for "a Russian people who made pogroms" against the Jews. Come to Palestine or go to America, he had said, not to Switzerland. As noted earlier (in chapter 1), Belkin converted Cahan into "a pro-American" idealist (*Education*, 185–86). The personalities of the historical Belkin and fictive Elkin differ markedly, to be sure, but once Pavel's status as a nihilist is confirmed, Elkin and he become compatible, and time confirms the soundness of Elkin's similar advice to Pavel (*WT&R*, 359ff).

The Jewish Heroine:
Embodiment of an Ideal and a Dream

It was to Elkin that Pavel had turned in Miroslav to learn more about a student protest that had occurred in the railroad station there when Pievakin was forced to leave. After a large group of students had gathered to encourage and support him, police were sent to disperse them, but instead of leaving under intimidation, they rallied as a girl courageously stood firm, taunting the gendarmes. Knowing nothing of the planned protest, Pavel had not attended, and when informed of it afterward, he despised himself for lacking the foresight of his classmates and those students who had come from the girls' gymnasium. He was especially intrigued by the unknown person who was said to have acted so heroically in front of the police, and to learn her identity he had turned to Elkin. But Elkin had then told him nothing.

For five years Pavel dreams of meeting this heroic young woman whom he has never seen and whose identity he does not know. By the time Elkin informs him that her name is Clara Yavner and that she, too, is one of the radicals, Pavel has fallen in love with the radiant portrait that the years have gradually painted in his imagination. His revolutionary zeal unites with this spiritual affection, thus giving his dual ideal a feminine aspect: "The word Woman would fill him with tender whisperings of a felicity hallowed by joint sacrifices, of love crowned with martyrdom, and it was part of the soliloquies which the sex would breathe into his soul to tell himself that he owed his conversion to a girl" (*WT&R*, 60). Nameless and faceless, she had been the catalyst that called forth his humanitarian spirit. When they meet at last, Pavel sees Clara as an attractive Jewish girl with light hair and eyes, an idealist like himself, and one who also combines the romantic qualities of self-sacrifice, courage, compassion, and ingenuousness. Pavel realizes that she embodies, after all, the phantom Woman of his dreams, and he loves her all the more once he has seen and spoken with her. As Ronald Sanders suggests, Clara's love becomes for Pavel "like the Revolution itself, a messianic promise" (Sanders, 343).

His developing relationship with Clara is idealized and sentimentalized, to be sure, as Jules Chametzky and David Engel note (Chametzky 1977, 121; Engel, 9:120), but it is more than simply the formulaic device that their criticism may suggest. Cahan wrote a decidedly historical novel in *The White Terror and the Red,* one concerned primarily with the revolutionary activities of the nihilists against the tyranny they perceived in the regime of Alexander II, not with the romance of a hero and heroine. Yet their love complements the larger theme rather than undermines or confuses it because the aim of the radicals was no less visionary and idealistic than Pavel's problematic courtship of Clara. Indeed, their prolonged love affair contains elements of the courtly romance, the innocent young warrior sighing and longing for the noble maiden who alternately charms and evades him. Eventually, it culminates in marriage, but by then the police are closing in on them; both have become "illegals" darting from one spot to the next with the eyes of their czarist foes and informers all around. They cannot elude their trackers for long, and because they refuse to heed the advice of more perspicacious friends, they are inevitably caught and imprisoned.

Through the narrator's omniscient insight, however, expressed over the course of their affair, the reader learns more about Clara than Pavel himself can apprehend, for it soon becomes clear that she, like him, is a dreamer. Longing for martyrdom, she envisions herself dying for the good of "the people," and she dotes on this vision whenever an image of suffering occurs to her. But the peasants to whose salvation she has dedicated herself are "like so many literary images," and the realities of Jewish life in her own family and community are unrelated to her "imaginary world" (*WT&R,* 137–38). Her naive idealism leads her to assume that "the era of undimmed equality and universal love would dawn almost immediately after the overthrow of Russian tyranny." Clara delays marrying Pavel because "[s]elf-sacrifice, not personal love, [is] what appeal[s] to her," and marriage would profane her moral vision, whereas sacrificing personal happiness brings her to exultation (*WT&R,* 165, 247, 251).

She sees herself as part of a great visionary scenario, disregarding the prevailing anti-Semitism both in the government and among her fellow nihilists. While the regime uses the Jews as a lightning rod, Cahan's narrator asserts, the radicals regard them as "revolutionary kindling wood"; their pamphlets link the Jews with the Czar as common enemies of the Russian masses (*WT&R*, 341–42). Among the most thought-pro-voking parts of the novel for Chametzky are those pertaining to the response of the Jewish revolutionaries to the prevailing anti-Semitism after Alexander's assassination. Like Clara, they try to rationalize and otherwise come to terms with it until it is impossible for them to con-tinue (Chametzky 1984, 33). Not until it is too late to change direction, then, when her own family is threatened by "the people" she would die to save, does Clara reassess her understanding of the Jews as an oppressed community themselves rather than as agents of the oppres-sors. At last she recognizes that they are truly victims of the revolution, a fear-ridden people persistently violated by the czarist government, including its ministers, army, and police. Until then, "[c]enturies seemed to divide [Clara] from her race and her past" (*WT&R*, 315). As for Pavel, never having associated with Jews outside of the underground movement, he remains detached from their plight until he observes the destruction and carnage of the Miroslav riot. Before that, "[h]e simply could not rouse himself to a sense of their being human creatures like himself at this moment" (*WT&R*, 367).

As narrator, Cahan points out that the "Russian Jews of 1881 felt themselves a living continuation of the entire tearful history of their people" (*WT&R*, 320). He follows this assessment of their seemingly endless despair with a description of the rampage in Miroslav, which in itself constitutes a graphic explanation for it. Once the violence com-mences, soldiers protect the houses of the richest Jews in Miroslav because the government fears that if the rioters are permitted to attack people of wealth and influence—even Jews—they may gain "a taste for playing havoc with 'seats of the mighty,' " and that soon could be dan-gerous to the nobility because such "Popular Fury was liable to confuse the Jew with the magnate, the question of race with the question of class" (*WT&R*, 386). Cahan's description of individual acts of brutality and the suffering they engender combine into a horrifying exposition of terror, yet they do not lose their distinctive clarity as single actions and responses that contribute to, without being lost in, the overall pattern of violence.

Jewish Life in the Pale

Although Pavel's love affair and revolutionary activities usually occupy the foreground, Cahan also devotes considerable attention to illustrat-ing Jewish life in Miroslav during the decade or so over which the action of the novel occurs, an existence reflective of his own days in Vilna. Clara's house on a small square in the Jewish quarter of Miroslav, for instance, resembles Cahan's first home in Vilna—both situated on a square amid a variety of merchants and artisans (*WT&R,* 138, 147–48; *Education,* 12). Her parents, like many other figures in *The White Terror and the Red,* are introduced by way of character sketches, stylistically similar to those identified earlier in *Bleter fun mayn lebn.* Both parents are individualized by Cahan's use of a few distinctive details that more effectively characterize than pictorialize them: Hannah, Clara's mother, is "a shrewd business woman, tireless, scheming, and not over-scrupulous"; and "Rabbi Rachmiel," as strangers address her father, is "a hot-tempered, simple-minded scholar, with the eyes and manner of a tiger and the heart of a dove." Hannah cares for him as if he were a baby and pays no attention to things he says about the mundane world, but she listens reverently and uncomprehendingly when he utters a few words from the Talmud (*WT&R,* 149).

Similarly, Makar's father, Reb Yossl Parmet, is characterized by his ambivalence, torn between adherence to piety and convention on the one hand and love for his imprisoned son on the other. Confronted by Clara, who travels to his home in the shtetl of Zorki to gain his help in enabling Makar to hide his real identity in prison, Reb Yossl shouts and argues but eventually succumbs to her quietly persuasive pleas. While she is there, all of Zorki is awaiting the visit of the "Good Jew" of Gornovo, a revered "Man of Righteousness" whose sagacity is known throughout the region (*WT&R,* 187). His visit draws pious Jews from many local communities, and Cahan's descriptions of their emotional behavior as they wait for him to appear and worship in his presence soon afterward provide the novel with some of its most vibrant and colorful scenes (*WT&R,* 178–95). Much later, his Dickensian portraits of individuals among the Jewish defenders preparing to confront the anticipated rioters are similarly detailed and realistic, though here the descriptions are more sharply pictorial (*WT&R,* 353). Many such distinctive images appear in the novel, to which they add an almost documentary sense of authenticity, as they do later throughout the autobiography.

Historical and Autobiographical Backdrop

Other glimpses from Cahan's life are represented as fiction in the novel but confirmed as fact in *Bleter.* For example, riding in the guise of a teamster atop a horse-drawn wagon while executing a plot to free

Makar from jail, Pavel is spotted by his mother before she learns that he has become a radical; she observes him with shock and astonishment as he passes, though she says nothing at the time. When she asks soon afterward if he had been where she had seen him, he glibly lies, confirming what she has begun to suspect of his unusual recent attitude and behavior. A little later, Pavel confesses, and the countess is drawn marginally into the movement (*WT&R,* 108). Similarly, Cahan's mother had seen him riding with a Gentile on such a wagon, but when she inquired about it later, he replied rudely. Soon she, like the countess, understood that her son was operating in radical circles (Pollock, 54).

Cahan's father is also partially represented in the novel through Alexander Vigdoroff, the well-to-do parent of Clara's cousin Vladimir, to whom she had been like a sister before identifying herself with the nihilists. The elder Vigdoroff has "the head of an agnostic and the heart of an orthodox Jew" (*WT&R,* 222). In *Bleter,* Cahan proposed that a secular friend might easily have influenced his father to become a freethinker: "My father feared and respected" orthodoxy and piety, says Cahan, but "he was irresistibly drawn to the secular books printed in Hebrew and he dreamed of helping me to become an 'educated man' according to worldly standards" (*Education,* 33). Such characterizations as well as his use of recalled incidents and settings verify that Cahan wrote *The White Terror and the Red* as much from his memory and heart as he did from his imagination and documented history.

By interweaving the momentous historical events and figures in power during the 1870s and early 1880s with the substance of his fiction, and by presenting the history in such analytical detail, Cahan was already writing an early version of the type of narrative to be developed much later in Meyer Levin's journalistic fiction and E. L. Doctorow's experimental *The Book of Daniel* (1971). A specific example of the way he draws history into the fiction occurs in the opening of chapter 26 ("On Sacred Ground"), where he refers briefly to the slaughter of 40,000 Jews by Chmyelnicki's Cossacks in the mid-seventeenth century. Bogdan Chmyelnicki, a Ukrainian, was one of the most brutal and merciless of the Cossack leaders in Russian history. Tens of thousands of Jews were slain by his hordes between 1648 and 1655; often entire cities and villages were razed and their inhabitants slaughtered. In 1655 his Cossacks, joined by the Russians, attacked Vilna, the likely model for Miroslav; they set the city in flames and destroyed its Jewish community (Cohen, 39–42). Cahan writes that the Jews of Miroslav were all slain in a small square that has since come reverently to be called "the Bloody Spot" (*WT&R*, 235).

In a synagogue built on that spot, Makar, having escaped from prison with Clara's help, is sitting with a volume of the Talmud before him, apparently studying. Of course, no one there knows his true identity. By virtue of recalling the Chmyelnicki massacre more than two centuries earlier and anticipating the riot soon to come against the Jews of Miroslav, a slaughter based at least in part on the recent Kishinev pogrom, Cahan put his fictitious characters and setting into the midst of an authentic and highly credible network of circumstances. Moreover, his abundant allusions to the Czar and his officers, including the political machinations among them, enhance the sense of authenticity to the extent that at times a reader cannot be certain where history ends and fiction begins.

For example, Count Loris Melikoff's thwarted attempts to promote cooperation with the radicals are presented in the novel as in Cahan's articles, and from the author's similarly sympathetic perspective. In *The White Terror and the Red*, however, Pavel and Clara completely misunderstand Melikoff's conciliatory role, thus making them appear to a knowledgeable reader as no less naive and short-sighted regarding facts than quixotically idealistic regarding principles (*WT&R*, 95, 255, 263, 266, 288–89). Although details are often altered, many allusions to imprisoned and executed revolutionaries in the essays and autobiography have their counterparts in the novel, and the specifics of such incidents as the bombing of the Winter Palace in February 1880, the establishment of a cheese shop to cover the digging of a tunnel beneath a wide avenue for a bomb to be exploded when the Czar's carriage passes over it, Alexander's assassination in March 1881, and the fomenting of pogroms afterward by hostile government officials—all correspond directly with references in *Bleter* and Cahan's recent articles.

With its intricate plot threading among materials drawn from history and Cahan's own background, Pollock praises *The White Terror and the Red* as "a tightly-woven narrative, Tolstoyan in concept if not in execution" (Pollock, 313). This is a fair assessment; the only other fiction from Cahan's pen to rank with this novel in magnitude and complexity is his next and final one, *The Rise of David Levinsky*, for which Pollock's Tolstoyan comparison may be more apt. Yet it also had the benefit of Cahan's experience combining history with a love story and presenting both with a pronounced socialist message in his panorama of prerevolutionary Russia.

"The Share of Count Brantsev": Origin of the Final Chapter

Ironically, the concluding chapter of *The White Terror and the Red* actually may have been the earliest part of the novel that Cahan wrote, antedating the Kishinev massacre by more than two years. In this chapter, Pavel is imprisoned in the Fortress of Peter and Paul, St. Petersburg, he and Clara having been arrested months before. She is equally isolated in another section of the prison, and Elkin, too, has been captured. Their only means of communication is rapping on the stone walls that separate one cell from the next, hoping that the coded messages will be passed along by other prisoners. When Pavel is not suffering from monotony and loneliness, his usual state, his mood alternates between joy over anticipating a successful revolution and total despair over his own hopeless situation, isolated in a dungeon vault with nothing in his future but a trial leading almost certainly to death in prison.

In this final portrait of Pavel, Cahan adapted the short fragment that he had brought out in *Ainslee's Magazine* in March 1901, more than four years before the publication of *The White Terror and the Red* (*Grandma*, 490–96). Entitled "The Share of Count Brantsev," it presents a situation nearly identical to that in which Pavel finds himself, an arrested radical trapped in his prison cell with communication limited to tapping on walls, though Brantsev can tap only to a prisoner he has never met. Less than a story, this short descriptive narrative lacks both plot and character development. The imprisoned count falls in love with a woman to whom he taps briefly, but her replies soon cease, possibly because she has turned her attention to a prisoner in the adjacent cell, and Brantsev, like Pavel, is left in despair. Before long he is sent to Siberia.

Pollock provides an apparent source for this sketch when he indicates that at the end of the century Cahan met one Natan Bogoraz, "a Russian writer and revolutionary" who was visiting the United States. Bogoraz had been imprisoned in Siberia, and Cahan asked him how he had responded mentally to an apparently hopeless situation. Bogoraz "described his state of mind while serving his sentence—the anxiety, the resort to philosophy, the contemplation of suicide, the inexplicable variation in mood, ranging from euphoria to stygian gloom." Pollock speculates on the possibility that Cahan "had so early been considering his novel of revolutionary Russia" and notes that the information gained from Bogoraz "undoubtedly" was used in the last chapter of *The White Terror and the Red*. He says nothing, however, about "The Share of Count Brantsev," with which he was evidently not familiar (290–91).[5]

Pavel and His Mother

Certainly Pavel, like Brantsev, undergoes these changes of mood. Occasionally, of course, he thinks of Clara and receives her tapped message of love, which he returns, but it is surprising what sustained attention he gives to thoughts "to-day" not of his wife but his mother, and "tantalising, heart-crushing thoughts" they are: "He pictured her committing suicide because of his doom, and the cruel vision persisted. . . . He tried to think of something else, but no, the appealing, reproachful image of his mother, of his poor dear mother . . . would not leave his mind. . . . He would not shake that image out of his brain if he could. It was tearing his heart to pieces, yet he would rather stand all these tortures than shut his mother out of his thoughts" (*WT&R*, 425–26).

Although the historical base of the novel is unaffected by Pavel's unshakable image of his mother in the closing chapter, his sudden regression at such times to a remorseful son rather than a yearning husband or inconsolable revolutionary calls for a reassessment of his maturity during the entire course of his young adulthood, from the time he elects to become associated with the radical underground to his imprisonment. The apparent domination of his mother's image over Clara's must lead readers to question whether Pavel's principal but unacknowledged and probably unconscious aim was initially to rebel irresponsibly against the countess to assert his independence or, as he believes, to promote reform in Russia and liberate the people. His utter despondency in the concluding sentence of the novel, when he throws himself on his bed and "burie[s] his face in his hands," implies that he has at last understood, as his mother's "reproachful image" alternates in his mind with thoughts of Clara, that he has gone too far in attempting to prove his sovereignty, and the enduring vision only confirms that her hold over him has never truly been broken. Indeed, his self-pity even leads him to picture the countess committing suicide over losing him, as if she cannot bear to live without him. Although one has no reason to doubt that Pavel's love for Clara is genuine, his mother's image appears to be the controlling manifestation of his loss and consequent despondency.

For readers of *The Rise of David Levinsky*, Pavel's indelible, affecting image of his mother should be particularly suggestive because, as the next chapter will explain, Levinsky is in a similar plight. He, too, unable to escape the vision of an idealized mother who has died for him, exists in his own solitary, loveless world: no real woman of flesh and blood can successfully compete with her.

Critical Reception

Although *The White Terror and the Red* differs distinctly from Cahan's earlier fiction, it was well received by reviewers, who generally recognized its limitations but nonetheless considered them to be outweighed by its strengths. With respect to Cahan's striking out on a different path with his fiction, perhaps the critics did not find the change altogether unexpected since he had been publishing articles, as noted above, on revolutionary activities and anti-Semitic rampages in Russia for the last several years. Therefore, although the novel was set a long way from the Lower East Side, its setting would have been considered to fall within the parameters of Cahan's expertise and journalistic interests.

In what is probably the most enthusiastic review received by the novel, Edwin Lefevre, writing for *Bookman,* admires it as "a work of art of the highest class." Lefevre, who had been a colleague of Cahan on the staff of the *Commercial Advertiser,* emphasizes and lavishly praises the realism of what he calls its brilliant narrative and lifelike character development.[6] Cahan must have felt gratified over such praise, as well as that of an anonymous reviewer in the *Critic,* who recalls Howells's prediction that Cahan would someday "do honor to American letters" and believes it "to be fulfilled in *The White Terror and the Red.*"[7] Other favorable reviews appeared in the *New York Times Book Review,* the *Reader,* and *Outlook;* in the last, the reviewer, again unnamed, praises the novel as "unexpected[ly] . . . well constructed, forceful, and ably sustained," but regrets that Cahan's Russian characters occasionally speak American slang. This leaves one to ask, of course, what other slang they might have been imagined to use in a novel written in English and published in the United States.[8]

As may be expected, Hutchins Hapgood, who also had recently worked with Cahan on the *Advertiser,* joined the other reviewers in admiring *The White Terror and the Red* for the way in which "the Russian realistic method and the Russian idealistic spirit have for the first time been applied to the direct and literal facts of the revolution." Also reviewing for the *Critic,* he recognizes that the "truthful and vigorous love-story forms a natural part of the book." Although he would have liked the novel to be longer so as to allow for fuller development of "the human story" and "the big historical theme," his reservations on this note are qualified by the observation that Cahan was writing a sequel ("The Chasm"?) in which he planned to bring the revolutionaries to the United States, where they would confront American problems and conditions.

Neither the manuscript of this sequel nor any part of it has ever been located. All told, Hapgood concludes that Cahan's new novel "is, in addition to its historical importance, a sweet, fully realized piece of fiction."[9]

Relatively little attention has been given *The White Terror and the Red* since shortly after its publication, and, as is true of the uncollected stories, it has not yet been reprinted. This novel deserves better. Moses Rischin noted that as of 1985 it was still the only novel in English he knew to describe the plot leading to the assassination of Alexander II and all that followed. Like the reviewers, he praised Cahan for portraying the revolutionaries as "models of heroic virtue, as historians generally have known them to be, and not as the subterranean grotesques who people two of Joseph Conrad's most brilliant novels" (Rischin 1985, xxxix). Similarly, Pollock favored *The White Terror and the Red* in comparing it with a roughly contemporary work, Henry James's *The Princess Casamassima* (1886), on the basis that Cahan knew the underground from experience whereas James did not, a difference which resulted in James's more limited authenticity (Pollock, 315–16). For Louis Harap, the most important aspect of Cahan's novel is the attitude of the Jewish radicals toward Judaism and their fellow Jews; he finds the writing "competent . . . [but] uninspired" and lacking in vitality, and so it is not surprising to him that the work should have nearly dropped from view (Harap, 509).

Probably the best criticism of the novel to date is by Jules Chametzky. Although he duly acknowledged it as excessively moralistic and sentimental, he put little weight on these shortcomings and praised the novel instead for effectively presenting a detailed view in fiction of the early revolutionary phase in modern Russian history. This aspect of the narrative is particularly important, he says, because Cahan's Gentile readers knew little or nothing about it. On a more personal level, Chametzky assesses *The White Terror and the Red* as "Cahan's act of homage to his past," for it centers thematically on the author's own "problem of reconciling a consciousness of Jewishness with the demands of the revolutionary spirit." Whereas Ronald Sanders, also recognizing its personal value to the author, believes that Cahan's Russian novel "suffers above all from his evident desire to dream out a course he had never followed," Chametzky praises it as an "ideologically sophisticated" work that both exposes Cahan's sympathy for the "courage and idealism" of the revolutionaries and constitutes a "serious critique of their methods and philosophy" (Chametzky 1977, 33, 115, 120–21; Sanders, 336).

Most points in these critiques but confirm what many thoughtful readers of *The White Terror and the Red* may perceive for themselves. The novel is tendentious, but it conveys, from the perspective of a marginal participant, an authentic account of the prerevolutionary activity in Russia during the late 1870s and early 1880s as well as the fearsome plight of the Jews there. If the love story is oversentimental and the nihilist endeavors seemingly quixotic, the exaggeration of these essentially romantic complementary themes effectively dramatizes them and thus helps to drive forward an exciting, engaging narrative. Although the novel met with favor among most of its reviewers, Cahan never published the sequel that Hutchins Hapgood had anticipated, probably because he had been reassessing his priorities. After seeing *The White Terror and the Red* through the press, he apparently intended to leave the writing of fiction behind him in order to devote full attention to the *Forward,* which in 1905 was still in a state of financial insecurity. Fortunately, he was dissuaded early in the next decade from following through with this aim, a reconsideration that led him to begin the first version of *The Rise of David Levinsky.*

Chapter Six
The Rise of David Levinsky

In the autumn of 1912, after a leisurely summer in Europe with Anna, Abraham Cahan was invited by *McClure's Magazine* to write a series of two articles on the success of the Jewish immigrant in the rapidly expanding garment trade. The invitation was unexpected. During the last seven years, since bringing out *The White Terror and the Red*, Cahan had been dividing his attention between labor and the *Forward*, which left him neither the time nor the inclination to return to writing for the English-reading market. Yet the idea of such a project had already germinated in his imagination; it strongly appealed to him as a means of publicizing the increasingly visible role of the Eastern European Jew in American life, and surely he knew that no one was in a better position to undertake it than he: a Jewish immigrant, labor leader, and accomplished writer.

Cahan soon decided favorably, chiefly because he did not expect to spend much time writing the two articles. As initially conceived, the series was meant to inform, not to entertain, the public; although *McClure's* had gained fame for its muckraking exposés of industry and city government in the previous decade, Cahan did not aim to resuscitate the movement with a contribution of that sort on the garment trade. Nevertheless, he wished to present the truth of the matter, and though aware of the danger of an "anti-Semitic backlash," he was willing to take the risk (Chametzky 1977, 127). He settled on using a fictitious first-person narrator whose account of his life would bear all the earmarks of verisimilitude as it conveyed what Cahan held to be a balanced exposition of the subject's early years in Russia, his immigration to New York, and his rise from poverty to commercial success in the garment trade. The series commenced in April as "The Autobiography of an American Jew: The Rise of David Levinsky."

Cahan was so successful with the first section that he was asked to extend the "autobiography" to four articles, which he agreed to do. Although he wrote quickly and well, he was under considerable pressure from his obligations to the *Forward* and to a group of garment workers participating in a strike that he was attempting to help settle. Moreover, he had developed an ulcer that had become so serious that immediate surgery was necessary to assuage the pain. Because of these problems, the four sections of Cahan's serial were written under strikingly different circumstances. He finished the first part before entering the hospital, the second while hospitalized, the third convalescing in New Jersey, and the fourth back in New York (Pollock, 382). In his introduction to the novel, Jules Chametzky points out that the author "specifically tied together the memory of the strike, the operation, and the origin of *David Levinsky*"[1]; although Cahan had intended to "trace the genesis" of the novel in a sixth volume of *Bleter fun mayn lebn,* he unfortunately never did so (Pollock, 381).

What Cahan probably did not know as he drafted the early part of his narrative was that in the issue preceding the opening of his series, Burton J. Hendrick, associate editor of *McClure's,* had arranged to publish in the magazine a long article of his own entitled "The Jewish Invasion of America," which details what he considered to be the Jewish acquisition of cultural and economic control in the United States. The inflammatory article appeared in March as scheduled. At the end of it, Hendrick announced the forthcoming series by Cahan as an illustration of how "the minute workings of that wonderful machine, the Jewish brain," has led the Jew to succeed over all other immigrant groups in America (Chametzky 1994, xxiv–vi). Although it is unlikely that Cahan knew of it before publication, the editorial epigraph introducing his series picks up the same idea: "Business is the Great Adventure of to-day. . . . Levinsky is, in fact, an actual type; his story reproduces actual characters, occurrences, and situations taken from real life. And his intense and complicated struggle shows, as no invention could do, the traits of mind and character by which the Jew has made his sensationally rapid progress in the business world of America."[2]

Thus it appears that without his knowledge, Cahan was set up to exemplify Hendrick's anti-Semitic thesis with the "autobiography" of David Levinsky, "an actual type," whose "traits of mind and character" underlie the rapid commercial success of the American Jew. As if to reinforce the point, Cahan's series is illustrated throughout by Jay Hambidge, whose graphics complement the text of the first two sections but deviate in the last two by emphasizing the stereotype of the gloating, lustful, long-nosed Jew and thereby maliciously undermining the truth of Levinsky's complex character as the author himself presents it (see Chametzky 1994, xvi–xviii). One longs to know if Cahan complained to the editor about these anti-Semitic illustrations; certainly, he had grounds for it, but I have found no evidence that he did so. Chametzky speculates that although Cahan was well aware of both latent and overt hostility to Jews in "the respectable mainstream of American publishing," he was less concerned over making an issue of it than with building a cultural bridge between Eastern European immigrant Jewry and Gentile America (Chametzky 1994, xviii).

Fortunately, the bridge led him inward as well as out. Ronald Sanders proposes that as Cahan developed the portrait of his narrator, he immersed himself so deeply in Levinsky's character that the personal aspects of the "Autobiography" became more engaging to the author than the original subject, the successful Jew in American business (Sanders, 423). But neither his editor nor his readers would have known that. For them, Levinsky's "Autobiography" evidently satisfied expectations as an exposure of "the minute workings of that wonderful machine, the Jewish brain," as it governed the transformation of a poor Russian-Jewish immigrant into a wealthy American industrialist. Had it not meant more than that to Cahan himself, however, he would never have revised and extended the narrative a few years later into a novel of more than five hundred pages. With the creation of Levinsky, he had initiated a process of self-exploration that had yet to be completed; consequently, he soon commenced working again on his Jewish American success story, polishing the prose style, adding characters and episodes, analyzing in far greater depth the moral and ethical complexities only introduced in the *McClure's* articles, and expanding on the ambivalence of his enigmatic narrator.

If "The Autobiography of an American Jew" served its basic purposes at the time of publication—that is, of reaching out to the American public for Cahan, and of exposing alleged Jewish business practices for *McClure's*—the complete novel published by Harper & Brothers in September 1917 as *The Rise of David Levinsky* did much more: it virtually dissects both the narrator's torn consciousness and his moral character. The difference between the two versions is almost the difference between a skeleton and a fleshed-out figure. Development, especially near the beginning, occurs through narrative reminiscence in the serial rather than through character portrayal and dialogue in the full-length novel. In the early version, several of the more arresting figures—such as Bender and Dora—are absent, and significant episodes—such as, to identify but a few, Levinsky's starting his own shop after spilling a bottle of milk at the Manheimers' factory, his entering the marriage market, his becoming engaged, and all but a passing reference to his stay in the

Catskills—are also missing. The prominent theme of sexuality in the novel is only touched on in the articles, where neither prostitutes nor attempted seductions are mentioned. Whereas the *McClure's* version contains the gist of Levinsky's success story, including his occasionally unscrupulous behavior, it lacks the drama and depth that give the full novel its compelling power. In place of the long meditation that concludes the novel, the serial ends with Levinsky's expression of resignation immediately after returning from his dinner with the tipsy Gitelson: "Such is the tragedy of my success" ("Autobiog," 128).

The Autobiography of an Alienated Millionaire

To contrast the serialized version with the book, it has been necessary to cite a few of the more important specifics from the novel before summarizing it. My intention in doing this has been to make it clear at once that the difference between the two versions is more than a matter of length gained in the book from Cahan's adding new but essentially similar episodes and characters, fuller descriptions, and more details. To be sure, these additions do constitute an important part of the transformation, for nearly everything in the book has been developed more substantially; however, it is a larger, tighter, and more fully realized work altogether.

Major Themes and Structure

Though episodic, Cahan's bildungsroman is comprehensive and well unified. Isaac Rosenfeld compares it structurally with the Talmud in that it "consists of an extended commentary on a single text." That text appears in the opening paragraph, especially the last few lines, in which Levinsky acknowledges that his "inner identity" has not changed in the past thirty to forty years and that his present life "*seem{s} to be devoid of significance*" (Rosenfeld's emphasis).[3] Jules Zanger notes that Levinsky himself is the chief "unifying device" for this novel "about the Americanization experience."[4] Although Cahan's novel is not limited to the process of Americanization, the key point here is to see Levinsky as unifier. As in the *McClure's* series, he is still the autobiographer looking retrospectively over his life at the age of fifty-two years, exactly Cahan's age when he began to write the first installment of his serial. Cahan melded essential elements of his own experience from three cultures—traditional Jewish life, especially among the Yiddish-speaking Jews from

Eastern Europe; a Russian artistic sensibility with its emphasis on realism; and the American initiative toward success.[5] The autobiographical content of *The Rise of David Levinsky* will be discussed later in the chapter, but for now this triad corresponds with three major themes of the novel: the Americanization of an immigrant Jew, the development of American industry and organized labor presented realistically in a literary format, and the apologia of a driven but irresolvably divided man. These complementary, mutually supportive strands integrate Levinsky's socioeconomic interests with the emotional and psychological pressures that distract him and create a complex pattern with a multitude of ambiguous implications. Ultimately, the novel is a moral tale that illustrates how not to live, a message that gains authority from Cahan's powerful representation of social, economic, and psychological forces at work.

The table of contents that precedes the text identifies by title the fourteen sections, or "books," of the novel. The list conveys a general idea of the stages of life through which Levinsky passes along the way from childhood poverty in the Pale of Russia to enormous wealth and power as a manufacturer of women's ready-made clothing in New York:

Most surprising about this list of section titles is that, despite Cahan's initial aim to write "an anatomy of Jewish business success in America" for *McClure's* (Sanders, 427), in the revised novel only the heading for book 10—"On the Road"—suggests anything at all about Levinsky's developing career as a businessman and industrialist. The other thirteen section titles pertain to the personal strand of his autobiography: his early life and education in Antomir, his preoccupation with sex, his immigration and rapid acculturation, his broken dream of a college education, and his persistent melancholy nourished by chronic loneliness.

Levinsky does not open his narrative with the time and place of his birth but with a confession that at his present age his external transformation from an immigrant pauper to a multimillionaire has no internal correspondence, for he asserts that no similar change has occurred in his "inner self," and with all his wealth and power, he finds his life essentially meaningless. Readers of his autobiography should keep this acknowledgment in mind, for from the very outset it is clear that his rise to commercial success will eventuate in a failure to achieve commensurate personal contentment. Moreover, his early confession, almost a lamentation, should lead readers to be less curious about Levinsky's success in business than his failure in life with so much money and worldly respect at his disposal.

Parental Loss and Early Duality

Born in 1865 in Antomir, a city in northwestern Russia similar to Vilna, Levinsky remembers losing his father as a child and living in a cramped cellar room in Abner's Court with his mother and three other families. For a time as a small boy, he sleeps with his mother, and when he becomes a little older, he uses his father's coat as a blanket. The Oedipal implications here are evident. Though poor, he receives a *kheyder* education from teachers well versed in employing sadistic disciplinary practices; oddly enough, on leaving the *kheyder,* he goes to a yeshiva but does not mention his bar mitzvah, a crucial episode in the life of a Jewish male. When he is eighteen, his mother is beaten to death by Gentiles when she leaves home to confront them in anger for having tormented David on his return from school. Working tirelessly for him over most of her hard life and finally dying for him, his mother anticipates the typical Yiddish mamas who became the butt of Jewish-American parody later in the century.[7] Grief-stricken, with her image embedded indelibly in his mind, he continues his yeshiva studies under the tutelage of Reb Sender, assisted with meals by charitable local people until 1885.

In describing the nature of his Talmudic reading, Levinsky focuses briefly on the theme of duality. This is a vital point; although it relates specifically to his consciousness while studying at the age of sixteen, it has implications that extend beyond this episode through the remainder of the narrative. Poring over the Hebrew text, Levinsky finds himself either in "an exalted state of mind or pining away under a spell of yearning and melancholy—of causeless, meaningless melancholy" (*RDL, 37*). His friend Naphtali, a former schoolmate from their *kheyder* days, explains that the duality comes because the mind is engaged with the meaning of the text while the heart is moved by the melody of the intonation, which "tells a tale of its own. You live in two distinct worlds at once," he says. This "singsong" creates a mystery in David because it seems the voice of another being inside him with a separate life (*RDL, 35, 38*). As Isaac Rosenfeld also notes, David's early longing for something unknown is a fundamentally Jewish characteristic, possibly traceable to the Jews' yearning for Jerusalem since their exile from the city by Hadrian early in the second century (Rosenfeld, 263). With this in view, David's enduring melancholia apparently has both a "self-inflicted" and a universal cause (Pollock, 395).[8]

Preoccupation with Sex and Power

By 1885, however, David's interest in the Talmud has waned, and when the possibility of a good life in America is mentioned to him, he decides to immigrate with money secretly given to him for that purpose by Matilda, the secularized divorced daughter of a wealthy Jewish woman who feels sorry for him and helps to support him after the death of his mother.

Matilda introduces David to sensual love and passion; though still too naive to comprehend her seductive purpose, he remains obsessed with her until long after he has arrived in New York. But even during his childhood years and early adolescence, David has experiences related to sex that he does not yet understand. At one time, he peeks through a fence along a forbidden street and asks his mother afterward what the half-naked women do with soldiers there; he tells her that one of the women who saw him gave him a piece of cake. Shocked, his mother warns him to stay away from that street because it is sinful, and he heeds her words. Also as a child he is teased sexually by Red Esther, a little red-headed girl from the family of a bookbinder living in the cellar with them. Though he detests her, he becomes so infatuated over Sarah-Leah, the daughter of one of his *kheyder* teachers, that he allows her to bite his finger as hard as she wishes, assuring her that he will not feel the pain, and he does not cry out though she draws blood. The oral and phallic suggestiveness of this episode foreshadows Levinsky's tendency toward erotic indulgence later on.

For example, several years afterward at the yeshiva, he cannot keep his eyes from young women who come to the building on errands. Although he notices their eyes and figures, he is "still more interested in their mouths" (*RDL,* 44), which he consciously associates with both biting and kissing, and less consciously with sexual aggressiveness and conquest. When nearly sixteen, David loves God "as one does a woman," but Satan also diverts his attention by bringing attractive women near him (*RDL,* 40). On one occasion, Reb Sender notices him looking at an especially pretty girl and quotes a Talmudic observation to David: "He who looks even at the little finger of a woman is as guilty as though he looked at a woman that is wholly naked" (*RDL,* 39). Early in his life, then, David is pulled in two directions regarding women, a conflict that leads to a sexual ambivalence he will never understand or overcome.

Further complicating this issue is his attraction to feminine young men. At the yeshiva, for instance, he intensifies his friendship with Naphtali, whom he admires for his polished manner and intelligence, though other boys at the seminary deride him for his "girl-like squeamishness" (*RDL,* 35). In New York some years later, he develops an even closer relationship with Jake Mindels, whose deep voice and manly physique are at odds with the soft-blue eyes and "effeminate psychology" that strangely fascinate Levinsky (*RDL,* 158). He attributes this adoration ("I adored him") to Jake's "good looks," but their intimate conversations on love suggest the presence of an erotic appeal of a deeper nature.

Another of Levinsky's features already evident during his school years is his developing sense of power, accompanied by a strong need to acquire control. While attending the *kheyder* of Sarah-Leah's father, he is "the strongest boy" in the school, and although the wealthiest pupil in a *kheyder* is normally "its king," David himself claims that he is "usually the power behind the throne," and he gains authority over the other boys by defeating one in a fight (*RDL,* 22–23). Later, while attending the yeshiva, he meets a Polish boy who has memorized hundreds of pages of Talmudic commentary and becomes jealous. Arrogantly, David commits himself to learning at least as many pages and commences to memorize them with this goal in mind rather than faith. When his profane aim is discovered, he is scolded by Reb Sender and ridiculed by his rival. Only because his mother is killed at this time does David avoid humiliating himself in this inane competition.

The first four books, which cover David's twenty years in Antomir from birth to young manhood, comprise but 81 pages, a little over one seventh of the 530 in the original edition of *The Rise of David Levinsky*. Yet they provide a foundation for the major themes of the novel: acculturation, the rise of a Jewish businessman to wealth and power, and alienation, governed by an ambivalent sexuality that vacillates between the ideal and the erotic. Not until Levinsky actually arrives in America does he consider how he will earn a living; in Antomir he thinks of the United States not only as a land of plenty but, more important, as a country "of mystery, of fantastic experiences, of marvelous transformations" (*RDL*, 61). It is with this romantic conception in mind that he immigrates, and the vague dream remains alive in him as he establishes a foothold in the New World, though initially it leads him to aspire to a college education, not a business, and the City College of New York becomes his "temple."

But Levinsky knows that such a goal is far beyond him until he works, saves enough money to support himself in college, and learns the English language. Books 5–7 cover the stages of his indoctrination into American life. His first source of assistance toward Americanization is Mr. Even, who purchases a haircut, a bath, and new clothes for him, arranges for a room and pays his first month's rent, then gives him five dollars and sends him on his way to a new life. "It [i]s as though the hair-cut and the American clothes ha[ve] changed my identity," he says, and all else seems part of "the remote past" (*RDL*, 101). At first, he tries a few odd jobs, which he soon finds unsatisfactory. As a peddler for a short time, he has modest success at best; much of his initiative goes into learning English, word by word and phrase by phrase, as Cahan himself did during his early years in America, and he seeks to achieve what he takes to be standard pronunciation. Levinsky believes that people "born to speak [English] [a]re of a superior race" and knows that fluency is essential to enter college.

Also as Cahan did, he attends an evening school, where he gains the admiration of his teacher, "a young East Side dude" named Bender, "hazel-eyed, apple-faced, and girlish of feature and voice"; before long, Bender has taught him much and made "a pet" of him (*RDL*, 129, 135). He learns American mores as well as the language from Bender, whose expression surprises him with its "unsmiling smile" (*RDL*, 130), or what Emerson called "the foolish face of praise."[9] Hence in rationalizing his own evasive and ambiguous behavior later on, he admits, "We are all actors, more or less. The question is only what our aim is, and whether we are capable of a 'convincing personation'" (*RDL*, 194). When told not long after his success in Bender's class that he has "a credit face"

(*RDL,* 202)—that is, he appears trustworthy—Levinsky applies this bit of personal information to great advantage. Of course, peddling gives him experience in business dealing—hawking merchandise, bargaining, making much of little, and so forth—and brings him into contact with other immigrants more experienced than he in street life on the Lower East Side. One of these peddlers is Max Margolis, whose salacious accounts of his sexual prowess both offend and fascinate Levinsky. It is Maximum Max who assures him that any woman can be seduced if the approach is right, a lesson Levinsky takes to heart and ultimately applies successfully in courting the peddler's own wife, Dora, the main subject of book 9, by far the longest in the novel.

Meanwhile, still dreaming of Matilda and no longer seriously restrained by religious scruples, Levinsky determines to gain sexual experience himself. His clumsy efforts to seduce his first two landladies are comical, but because the second is a Mrs. Levinsky, a matronly woman to whom he is not related, his efforts to win her echo earlier Oedipal overtones, a suggestion reinforced by the image of his mother that comes to him immediately after he mentions his landlady's name. Quickly squelched by both women, he loses his virginity to a prostitute, and once he has enjoyed "the novelty of yielding to Satan," he enters an extended period "of debauchery and self-disgust" (*RDL,* 125). Among the "girls" he visits, Argentine Rachael becomes a favorite; although he finds her "repellent," he also cannot "help liking her spirit," and she becomes an early source of streetwise information for him on local politics. Consequently, he cannot despise her as conventional values may dictate; indeed, he says, echoing Stephen Crane's note to Hamlin Garland in a copy of *Maggie* that Crane presented to his friend: "I knew that at heart she was better than some of the most respectable people I had met" (*RDL,* 128).[10] Levinsky continues to patronize brothels while pursuing Dora, whom he claims to love (*RDL,* 288). For him by now, though, love has become a clash of opposites, a discordant fusion of the sensual and the sublime.

It is Maximum Max himself who brings Levinsky to his flat and introduces him to Dora; they become friends, and soon Levinsky begins taking his meals with them; later he becomes their boarder. By this time, he has given up peddling in favor of the sewing machine. A nervous young tailor named Gitelson, who clung to Levinsky "like a lover" as they crossed the Atlantic (*RDL,* 88), helped him to enter this craft soon after arriving in New York; when they meet on the street sometime later, he convinces Levinsky that the machine could be far more lucrative for him than peddling. Gitelson arranges for Levinsky to be apprenticed to an experienced operator who trains him, and before long he is quick and adept in using the Singer. Recognizing himself as one of the workers now, rather than the businessman he was as a peddler, Levinsky joins the union. Determined to gain a college education, he gives increased attention to the acquisition of fluent English, poring over volumes of Dickens and Thackeray.[11] Unlike Cahan himself, Levinsky favors Dickens over the more realistic Thackeray (RDL, 165). In his eagerness to fund his studies, Levinsky turns to Gussie, a sensible but unattractive coworker in his shop, in an attempt to marry her for the money she has saved. Although he seduces the lonely woman one evening in the moonlight, she rejects him the next morning, fully aware of his exploitative intentions.

Also during this period, he and Jake Mindels often attend the Yiddish theater; again unlike Cahan himself, Levinsky approves "unnatural speech" on stage rather than realistic theater. That is "one of the principal things an audience pa[ys] for," he says to Jake (RDL, 161). Affecting a lovelorn devotion to Madame Klesmer, one of the leading Yiddish actresses, the two young men converse and write emotionally of their love for her, though beneath the surface Levinsky seems to be using Madame Klesmer as a means of displacing his attraction to the masculine appearance and "effeminate psychology" of Mindels himself (RDL, 158).

The Drive toward Wealth

As his skill on the Singer increases, Levinsky grows dissatisfied with the conditions and pay in the shop where he learned his trade, and after initiating a disagreement with his contractor, Levinsky leaves to work in a larger factory run by the Manheimer Brothers, of German-Jewish heritage. For a short time he also supplements his income at the shop by teaching English to Meyer Nodelman, a wealthy clothing manufacturer who is the son of the elderly couple from whom he rents his room.

Levinsky's change of employment leads to what he calls in the title of book 8 the destruction of his temple. Though working for the Manheimers brings a decided improvement in pay over his previous earnings, he resents their treating the Russian-Jewish workers as inferior, which was then characteristic among Jews of German background. It is not their occasional denigration of the Russians that causes him to leave, however, but a small accident, "a mere trifle," that sours him on his employers and completely changes the direction of his life (RDL, 187).

When he spills a bottle of milk over a few silk coats on the floor, Jeff
Manheimer, enraged, calls him "a lobster," which Levinsky possibly
"feels subconsciously" to be a gross insult, for the lobster is not only
clumsy with its huge claws but also tref (not kosher),[12] and he threatens
to cut the cost of the garments from Levinsky's pay.

Like the accidental closing of his firm's safe that leads George Hurst-
wood to flee from Chicago as a thief and adulterer in Dreiser's *Sister Carrie,* the spilling of a little milk induces Levinsky to reconsider his
options. He suddenly realizes that among them is the possibility of
establishing a shop of his own, and after a short time he decides that
with a little capital and a good designer he can do it. Excited about the
possibilities rather than fearful of the risk, Levinsky sees his plans as not
simply an attempt to become rich but to play "a great daring game of
life" or, as he alludes to it near the conclusion of his narrative, as "good
sport" (*RDL,* 189, 523). Shrewdly he persuades Ansel Chaikin, a superb
designer with the Manheimers, to work for him as a nonpaying partner
without leaving or informing his present employers. It is difficult for
him to gain the approval of Chaikin's skeptical wife, though by mislead-
ing her into assuming that his "factory" is already being set up and that
the necessary money to begin is available, he satisfies her doubts sufficiently to allow her husband to try.

Books 8–10 constitute the heart of Levinsky's ascension to success in
the garment manufactory. They detail his shady practices, his art of
manipulation and deception, his readiness to take serious risks on the
chance of lucrative profits, and his capacity to learn as he goes. He turns
successfully to Meyer Nodelman for money to help start the business;
indeed, he and Nodelman share an interest in becoming educated, but
both alike put money first. "What is a man without capital?," Nodelman rhetorically asks him and answers without pause, "Nothing!"
(*RDL,* 181).

On the road, Levinsky ingratiates himself with managers and pur-
chasing officers, and he slyly copies successful designs by competitors,
passes them off as his own, then sells them at a lower cost by keeping his
labor expenses below those of other shops. This he does by leaving his
Jewish workers free on Saturday, the Hebrew Sabbath, whereas other
employers refuse; when the unions apply pressure for a maximum number of hours in the workweek, Levinsky quietly allows his laborers to go
beyond the maximum; they work for a smaller wage but for more hours,
thus earning more with him in a week than they could with his competition. These are the tactics promised in the original announcements for

the *McClure's* series. And Cahan does, indeed, expose "the minute work-ings of . . . the Jewish brain," as Burton Hendrick promised; the exposé does not paint an attractive portrait of the successful businessman in action. But this is the truth of the matter as Cahan himself recognized it from experience among workers, contractors, and manufacturers alike, and for him, as for Howells, the truth in itself had an intrinsic value that transcended the merits of popular approval.

Whereas book 8 opens with Levinsky still sewing for the Manheimer Brothers, a proud worker and union man preparing for a college educa-tion, by the end of book 10 he has achieved the success and prosperity he was after. These books detail "the rise" of David Levinsky as a man governed by economic values who evolves into a commercial success; book 8 focuses on his early struggle to establish an independent shop, and the latter two convey an account of its expansion.

Central in book 9, however, is not his business but a long episode in which Levinsky meets, courts, seduces, and ultimately loses Dora, with whom he claims to have fallen in love. Like Jake's wife, Gitl, in *Yekl,* Dora represents the nobility of life that could be found among the poor immigrant Jews on the Lower East Side, an unfamiliar and unexpected aspect of their existence to most contemporary Gentile readers, and Cahan sought to depict it through his realistic fiction. Dora's benignity and profound suffering contrast sharply with Levinsky's hypocrisy and materialistic aims, yet the two are drawn together by mutual longing for some inexpressible romantic need, he for an idealized woman to fill the combined role of mother and harlot, she for a savior to rescue her from the mundane existence of a vulgar peddler's wife without losing her self-respect or her undeserving daughter, Lucy, to whom she has devoted her life. Dora endures the arduous, selfless life of typical ghetto wives whom Cahan had described in an article for the *Commercial Adver-tiser* fifteen years earlier (*CA,* 29 June 1902; *Grandma,* 602–9).[13] Lucy, in contrast to her mother, is merely "an interesting study" to Levinsky (*RDL,* 288), as she adopts American ways and sloughs off, layer by layer, the influences of her Yiddish past until she virtually sells herself in marriage to a wealthy suitor who will enable her to live in comfort and style.

The Social Darwinism of an Incipient Millionaire

Cahan's compassionate portrait of Dora accentuates Levinsky's cold, cal-culating manipulation of her, her husband, and virtually everyone with whom he enters a relation, personal or commercial, in his egocentric drive for conquest. As an employer now rather than an employee, Levinsky reassesses his role in society largely on the basis of his readings in Emerson and Herbert Spencer among other books to which he turns while drumming up sales as he travels through the country (*RDL*, 326). Through Social Darwinism, he sees himself as "one of the 'fittest.' It [is] as though all the wonders of learning, acumen, ingenuity, and assiduity displayed in these works ha[ve] been intended, among other purposes, to establish my title as one of the victors of Existence" (*RDL*, 283). These lines appear in book 9, shortly before Levinsky overcomes Dora's weakening resistance, where they document his will to personal as well as economic power. They are reinforced with reference to his position several years later; by then, he is a millionaire industrialist convinced that society is a sham, fundamentally a brutish, selfish jungle.

No doubt, society at large presents an accurate reflection of his own corrupt values, and, peering outward, he but sees himself. Lacking faith and ideals of any kind, he believes only in "the cold, drab theory of the struggle for existence and the survival of the fittest. This could not satisfy a heart that was hungry for enthusiasm and affection," he says, "so dreams of family life became my religion" (*RDL*, 380). His wealth and social stature by this time have made him a target of matrimony among eligible young Jewish women, and in book 11 he describes his quest for a wife in "the marriage market" to help him establish a home and family. By the end of that book, he is engaged to Fanny Kaplan, the daughter of a patriarchal man of sixty prominent in the new Antomir Synagogue, whose appearance gives the impression of "Talmudic scholarship and prosperity" (*RDL*, 389). At the synagogue on the anniversary of his mother's death, Levinsky combines his lamentation for her with the thought of his forthcoming marriage to a young woman he does not love, and incongruously gloats over his commercial and social success (*RDL*, 389).

But his engagement does not lead to marriage after all. On the way to spend a weekend in the Catskills with the Kaplans at their summer home, Levinsky is delayed and unable to leave as expected on Friday, so he stops overnight at the Rigi Kulm House, a resort on the way, to avoid giving Mr. Kaplan the impression that he was riding on the Sabbath, forbidden by Hebrew law. As Levinsky describes it, the Rigi Kulm is "a babel of blatant self-consciousness," whose boarders include Jewish vacationers from all backgrounds, *olraytniks* freed from their urban responsibilities for a couple of weeks, young single women seeking husbands, workers, employers, and tradesmen of all descriptions (*RDL,* 404). Levinsky expects to remain through Saturday and catch a train the rest of the way to the Kaplans' cottage on Sunday morning, but while leisurely watching two young women playing tennis, he finds himself strangely attracted to one of them; within a few hours, the attraction has become an obsession that keeps him at the Rigi Kulm for the next two days and assures the breaking of his engagement.

Unrequited Love

He soon learns that the name of this captivating young woman is Anna Tevkin, whose surname first came to his attention almost immediately after the death of his mother, when "the face of my martyred mother would loom before me" at prayer. In Antomir, Naphtali told him the romantic story of an admired Jewish poet, Abraham Tevkin, who had gained his bride by writing long letters to her father expressing devotion for the daughter and thus winning parental approval for their marriage (*RDL,* 56–57). No sooner has Levinsky associated the girl on the tennis court with this romantic tale than "a halo of ineffable fascination" is cast around her, and again he is obsessed with an elusive woman, the daughter of the romanticized poet and his wife (*RDL,* 413). His craving for Anna relates directly to his sentimentalizing of the past, and her image merges with the indelible one of his dead mother to intensify the aura of his idealized woman, the impossible quest of his dreams.

Almost the whole of book 12 traces the course of his clumsy attempts to become acquainted with Miss Tevkin at the Rigi Kulm and its grounds. Unlike most of her single female contemporaries there, Anna is not a husband-hunter but simply a stenographer enjoying herself on a vacation with companions. Obviously disgusted with the imposing boorishness of this would-be suitor far older than she, Anna rejects him outright, a rebuff, he says, "that [lies] like a mosquito in my soul" (*RDL,* 447). In conversing briefly with Anna earlier, Levinsky attempted to employ poetic imagery to describe a sunset (*RDL,* 437), and his ludicrous mixed images then, as in the "mosquito in my soul" passage, expose a surprising insensitivity to the inappropriate use of language for expressing thoughts inspired by the spirit or the imagination.

Levinsky's courtship of Anna Tevkin continues in book 13 as he attempts to apply the same methods toward winning her that enable him to succeed in business as he courts buyers to gain sales over competitors. His approach resembles that of her father years before, as

Levinsky traces the aging poet to an East Side coffee shop, introduces himself, and praises the old man's poetry, long out of fashion, after reading examples of it in the Astor Library. It does not take long for him to ingratiate himself with Tevkin, who hungers for such praise and, like Rabbi Eliezer and Tzinchadzi in two of Cahan's uncollected stories, misses the old life in Russia as he believes that he remembers it, with its slower pace and artistic sensibility.

In America, little of Tevkin's time is given to writing; instead, he has become involved in real estate speculation, which had attracted vast sums of borrowed money around the turn of the century. When Levinsky asks him why he no longer writes beautiful Hebrew poems, Tevkin replies, as Meyer Nodelman did years before vis-à-vis education in relation to his factory: "Business is business and poetry is poetry. I hate to confound the two" (*RDL*, 457). Then Levinsky expresses an interest in Tevkin's investments as a tactic to help him gain access to Anna, though he insists at first that he does not intend to invest. The tactic works, and when Tevkin invites him to visit his home, Levinsky informs him of his desire to see Anna. Though taken aback, Tevkin agrees when the millionaire says that his only motive is to convince the young woman that he was not really the boor he seemed to be in the Catskills.

Of particular interest in book 13 beside Levinsky's unsuccessful pursuit of Anna is the array of friends and relatives who appear at Tevkin's home, proponents of various radical social views and modern literary ones. Anna herself supports realism in the theater, especially the plays of Ibsen; although Levinsky says that she is simply reiterating the opinions of others, her observation that Ibsen's plays are "full of life" and that they include a "moral force and beauty" superior to the plots in traditional drama clearly corresponded with Cahan's own views (*RDL*, 415–16). Her father is an outspoken Zionist, an important movement of the era, though it is given little other attention in *The Rise of David Levinsky*. For the most part, Levinsky recalls being more amused and bewildered over the constant bickering that occurs among Anna's family and acquaintances than seriously interested in the subjects of their discussion. His only concern there is Anna herself, and when he finds an opportunity at last to ask for her hand, she rejects him even more forcefully than she did earlier.

Thus ends the third and last of Levinsky's major love affairs, all of which, as Bonnie Lyons perceptively observes, were motivated chiefly to help him escape his orphaned state. Each of the three women involved—Dora, Fanny, and Anna—represents different cultural aspects of the Lower East Side. Dora symbolizes sacrifice for the family, Fanny embodies traditional Judaism and authority, and Anna represents art, socialism, and Zionism—"the whole intellectual Lower East Side."[14]

A Meaningless Life

Shortly before Anna's final rejection of him, Levinsky succumbs to the fever of real estate speculation, and once he has done so, he commits increasingly large sums of money. Many years earlier, he had hired Bender, his old evening-school teacher, to work in his office, and over the passage of time, Bender's value as an assistant and consultant has increased many fold, to the extent that Levinsky entrusts him with considerable responsibility in the firm, as he does when he leaves to court Anna.

Bender understands that Levinsky is investing irrationally and pleads with his employer to return to the office, but his pleas are disregarded. To be sure, Levinsky himself realizes that his extravagance is not simply a matter of greed or lust for money; instead, his investing has become a "gambling mania [that is] really the aberration of a love-maddened brain" (RDL, 483). Anna's final refusal awakens him to the fact that he has so heavily committed himself in speculation that he is in serious danger of bankruptcy, and he can regain financial stability only by borrowing from a wealthy Gentile supplier of wool, who lends him the necessary funds because Levinsky is one of his best customers.

With the restoration of his solvency, Levinsky's account of his past is over but for a few incidents that he recalls in the anticlimactic closing section, book 14, which further emphasize the loneliness and prevailing sense of meaninglessness that characterize his life as an alienated millionaire. In the most poignant of these recollections, he remembers having owed ten dollars to Gitelson, who sailed with him to America exactly twenty-five years earlier and arranged for him to learn how to operate a sewing machine. Consequently, Levinsky invites his old shipmate to an anniversary dinner with champagne in a lavish hotel restaurant. Unaccustomed to alcohol, Gitelson becomes intoxicated, and Levinsky repays him the money with extravagant interest, disgusted over the failure of what he expected to be a gratifying nostalgic evening. But the vast social and economic gap that has grown between them is impossible to bridge with an expensive dinner, as Levinsky realizes too late, and his sense of alienation afterward is more pronounced than ever.

A single incident near the end of the novel brilliantly exposes the extent of Levinsky's ambivalence, hypocrisy, and alienation at this stage of his life. On a street in New York he sees Shmerl the Pincher, a former *melamed* whom he and the other boys had detested for his torturous pinching, and his first thought is to exact the revenge for which he had longed as a child. But his ancient teacher is obviously impoverished and alone, and Levinsky cannot bring himself to vengefulness after all. Instead, he decides to help the old man, but then makes no effort to do that, either, realizing the spell of the past is "broken irretrievably," as if it were a revelation (*RDL*, 504).

Levinsky's Essential Ambivalence

Throughout his autobiography, Levinsky's ambivalence is evident, as is the hypocritical rationalizing by which he justifies and explains both his manipulative strategies and his irresolvable, allegedly undeserved longing.

He begins the closing chapter of his narrative with a rhetorical question: "Am I happy?" Of course, much of the preceding text from the opening paragraph onward makes his answer a foregone conclusion. No one exists who can inspire or serve him, he says, and the "gloomiest past is dearer than the brightest present. . . . My sense of triumph is coupled with a brooding sense of emptiness and insignificance, of my lack of anything like a great, deep interest" (*RDL*, 525–26). Levinsky regrets not having followed his original intentions of pursuing an intellectual life, for that, he believes, is what would have best suited him. "I pity myself for a victim of circumstances," he laments, then concludes, "I cannot escape from my old self" (*RDL*, 530).

What he says here no doubt is true for him at the time, but he does not recall that his "old self" is decidedly other than the poor, devout lad at his Talmud studies whom he envisions in his shadowy, romanticized recollection of the past. His arrogance and pride, his quest for power, his sexual curiosity followed by lustful urges, all of these are already apparent in the youthful David during his years in the *kheyder* and the yeshiva.

Much of the ambiguity in the pattern of the narrative is attributable to the character of Levinsky himself. In his putative confession, he alleges frankness, but what he really offers, as Sanford Pinsker suggests, is a combination of "selective memory" and the desire "for consolation."[15] In creating the character of Levinsky as narrator, Cahan may have adapted a method used by Howells in *The Rise of Silas Lapham* (1885), from which he obviously borrowed the title for his own novel. Everett Carter hypothesizes that in *The Rise of Silas Lapham* Howells appears to have employed Anthony Trollope's method of "using his characters' thoughts and words as self-indictments."[16] Carter refers here to a specific conversation in the novel that many readers have interpreted as anti-Semitic, not only on the part of the characters but possibly the author himself; perhaps Howells's irony, he suggests, was too subtle for his readers to penetrate.

Cahan's use of this method of narrative self-denigration is also apparent throughout Levinsky's autobiography, leaving readers uncertain as to how he expects his allegedly candid apologia to be received. Is Levinsky truly filled with "self-pity"? Does he really believe that he is "a victim of circumstances"? Having recalled his sensual behavior as a *yeshive bokher,* is it possible that at fifty-two he nevertheless envisions himself in his youth as a devout Talmud student? What exactly does he mean when he says at the outset of his narrative that his "inner identity" is "precisely the same" as it was three or four decades earlier, and in his closing paragraph, "I cannot escape from my old self"? While openly acknowledging the sins of his past, does he yet remain blind to his essential egoism, a sense of self so all-consuming that it has rendered him emotionally and spiritually vacuous? Because genuine love and compassion are beyond not only Levinsky's grasp but his ken, his quest for a profound emotional relationship is futile, so time and again he is rejected. But it remains uncertain how much of this Levinsky himself perceives.

Cahan versus Levinsky: A Dissonant Autobiography

Because Cahan incorporated so much of his own life and experience into *The Rise of David Levinsky,* many readers have assumed that the novel is more autobiographical than not and that to a large extent the author and his central character are identical. Although W. D. Howells, for example, thought *Levinsky* "too sensual in its facts," he still considered it "a pretty great autobiographical novel."[17] Louis Harap said simply that "Levinsky is a thinly disguised Abraham Cahan" and considered him a "fictionalized evaluation of [Cahan] as a conflicted person who chose success over integrity" (Harap, 518, 524). According to Ronald Sanders, "The young Levinsky is, in fact, so much like the young Cahan . . . that it must have been extremely difficult for Cahan to formulate the crucial point at which Levinsky's life and career diverged from his own" (Sanders, 420). Moreover, from John Higham's viewpoint, Cahan "never steps beyond Levinsky's angle of vision" (Higham, vi), an observation suggesting that Higham apparently missed much of the irony in Cahan's portrait. As Irving Howe understood the relationship between them, the author and narrator alike longed for things that no culture, with its inevitable limitations and imperfections, could possibly satisfy. The being of "Cahan-Levinsky" derives from self-conflict, Howe says, and Levinsky's endless seeking underlies Cahan's own "foreboding of unfulfillment" (Howe, 523; Pinsker, 2–3). Like Sanders, Jules Chametzky believes that part of the cause of the more melancholy tone of the full novel was Cahan's own darkening mood as a result of the anti-Semitic persecution evident in the Leo Frank "trial" in Atlanta (1913–15) and that of Mendel Beiliss in Kiev (1914) (Chametzky 1994, xix). Making the case for contemporaneity more broadly, Richard S. Pressman plausibly observes that the novel should be regarded as a product of the time in Cahan's life when it was written rather than as a reflection of his past, for it depicts both the 1910s and his own success story at that time.[18]

Harap and Sanders, in particular, offer many valuable insights into the novel, but with respect to the correspondence between author and fictive autobiographer, their readings are too reductive. For Harap the fundamental similarity is ethical and moral, whereas for Sanders the parallels are established chiefly through specific facts. Many details and allusions in the novel do, indeed, seem to confirm the latter's view. Anna, for instance, was the name of Cahan's wife and of Tevkin's daughter, and Cahan himself has the same first name as Tevkin (Pressman, 16n11). Also like Cahan, Levinsky has a remarkable memory for childhood details; as children, both were fascinated with the soldiers stationed nearby, and both had neighbors with daughters named Esther. Both Levinsky and Cahan studied English intensively, attended public school to learn it more quickly, and taught English; both held a passionate interest in the Yiddish theater; and both were equally surprised by the immensity and variety of America when they first traveled outside of New York. These parallels and many others are beyond question; indeed, Isaac Rosenfeld and Joan Zlotnick are correct when they indicate that because the voices of Cahan and his narrator seem to have so much in common, confusion occasionally results (Rosenfeld, 265–66).[19]

But as Jules Zanger cautions, one must not confuse Levinsky's language with Cahan's (285) because the differences between the author and his central character are far more important than the likenesses. Their priorities were diametrically opposed. The similarities in their personalities notwithstanding, whereas Levinsky is absolutely egocentric, Cahan worked chiefly and tirelessly to improve the lives and futures of Eastern European immigrant Jewry. Although the Cahans had no children, their marriage lasted more than sixty years, while Levinsky never marries at all. Levinsky exhibits a superficial interest at best in the fiction he reads and the theater he attends, but Cahan contributed significantly to both as a writer and critic, loved music, and showed a decided interest in painting as well. Moreover, unlike Cahan's diversified English writing, which suggests a style of genuine engagement, Levinsky's language seems contrived. Chametzky astutely observes that it lacks emotional authority and therefore dramatic intensity; his language is reportorial and "lifelessly stiff" rather than truly expressive of an emotional state, like Cahan's.[20]

One of the crucial differences between them, too, is that Cahan knew his own mind far better than Levinsky knows his. Whereas Cahan was drawn alike to writing fiction in English and to Yiddish journalism, he was highly competent and successful in both endeavors, as his enduring reputation as author of *The Rise of David Levinsky* and editor of the *Forward* for half a century testifies. "It is a fine feat to write a first-rate novel," H. L. Mencken wrote for Cahan's eighty-second birthday, "but it is also a fine feat to steer a great newspaper from success to success in difficult times. [Cahan] has done both."[21] For many years, he was engaged with and committed to both aspects of this dual career, which together constituted the core of his life. Levinsky, on the other hand, is never clear on what he really wants; his success in business feeds his vanity, but it does not satisfy his longing, for he is motivated simultaneously toward loving and conquering, as in his pursuit of Dora and Anna. Consequently, at fifty-two, this melancholy magnate remains alone, believing that he would have been happier as an artist or intellectual, though once in America, he remained preoccupied with sexual adventures and business. These are among the most apparent disparities between the author and his narrator, but readers familiar with both Cahan's biography and Levinsky's narrative will perceive many more.

In addition to autobiographical correspondences, there is a biographical one as well. Although Irving Howe does not propose that Cahan based the character of his narrator on a specific historical figure, he outlines in *World of Our Fathers* the life of Louis Borgenicht, whose dates of birth and death (1861–1942) and career roughly correspond with Levinsky's. Borgenicht became wealthy twice in the garment industry. Near the end of his life, like Levinsky, he devoted much of his time to charity and society, but "[t]orn between the social possibilities created by his wealth and the pieties he still felt toward the East Side, Borgenicht ended as a man not quite comfortable in any world, . . . a stranger, perhaps, even to himself" (Howe 159, 161). Cahan may have known personally or at least known of Borgenicht when he decided on the nature of his central character, but I have seen no evidence to confirm that Levinsky is in any way based on his life.

The American Cultural Context

In any case, Cahan's grand novel unquestionably offers far more than a fictionalized biography, autobiography, or psychological case study of either the author or the narrator. As John Higham suggests, the insights and psychological portraits Cahan conveys through Levinsky "emerge . . . from a rich context of social history" (Higham, vii). If Levinsky himself is the unifying center of the novel as both narrator and participant, his encyclopedic coverage of the historical context through which he passed from stage to stage of his life constitutes a description of two vastly different social worlds that merge in a verbal panorama of New York's Lower East Side. Because Cahan graced Levinsky with his own phenomenal memory for details, the narrative is energized with the scenes, incidents, names, and voices of Levinsky's past, from the cellar and *khadorim* of Antomir to the peddlers and tenements of the East Side ghetto.

For Cushing Strout, *The Rise of David Levinsky* confirms that a novelist with "a strong sense of time and place, combined with perception into the individual motivations of his characters" will write fiction in which history and culture come alive. Of special importance, he proposes, is the way the novel illustrates "the complex transactions between the self and its culture in a historical moment."[22] Of course, this is precisely what literary realism demands, as Joan Zlotnick stated more than two decades ago. Cahan was a realist not only because he represented "reality as he saw it," she said, but also because he "modified the convention of happy endings and poetic justice, . . . created complex characters, . . . employed the international theme, expressed an interest in social and political issues, and experimented with point of view as well as vernacular, colloquial, and dialectical speech" among ordinary people (Zlotnick, 34).

To be sure, the small-scale individual scene authentically presented in a given time and place is a crucial component of literary realism, as evident in such detailed descriptions as those of Yampolsky's Bohemian café on the East Side and the Tevkins' Passover seder table (*RDL*, 455, 494). But such glimpses of quotidian existence without a grander context are the stuff of local color, appealing and engaging to a point but lacking the power of the grand spectacle, the full program in its various stages of development and transformation.

Cahan provides this colossal scope in Levinsky's depiction of the rapid expansion of the ready-made clothing industry by the Russian-Jewish immigrants on the East Side. First, Levinsky depicts the lower echelon of the business, the lives of the peddlers and shop laborers as he and they drudge daily and uncertainly for a few dollars a week. Then, once he has described the establishment of his own business, he periodically turns aside from his personal dilemmas to explain what changes have been occurring in the garment manufactory and their overall effects on American culture, particularly on fashions as style becomes democratized among American women. In book 8 he describes the first part of this process as the Eastern Europeans move into the industry with the greater inflow of immigrants into New York; then he follows up with their gaining control of it from their German-Jewish predecessors; and, finally, he specifies the unperceived impact that Russian-Jewish immigrants like himself have had on the lives of ordinary American women (*RDL*, 201–2, 372–74, 442–44).

With such information as this in mind, Phillip Barrish suggested that the overview given by Levinsky can readily be extrapolated: "*The Rise of David Levinsky* should be read as a powerfully distilled performance of the far more general historical mechanisms of capitalism, the formation of modern bourgeois subjects, and the socio-cultural hierarchies instituted in both phenomena."[23] In sum, Levinsky the alienated melancholic may engage and disturb readers who find it difficult to gain insight into his peculiar state of mind, but Levinsky the ambitious, amoral industrial magnate fascinates because readers see him as representative of the impoverished immigrant Jew who has "made it" in the Golden Land, an achievement that seems to Sam B. Girgus "more diabolical than miraculous."[24]

As pointed out in earlier chapters of this study, once the East European Jews recognized that the possibility of a better life was available to them in the United States, they began to reach for it (Howe, 120).[25] Levinsky learns this soon after his arrival. The new immigrant passes through "a second birth" on entering America (*RDL*, 86, 93), he says, acknowledging his own virtual change of identity—an American haircut and new clothes provided by Mr. Even (*RDL*, 101).[26] Everything becomes subject to reversal in this "topsy-turvy country," he is told by an elderly man in a synagogue on the very day he arrives; it transforms "the immigrant shoemaker into a man of substance, while a former man of leisure [is] forced to work in a factory," a statement directly echoing *Yekl,* though in the earlier novel Cahan used the Yiddish *shister*[27] instead

of the English "shoemaker" (*RDL,* 97). Fully aware of his lack of refine-
ment by American standards, Levinsky struggles to correct this short-
coming day by day. He learns dining etiquette from Charles Eaton, a
Gentile buyer whom he takes to dinner, and to whom he acknowledges
his ignorance of the menus and use of fancy silverware in a stylish
restaurant. In this way, he discovers the difference "between taste and
vulgar ostentation," thus avoiding the pitfalls of an *olraytnik* (*RDL,*
259–60).

As Levinsky becomes acculturated and finds the secular world
increasingly complex, heartless, and "interesting," his waning piety dies,
an essential step, he believes, if the immigrant is to become Americanized and gain commercial success (*RDL,* 110). For this reason, Levinsky
retains his Hebrew affiliations, exploiting them as needed, but he leaves
Yidishkayt behind with his lost faith and piety. Charles Liebman found
such an abandonment uncharacteristic of most East European immigrants,[28] who held ethnic rather than religious ties with their fellow Jews
and therefore often continued to conform with Jewish traditions without struggling to retain their Hebrew practices, a theory Bonnie Lyons
has affirmed with respect to Cahan's own views (Lyons, 90).

America is a major topic in *The Rise of David Levinsky,* and the process
of Americanization is an essential theme; for good and for bad, Cahan
treats both with unblinking realism. In dealing so thoroughly with "the
immigrant experience," Chametzky asserts, this novel is "a quintessen-
tially . . . American book" (Chametzky 1977, 141). The idea is high-
lighted when Levinsky observes the vacationers in the dining room of
the Rigi Kulm House. As soon as the band begins playing "The Star-
Spangled Banner," the diners all arise, enthusiastically applauding. Even
of himself, Levinsky recalls, "Love for America blazed up in my soul"
(*RDL,* 424). Again like Stephen Crane, who had made the same point in
Maggie more than two decades earlier, Cahan used this scene ironically
to suggest the difference between genuine patriotism based on American ideals and mere flag-waving based largely on sentiment. But Cahan
probably felt more deeply than Crane the opportunities America provided for immigrants because by the time he began writing *The Rise of
David Levinsky* he had taken full advantage of them, whereas Crane,
then dead for more than a decade, had expatriated himself during his
final years of life.[29]

In this respect, Cahan's candid realism again takes his novel beyond
the limitations of ethnic writing into the wider realm of American fiction through the narrator's telling confession that although he remains

"an atheist," he lives in a hotel with mostly German Jews and belongs to one of their synagogues; of course, his prosperity separates him from most Russian Jews. "I often convict myself of currying favor with the German Jews," he admits, then adds, "But then German-American Jews curry favor with Portuguese-American Jews, just as we all curry favor with the Gentiles and as American Gentiles curry favor with the aristocracy of Europe" (*RDL,* 528). With such a comment as this, Cahan provokes non-Jewish-American readers to consider their own inclinations to "curry favor" with groups a level or two higher than their own in the social hierarchy of and beyond our democracy.

Despite Levinsky's failure as a human being, he is a remarkable success as a businessman, and that is surely one of the main points Cahan intended to document with this novel of immigrant achievement. As Lothar Kahn notes, *The Rise of David Levinsky* emphasizes American impatience—the desire for quick success—through schemes, speculation, however it can be achieved (Kahn, 5). Indeed, in the midst of the madness to grab millions from real estate speculation, Levinsky veritably shouts: "Success! Success! Success! It was the almighty goddess of the hour" (*RDL,* 445). But his failure as a man of compassion and emotional attachment has led several critics to find fault with America for making such driving materialism possible. Given Levinsky's personal limitations before he ever sets foot in the United States, this conclusion seems incredible, but it is by no means uncommon.

Theodore Marvin Pollock, for example, alleges that Cahan's "favorite theme" is "the tragedy of success," and Levinsky personifies it, a person "who has been thoroughly imbued with—and corrupted by—the American dream of material success" (Pollock, 384). Sanders agrees when he proposes that from the beginning of the novel "there are signs that the source of the trouble is America itself, or rather, the uprooting that America represents, undertaken for the sake of a more glorious-seeming future, but at the expense of whatever is beautiful about the past."[30] For David Engel, too, Levinsky's ultimate unhappiness implies that "America fails on its own terms"; instead of a haven it is a source of alienation for immigrant and native-born American alike.[31] According to Sam B. Girgus, Cahan used Levinsky as a contemporary Jeremiah to attack those who had either lost faith in the basic ideals and principles of the United States—which call for "political, economic, and cultural democracy"—or had failed to uphold them. To Girgus, Cahan's novel is "part of the traditional ritual of renewal of the American Way," but in distinguishing between author and narrator, he, too, inculpates "the other side of the American Dream, . . . the nightmare of conformity, materialism, and dehumanization that corrupts the idea of America," as the source of Levinsky's dissatisfaction and alienation (66, 91).

It is difficult to understand how such conclusions can be drawn by critics who are as familiar with Cahan's novel as these. In attempting to account for it, one can only assume that they have not given sufficient attention to the molding of Levinsky's personality and character in his early years. His youthful desire to be "the power behind the throne" in his *khadorim;* the vanity that drives him to absurd lengths in his attempt to prove his superiority as a Talmud student; his self-pity over the death of his mother, whom he makes no real effort to protect though she is beaten to death trying to defend him from anti-Semitic persecution; his increasing preoccupation with the pretty faces of young women visitors in the prayer room rather than Scripture or Talmud; his passionate "love" for Matilda—all of these among other unattractive traits are evident during his Russian years. When immigration to America becomes a real possibility for him, he can think of nothing else, certainly not the traditions of *Yidishkayt,* Hebrew scholarship, and piety.

Levinsky's Mind and Character

Why blame America for the freedom it offers to someone lacking the values and principles to use it appropriately—with wisdom and compassion? As a youth in Antomir, Levinsky never develops a set of values that extend beyond his own self-interest; the I-Thou relations that Martin Buber proposed as a guide to life would have been beyond Levinsky if such a philosophy could have come to him instead of Spencer's Social Darwinism. He recalls reading Emerson as a salesman on the road but does not identify titles; one suspects that he read "Self-Reliance" but missed the core of it, which deals with the all-important moral spirit or sentiment of virtue that nourishes self-reliance through building character, and therefore he understands the self only in terms of the ego, not the spirit. Had he read *Nature,* in which Emerson rises to a mystical state as "all mean egotism vanishes," Levinsky would not have understood it because his ego constitutes his self, and he cannot transcend it. No, it is not America that undermines Levinsky's psychological and moral life; it is already in a disoriented, degraded state before he leaves Antomir.

Perhaps his basic problem is Oedipal, or perhaps it is a neurosis evolving from an early trauma that generates increasing tension in Levinsky's psyche from that time forward, thus precluding normal psychological development. Karen Horney's analysis of neurosis is especially pertinent here. She proposes that the "actual self" and "ideal self" are at war with each other in the consciousness of a neurotic as the "actual self" interferes with the progress of the proud idealized self, thus inhibiting its attempts to achieve its goal of perfection.[32] The neurotic is hindered by pride from true self-realization, she says, illustrating with a highly ambitious person who may invest enormous energy toward fulfilling a drive to "eminence, power, and glamor" yet leave none for a "personal life and . . . development as a human being." Hence the proud neurotic, when under the control of the "ideal self" and assured of superiority (for example, being "one of the fittest"), becomes convinced of being able to achieve anything and thus grows arrogant and disdainful toward others.

But when the "ideal self" gives way to the "subdued self," as it occasionally must, for such tension in the consciousness cannot be sustained without pause for relief, the neurotic "tends to feel helpless, is compliant and appeasing, depends on others and craves their attention," like Levinsky, who strives to gain the affection of Dora and Anna, among others. For the proud neurotic, the feeling of "helplessness . . . is the most poignant dread" (Horney, 166, 189, 192). Levinsky exposes this fear twice near the end of his narrative; first when his irrational craving for Anna leads him to overinvest in real estate speculation, and later when he admits: "At the bottom of my heart I cow before waiters to this day." They make him feel as if he were being ridiculed and out of his element wearing expensive clothes and affecting American manners (*RDL,* 515).

This fear "may follow a feeling of shame without the latter being experienced as such," according to Horney; in this case the unacknowledged shame is not only awakened by but externalized in whatever seems intimidating (such as waiters in elegant restaurants), temporarily overwhelming the "proud self" (Horney, 101–2). Perhaps the trauma is initiated by the eighteen-year-old Levinsky's shame over neither stopping his mother nor running after her when she dashes in anger from their Jewish neighborhood to confront the Gentiles who have abused him. Levinsky's humiliation over being called "a lobster" after spilling a little milk on some clothes at the Manheimers' shop reinforces this possibility because of the direct association between mother and milk.

To be more accurate and more certain regarding the applicability of Horney's psychoanalytical theory or those of others would probably require additional information about Levinsky's past, especially from an outside source or sources, and that is obviously unattainable. So conclusions about the actual—rather than probable or possible—cause of Levinsky's enduring malaise are not likely, except insofar as the essential problem inheres in him, not in American freedom or corruption. Diane Levenberg expresses the idea especially well when she concludes that Levinsky's desperate problem cannot be attributed to American wealth and corruption; instead, the early death of his mother, "his grief, perhaps even his guilt, and his own broken heart" leave him a hopeless captive of his "old self."[33]

The Rise of David Levinsky as a Prophetic Novel

The exact cause of the narrator's maladjustment notwithstanding, *The Rise of David Levinsky* is regarded by many readers as a decidedly prophetic novel partly because of it. Alienated and hypocritical, uncertain of his identity in a country where he never comes to feel quite "at home," Levinsky represents the contemporary American drawn nostalgically to a romanticized childhood past when values and goals seemed clearer, but one who is restrained from making deep commitments for the present and future, a future that appears cloudy at best. Jules Chametzky perceives that Levinsky's "spiritual malaise" was evident "at the heart of . . . more or less affluent Jewish existence" in the 1960s,[34] and David Engel suggests more broadly that in tracing the change from shtetl life to that of contemporary American openness, urbanity, and industrial labor, *Levinsky* is essentially "absorbed with the issue of what it means to be modern" (70). For Bonnie Lyons, his narrative offers "a surprisingly modern parable" of the alienated contemporary; it predicts "the malaise of the post-immigrant generations: the loss of values that accompanied the normalization and *embourgeoisement* in suburban America. . . . [*Levinsky*] probes the condition of modern man in a world where God is dead, where homes are transitory or absent, where authority is specious or at best dubious" (Lyons, 86, 93).

Critical Reception

As with Cahan's earlier fiction in English, *The Rise of David Levinsky* received a generally favorable response from reviewers, though some found it realistic to excess and bordering on gross anti-Semitism. According to Milton Hindus, however, it was the first book about Jewish immigrants to be reviewed on the front page of the *New York Times*

Book Review, and eight thousand copies were sold in 1917 and 1918, which Hindus indicates "was very good for that period." After being cheaply reprinted by Grosset and Dunlap in 1928, it sold "fairly well" for a while before going out of print more than ten years later.[35]

A critic going by the initials R. B. reviewed it jointly with M. E. Ravage's *An American in the Making,* highly recommending both: by virtue of their similar themes, "Each gains significance from the other." As a character, Levinsky is assessed sympathetically, for the reviewer suggests that despite his materialism, he is neither altogether without honor nor "wholly unattractive." Instead, like several later critics mentioned above, R. B. casts more blame on American society as a whole than on Cahan's narrator, whose meticulous observations of his culture constitute a "corroding criticism of . . . this pushing, primitive society."[36] John Macy takes a similar stand in his review for the *Dial,* where he is unusually perceptive in identifying Cahan's intention with the novel. Macy praises Cahan as an "artist and a seer," whose narrator represents the whole of American society and not simply the Jewish members of it or those who reside in New York; he proposes, moreover, that "the Great American Novel" may well be within Cahan's reach.[37] An anonymous reviewer for *Call* agrees, asserting that in this novel, "Cahan shows us the world under capitalism as a world of chance"; as one of the few American authors "who do not write for the market," Cahan has written a novel that "is not a commodity, but a piece of art, full of life's unvarnished truths."[38] A quarter-century later, H. L. Mencken called the publication of *The Rise of David Levinsky* "one of the great literary events of the last war" and praised the book itself as "one of the best American novels ever written" (9).

Among the sharpest attacks, on the other hand, were those by H. W. Boynton and Kate Holladay Claghorn. For Boynton, Cahan's novel is about "the predatory immigrant," and Levinsky himself is a "spiritual obscenity."[39] Claghorn, too, finds Levinsky's character repulsive. To her the novel "reveals with crude and unashamed realism" the reversal of acceptable priorities in Levinsky's life. Akin to the other figures, he is sensual, egocentric, and materialistic, and all alike are foolish, ignorant, ambitious, and "above all tasteless!" She concurs with Boynton that the novel seems anti-Semitic, and she finds the only decent portraits in it to be those of the Socialists![40] The language of another anonymous reviewer, this one for the *Nation,* is vitriolic: Cahan is excoriated for portraying so despicable a creature as Levinsky, who resembles "a sneaking malodorous animal" and whose "fumblings with friendship and love are nauseating." He is "that type of Jew who raises the gorge of all decent human beings." Yet the reviewer admits that Cahan's "naturalism is appallingly spontaneous and sincere," an assessment of method that the author must have appreciated.[41] Some four decades later, in a more moderate evaluation, Leslie A. Fiedler praised aspects of the novel but also estimated Cahan's fiction as lacking excellence and being "irrelevant to the main lines of development of fiction in the United States" (Fiedler, 4).

Time has confirmed that John Macy's review was much closer to the truth than Fiedler's dubious judgment, for not only is the novel distinctively American in its content, but its naturalistic method and psychological theme, including the complex ambivalence of its narrator, carried it into the main literary current of American fiction for at least two generations after its publication. As Bonnie Lyons and other contemporary critics suggest, Cahan's novel is prophetic, a foreshadowing of current modernity as well as a realistic analysis of its own period. By now, as we approach the end of the twentieth century, *The Rise of David Levinsky* has found a distinctive place in the historical canon of American literature.

Chapter Seven

"The Thrill of Truth": Legacy of a Jewish American Realist

With the publication of *The Rise of David Levinsky* in 1917, Abraham Cahan ended his fiction-writing career. During most of the nearly thirty-five years that remained to him, he served as editor of the *Forward*—a post that perhaps gained in prestige but declined in influence as the midcentury approached. One reason for the waning popularity of the daily was the diminishing use of Yiddish among Jews of younger generations. Another prime reason that the authority of the *Forward* abated in the 1930s and 1940s was the success Cahan had achieved in helping to Americanize the millions of Jewish immigrants who had followed him from the Pale through the doors of Castle Garden and Ellis Island. Americanization—this became his principal aim when he returned to the *Forward* in 1902, and he directed the daily toward fulfilling it. By the time he died in 1951, Jews whose families had originated in the shtetlekh of Eastern Europe thrived and worshipped in heterogeneous communities across the country. If their grandparents and parents still spoke Yiddish, the second and third generations of American Jews had English as their native tongue. Although many still felt the strong influence of the past on their lives, most were no longer governed by it; their mores, their values, and their aspirations were chiefly American. Cahan's voice and the pages of the *Forward* had been major instruments in making this dynamic transformation occur.

No small part of this process of Americanization, however, is also attributable to his extensive contribution in English to newspapers, popular magazines, and books between 1895 and 1917, especially his fiction. Initially, his English stories of the 1890s and first few years of the new century, along with his hundreds of articles and sketches in the *New York Commercial Advertiser,* appealed at least as much to Gentile as to Jewish readers. If they occasionally betray stylistic echoes from his readings of American romantic authors, especially Hawthorne and Irving, Cahan's accounts of the East Side are nonetheless authentic. His English writing not only brought the tribulations of daily existence among the

Jewish immigrants to the attention of a non-Jewish readership, but his lifelike descriptions also relieved the Jews of the exoticism that accompanied them in the minds of many native-born Americans. Equally important, he humanized them; Cahan portrayed the Jews realistically, without attempting to omit or hide their blemishes. Indeed, he did it to so great an extent that the intrinsic nobility he recognized in their lives was often obscured, and he was occasionally vilified by his own people for presenting them to a Gentile American public largely ignorant of Jews and Judaism or hostile to them for all of the reasons embedded in conventional anti-Semitic stereotypes.

That Cahan's attitude toward Judaism was inconsistent when he considered it from different perspectives is evident to anyone familiar with his life and writings. Indeed, the value of Judaism varied dramatically for him depending on whether he was regarding it at any given time as an organized religion, a spiritual faith, an ethnic heritage, a basis for Zionism, a pattern of daily behavior, or a body of traditional laws and practices. From soon after his arrival in America, Cahan sympathized and identified himself with the Jewish people without accepting their theology or observing their rituals. Seeing himself as a secularized Jew by the time he was fourteen, he would have preferred as a teenager to slough off his Jewishness, were it possible.

Yet after his immigration, he never attempted to alienate himself from his people. He understood too well the educational and cultural differences of the immigrant Jews in America, a multitude who, only because they were Jews, had been reared in Eastern Europe under especially harsh conditions, including governmental discrimination, popular hostility, enforced isolation of community, and brutal poverty—all topics that find their way into his fiction. Cahan realized that Jews did not suffer from some of the same circumstances in the United States, not even on the East Side, but he perceived that the effects on the personalities, on the daily behavior, on the popular values of people who had struggled for existence under such circumstances for centuries could not possibly change in the course of a few days or years in the New World. That is why he made so decided an effort to Americanize the immigrant Jews through the pages of the *Forward* when the opportunity came.

Moreover, as a literary realist, these limitations and foibles became the substance of his portraiture, the very qualities that idealistic romantic critics condemned in his work, Jews and Gentiles alike. It should be too obvious to mention that the many unattractive characters in "A Providential Match" and elsewhere—including *Yekl* and *The Rise of*

David Levinsky—do not necessarily reflect Cahan's personal attitude toward Jews or Judaism. Cahan had no intention of using individual figures to characterize or represent Jews as a whole but to convey human truths as they manifested themselves under cultural conditions with which he was familiar by virtue of his background and experience. Personally ambivalent? Perhaps he was, but little if anything beyond a few magazine illustrations exists to suggest that whatever ambivalence he might have felt leaned toward the gross anti-Semitism they seem to expose, and it is doubtful that he had anything to do with them beyond giving his characters qualities that the illustrators could exaggerate.

Whether or not in some way these unsavory portraits reflected Cahan's possible ambivalence, there can be no question that his English writing, the expository prose as well as the fiction, helped to open doors for Jewish immigrants that encouraged them to leave the urban ghettos for more promising and productive lives than such closely knit and largely impoverished communities could support. Cahan's fiction illustrates both the way it could be done and the impediments the immigrants faced in attempting to achieve it. To Americanize according to Cahan's guidelines required a virtual transformation of identity, and for a long time after this dramatic process of acculturation had occurred, it often left the new American Jew uncertain of exactly who he or she really was. After attaining a "normal" American life like that of other citizens, the Jew was persistently badgered by the questions, as Irving Howe phrases them: "who am I and why do I so declare myself?" Howe recognized this "crisis of identity" as the primary dilemma of these East European Jews in America. In "bearing the troubles of an unfixed identity," he said, "they had finally entered the American condition," for no less than the Jews, most other citizens of the United States had come, one or two or three generations back, from somewhere else and left their past behind them (Howe, 642). "Where is my head," they asked themselves, "and where is my heart?"

According to Lewis Fried, "Part of our national sensibility [as Americans] involves the belief that a migration—spiritual, cultural, or physical—to the past and its places is part of a drive for 'characterization.'" In fiction, "[t]his quest can also be the task of memory, liberating the novel's characters or narrators into a present that fits well with a past that has become therapeutic."[1] For David Levinsky, however, financially successful but alienated and suffering under a chronic malaise, this insatiable quest for the past has an antithetical effect, for it eschews the possibility of his ever achieving wholeness.

Perhaps partly with Cahan's narrator in mind, Fried also points out that the struggle for identity in Jewish American literature is often underscored by "the idea of orphanhood"; a central figure such as Levinsky, morally supported by neither parents nor siblings, may repudiate his faith but not his people, and the same may be said of Cahan himself. Fried proposes that a primary goal for Jewish American authors, as Jews under the covenant in "the promised land," is to foster those aspects of their culture "that make for self within community," and for these writers "the *idea* of community must be *envisioned* again and anew" (24, 19; Fried's emphasis). The vast chasm between Levinsky and Cahan in this respect exists in the antipodal motives that link "autobiographer" and author to their respective communities. Whereas Levinsky conscientiously sustains his association with other Jews—German, however, not his Russian landsleit—to nourish his business and his vanity, Cahan's aim was essentially philanthropic, though it would be shortsighted to overlook the personal satisfaction he gained from progressing toward the economic, social, and cultural targets he identified for Eastern European Jewish immigrants.

In Cahan's early English fiction, *Yekl* and the four published stories collected with "The Imported Bridegroom," a tightly constrictive ghetto setting reinforces the emotional tension of two or three characters in conflict, sometimes with each other and usually within themselves as well. But in the novelette "The Imported Bridegroom," the last of the works in the collection to be written, the setting expands, and money is no longer a concern. In this story, the East European Jewish immigrant has achieved economic success in America, but the vanity he can now afford to nourish leads to alienation amid secular intellectual and social views that had held no place in the circumscribed lives of Old World Jewry.

Most of the stories that follow also extend the setting from the confining limitations of the ghetto into the wider communities around it. Even "Rabbi Eliezer's Christmas," set on the East Side, draws into its Jewish sphere of poverty and commerce two Gentile ladies from the nearby settlement house, an intrusion altogether foreign to the earlier fiction; and another story, "The Apostate of Chego-Chegg," published but a month earlier, deals with intermarriage and apostasy. Moreover, of his six uncollected stories published after *The Imported Bridegroom,* only one—"The Daughter of Reb Avrom Leib"—deals exclusively with Jewish characters, and three of the remaining five include no specifically Jewish figure at all. Clearly, Cahan had widened the horizons of his fiction, as Howells had advised.

His penultimate novel, *The White Terror and the Red,* is an anomaly in Cahan's English canon because it is set in its entirety outside the United States. His most autobiographical work, it describes prerevolutionary activities in czarist Russia, in which Cahan had participated marginally as a young man. Despite the romantic love affair at its center, the historical context is so realistically supported with data from his recent essays on the pogroms and radicals that one can hardly doubt its authenticity.

His final novel, *The Rise of David Levinsky,* begins in the Russia Cahan had known in his early years, but most of the action occurs in the familiar setting of New York's Lower East Side. Here, however, instead of limiting his interest to the economic or emotional struggles of two or three characters, he placed his alienated millionaire amidst the vast social, cultural, and economic transformation occurring in turn-of-the-century America, then passing through a period of massive immigration that ultimately included some two and a half million Jews from Eastern Europe. *The Rise of David Levinsky* dramatically reveals how America accommodated those newcomers, whom Emma Lazarus had called the "wretched refuse" of Europe's "teeming shores."

Though not farmers, these immigrants otherwise resembled the new Americans whom Crèvecoeur had described in 1782, precisely a century before Cahan arrived at the gates of Castle Garden: "From . . . servile dependence, penury, and useless labor," the new American "has passed to toils of a very different nature, rewarded by ample subsistence."[2] The urban Jewish immigrants of whom Cahan wrote, people in many ways like himself, followed their dream as Crèvecoeur's farmers had done; similarly, with luck and work, many eventually brought it to life. Their trials on the way to success or failure became the substance of Cahan's diverse contributions to American letters in both Yiddish and English. If he represented the breadth of this cultural transformation with his panoramic expositions of life in the Jewish communities of Russia and New York, he plumbed the depth and complexity of its effects on the individual best in his enigmatic characterization of David Levinsky, whose unsatisfied quest for identity in the United States is persistently thrown off course by his unresolvable ambivalence. That Levinsky's dilemma reflects the instability felt by thousands of the Jewish immigrants whom Cahan addressed in the *Forward* is suggested through countless letters published in the *"Bintl briv"* for decades early in the century.

All told, Abraham Cahan was more than an advocate, a journalist, and a writer of fiction. He was a force, a dynamo, a man of lofty aspirations who initiated grand events and took a commanding post in following them through. Opponents complained of his arrogance and fault-finding, for Cahan was neither easily pleased nor inclined to suppress sharp criticism when he felt it warranted. But millions of Jewish immigrants from hovels in the Pale, and their children and their children's children, were immensely indebted to this "friend of the ghetto," as are the countless readers who have praised his fiction over the many years since its publication. Through it, Cahan presented a new image of his people and gave them a voice that eventually could be heard across the continent.

Here, then, at least in part, is the legacy of Abraham Cahan, an American by nationality, a socialist among the multitude, a Jew throughout his life, and a literary realist at heart.

Notes and References

After their first citation below, all sources are cited parenthetically in the text.

Chapter One

1. Abraham Cahan, *The Education of Abraham Cahan,* vols. 1 and 2 of *Bleter fun mayn lebn,* trans. Leon Stein, Abraham P. Conan, and Lynn Davison (Philadelphia: Jewish Publication Society of America, 1969), 216; hereafter cited in text as *Education.*

2. The Pale of Jewish settlement was initially established by Catherine II in 1791 to prevent an influx of Jews into Russia from the section of Poland over which her empire had assumed control after the partition of that country. Within its bounds the movement and living conditions of Jewish inhabitants were sharply regulated; only with permission of the government were occasional Jews allowed to leave and work outside. Even within it, however, they could not own land, they were confined to living in designated areas, their means of livelihood were restricted to certain trades and vocations, and they were subject to harassment and abuse by local peasants with minimal government protection.

3. Sholem Aleichem is the pseudonym of Solomon Rabinowitz (1859–1916), who established his reputation as an author before emigrating from Russia in 1906.

4. Yiddish (which means "Jewish") was first spoken by European Jews about a thousand years ago, having originated in west central Germany. Initially a combination of Hebrew with Old French, Old Italian, and various early German dialects, it eventually absorbed elements of Slavic, Bohemian, Polish, and Lithuanian. Early European Jews read Hebrew but spoke Yiddish, and in developing a written language, they used Hebrew letters to represent the sounds of their vernacular. Therefore, although Hebrew and Yiddish may appear identical on paper, they are very different. The modern form dates from the mideighteenth century, though English additions merged with the language as Yiddish-speaking immigrants from Eastern Europe adapted English words and phrases into their tongue. See Emanuel Goldsmith, *Architects of Yiddishism at the Beginning of the Twentieth Century* (Rutherford, N.J.: Fairleigh Dickinson University Press, 1976), 29–30, and Leo Rosten, *The Joys of Yiddish* (New York: McGraw-Hill, 1968), 436).

In the Pale, for a Jew to speak even Russian, much less German or French, implied a movement outward, an introduction to secular learning, and a gradual loosening of traditional ties. Most Jewish intellectuals of Vilna, however, regarded Yiddish as "a jargon for the illiterate" and influenced the *melamdim* (teachers of Hebrew) to avoid it in teaching Hebrew and the Bible (*Education,* 25).

5. *Education* gives the name as Isaac (55), but Ronald Sanders, in *The Downtown Jews: Portraits of an Immigrant Generation* (New York: Harper & Row, 1969), refers to him as Isador (text pp. 155, 390) and Isidor (index p. 469); in Hebrew, both names are translated as *Yitskhok.*

6. Vilna, capital of the Vilna district, had a population of about 80,000 in the midnineteenth century, about a third of whom were Jews. Its Jewish history dates at least to the end of the fifteenth century. The city became a center of Jewish learning, also called "the city of the Vilna sage," identified with the *Gaon* (Eminence), Rabbi Elijah, one of the most articulate opponents of the new Hasidism (*Education,* 30; see also Israel Cohen, *Vilna* [Philadelphia: Jewish Publication Society of America, 1943], 3, 36–37, 333).

7. In the closing decades of the eighteenth century, the traditional Talmudic scholars of Vilna fought a losing battle with the recently established Hasidim, emotionally charged enthusiasts and occasional mystics who held that God communicated directly with the people and that historical scholarship was unnecessary to determine His will.

8. See also Theodore Marvin Pollock, "The Solitary Clarinetist: A Critical Biography of Abraham Cahan," Ph.D. diss. (Columbia University, 1959), 170, 308, 336.

9. To be kosher, the animals had to be killed according to specific rules.

10. Ralph Waldo Emerson, *The Journals and Miscellaneous Notebooks,* ed. A. W. Plumstead and Harrison Hayford (Cambridge, Mass.: Harvard University Press, 1969), 7:202.

11. The pamphlet had been written by Aaron Lieberman, editor of the first Hebrew Socialist newspaper.

12. Jules Chametzky, *From the Ghetto: The Fiction of Abraham Cahan* (Amherst: University of Massachusetts Press, 1977), 3.

13. Under the liberal rule of Alexander II (Czar, 1855–81), Jews were treated relatively well by the government, which was not the case during the regimes of his two predecessors, Alexander I (Czar, 1801–25) and Nicholas I, the "Iron Czar" (Czar, 1825–55). Alexander II attempted to modernize Russia by ending serfdom in 1861 and making secular education available to the Jews for the first time. Instead of fostering their assimilation, however, this opportunity made them aware of revolutionary authors who advocated replacing the czardom with socialism or anarchy. Alexander's sustained attempt to modernize without relinquishing his authority as czar led to increasing turmoil in Russia.

His assassination in March 1881 by the terror faction of the revolutionaries, the Will of the People Party, with whom Cahan was not affiliated, led to the accession of his son, Alexander III, who reacted sharply against the underground movement. The Jewish people again became scapegoats and the easy prey of government-fostered pogroms that produced mobs, riots, and wholesale slaughter in city after city—Elisavetgrad, Kiev, Nizhni-Novgorod (now Gorki), Odessa, Kishinev, and others—often beginning around Easter. Simultaneously, some Jewish revolutionaries had considered anti-Semitism to be "a good omen," reasoning that in attacking Jews, the people were fighting their oppressors—the czarist government and the Hebrew pawnbrokers and tradesmen whom they resented for taking their goods or money. Thus the Jews were universally squeezed: by the government that restricted them, the masses who despised them, and the revolutionaries—even the Jewish ones—who exploited them.

14. Moses Rischin, *The Promised City: New York's Jews, 1870–1914* (Cambridge, Mass.: Harvard University Press, 1962), 270.

15. At the end of the century, Cahan identified three other New York ghettos beside that on the Lower East Side: one existed uptown between 98th and 116th Streets east of Central Park, another was Brownsville in Brooklyn's 26th Ward, and the third was Williamsburg in North Brooklyn.

16. Arthur Bartlett Maurice, *New York in Fiction* (1901; Port Washington, N.Y.: Ira J. Friedman, 1969), 70.

17. Milton Reizenstein, "General Aspects of the Population (A) New York," in *The Russian Jew in the United States: Studies of Social Conditions in New York, Philadelphia, and Chicago, with a Description of Rural Settlements,* ed. Charles S. Bernheimer (Philadelphia: John C. Winston Co., 1905), 46.

18. Andrew R. Heinze, *Adapting to Abundance: Jewish Immigrants, Mass Consumption, and the Search for American Identity* (New York: Columbia University Press, 1990), 45–56.

19. Cahan himself notes that he and Anna were married in February (*Education,* 306), but Pollock, citing *Who's Who in American Jewry* (1938), gives the date as 21 March (102n1); without documentation, James Glen Stovall puts the date much later, as 11 December 1886 ("Abraham Cahan," in *American Newspaper Journalists, 1901–1925,* ed. Perry J. Ashley, vol. 5 of *Dictionary of Literary Biography* [Detroit: Gale Research, 1984], 32).

20. Although published comments on the alleged strains in their marriage are speculative and vague, Cahan's stubbornness, intensity, and assertiveness could well have overwhelmed Anna's more refined nature and probably more subtle aesthetic sensibility, thus generating tension between them. Nevertheless, one should be cautious about assessing the integrity of their marriage on the assumption that a hypothetical personality conflict made them incompatible. See Sanders, 75, 227, 272, and especially 449–50, and Chametzky 1977, 40. Cahan's autobiography conveys few references to his wife and no specific information on the state of their marriage.

21. In *From the Ghetto,* Chametzky examines Cahan's acquisition of English in relation to his use of both that language and Yiddish; Chametzky's analysis testifies that it is a subject deserving close scrutiny.

22. Quoted by Melech Epstein, "Abraham Cahan," in *Profiles of Eleven: Profiles of Eleven Men Who Guided the Destiny of an Immigrant Society and Stimulated Social Consciousness among the American People* (Detroit: Wayne State University Press, 1965), 63.

23. With the influx of Eastern European Jews into the American clothing manufactory late in the nineteenth century, the entire garment trade underwent a colossal transformation as relatively inexpensive ready-made clothing gained precedence over individualized tailoring (see Irving Howe, *World of Our Fathers* [New York: Harcourt, Brace, Jovanovich, 1976], 139). By 1900, more than 90 percent of the industry was in Jewish hands, and the East Europeans were rapidly pushing out their German predecessors. Isaac M. Rubinow estimates that in 1915 almost 53 percent of Russian-Jewish male workers and 77 percent of Russian-Jewish female workers were employed in one sector or another of the garment manufactory (Rubinow, "Economic and Industrial Condition (A) New York," in *The Russian Jew in the United States,* ed. Bernheimer, 112).

Meanwhile, use of the Singer sewing machine was becoming so widespread in the United States that it "began to revolutionize the Jewish home"; by 1881 Singer was selling an average of 1,700 machines a day (Rischin 1962, 27, 62). The machines were priced modestly, could be purchased with small installments, and were easily portable, which was a crucial advantage in the early years because work was uncertain from day to day and the workers had to carry their Singers along with them between home and workplace (Sanders, 93). Equally important was the fact that one could learn to use a Singer—and thereby profit from it—quickly.

The proliferation of Singers led to the rapid expansion of the sweatshop clothing manufactory, in which specialized tasks were allocated to different workers in the tailoring of women's cloaks and shirtwaists and men's suits, step-by-step, piece-by-piece—pants, sleeves, collars, and so forth. The pieces would then be gathered and sewn together. Sanders describes the manufacturing process: the owner-merchant bought the cloth and cut it to size in his shop. He gave the pieces to a contractor (called the "sweater"—the one who made the workers "sweat"), who distributed them to the sewers; the pieces were sewn, tailored, stitched into finished garments, and pressed in the sweatshops. The contractor then took the clothes back to the owner-merchant, who sold the garments to wholesale and retail commercial outlets (Sanders, 49).

Workers were paid at times by the piece, at times by the hour, and at times by the task, but the latter was the most pressing because contractors increased the number of items per task without a commensurate increase in pay, and some workers could tailor more garments than others within the same span of time. The sweatshop manufactory was a grueling, hard-paced way to earn a living, highly competitive and seasonal. When jobs were available, the six-day work-week could be anywhere from sixty-four to eighty-four hours—plus overtime. In the 1880s wages varied from about seven to twelve dollars weekly for men to less than half of that for women and a little over half of that again for children (Howe, 82–83; Rubinow, 111, 119). Indeed, the sweatshop was often a family affair, and when the contractor did not provide a workplace, the family worked at home in a cramped, airless, tenement flat.

Except on the Sabbath, there was little time but to work and sleep, the latter for a few hours only; hence in 1899 Cahan wrote in the *Commercial Advertiser:* "Here is America, where everything is done on the 'hurry-up' principle" (see *Grandma Never Lived in America: The New Journalism of Abraham Cahan,* ed. and intro. Moses Rischin [Bloomington: Indiana University Press, 1985], 375; selections of Cahan's writings from this volume hereafter cited in text as *Grandma;* Rischin's introduction hereafter cited in text as Rischin 1985; for a description of this volume, see chapter 2, note 7). This remark would echo in one of his stories of the same period, "Rabbi Eliezer's Christmas." But as he also pointed out in a later essay, the sweatshop system was already established in American industries when the Russian Jews arrived—and according to Melech Epstein the sweatshops were worse in Chicago than New York (see Abraham Cahan, "The Russian Jew in America," *Atlantic Monthly* 82 [July 1898]: 135; Melech Epstein, *Jewish Labor in {the} U.S.A.: An Industrial, Political, and Cultural History of the Jewish Labor Movement, 1882–1952* 2 vols. in 1 [1950; Hoboken, N.J.: KTAV, 1969], 1:94).

24.   Alfred Kazin, "Jews," *New Yorker,* 7 March 1994, 72.

25.   The riot occurred in Haymarket Square when a large assembly of striking workers and anarchists were ordered by the police to disperse, though they had been authorized to hold their meeting. When an unidentified anarchist threw a bomb, the police opened fire, and several people on both sides were either killed or wounded. Consequently, eight anarchists were arrested and tried in a highly biased court, which found them guilty; four were executed, though the person who threw the bomb remains unknown.

26.   On Cahan's naturalization: Card #500, Film #1420102, U.S. Naturalization Records, Family History Library, Church of Jesus Christ of the Latter-Day Saints, Salt Lake City, Utah; on representing the United Hebrew Trades at the Second International: Epstein, 1965, 68.

27.   David Engel, "Abraham Cahan," in *American Novelists, 1910–1945, Part 1: Louis Adamek-Vardis Fisher,* ed. James J. Martine, vol. 9 of *Dictionary of Literary Biography* (1981), 119.

28.   "Abraham Cahan, Editor, 91, Is Dead," obit., *New York Times,* 1 September 1951, 11.

29.   The "muckrakers" were journalists whose graphic exposures of the devastating social ills in America, especially in business, finance, and politics, were intended to promote large-scale reform by engaging the emotions of the public.

30.   Moses Rischin, "Abraham Cahan and the *New York Commercial Advertiser:* A Study in Acculturation," *Publication of the American Jewish Historical Society* 43 (September 1953): 35.

31. Louis Harap, *The Image of the Jew in American Literature from Early Republic to Mass Immigration* (Philadelphia: Jewish Publication Society, 1974), 491; Paul Novick, "Abraham Cahan and the *Forward,*" *Jewish Life* 6, no. 1 (November 1951): 14–16.

32. Milton M. Hindus, ed., "Abraham Cahan," in *The Old East Side: An Anthology* (Philadelphia: Jewish Publication Society of America, 1969), 20.

33. Abraham Cahan, "The Russian Jew in the United States," in *The Russian Jew in the United States,* ed. Bernheimer, 36.

34. Michael Emery and Edwin Emery, *The Press and America: An Interpretive History of the Mass Media,* 6th ed. (Englewood Cliffs, N.J.: Prentice Hall, 1988), 250.

35. See also J. C. Rich, "60 Years of the Jewish Daily *Forward,*" *New Leader,* 3 June 1957, sec. 2, p. 26.

36. "10,500 Pay Tribute," *New York Times,* 6 September 1951, 31.

Chapter Two

1. Ephim H. Jeshurin, *Abraham Cahan Bibliography* (New York: United Vilner Relief Committee, 1941), 11, 13.

2. See also George Tucker, "Bits of History," in *Hear the Other Side: A Symposium of Democratic Socialist Opinion,* ed. Abraham Cahan (New York: Forward Publishing Assoc., 1934), 66–71.

3. The *Minerva's* first editor was Noah Webster, who wrote much of its text in support of the new American government, but he left to continue his work in politics and language in 1797, soon after the name of the newspaper was changed to the *Commercial Advertiser.* In the early nineteenth century, its circulation was the highest of all the popular commercial dailies. At that time its title was appropriate because most of its space was devoted to advertising. Of course, its influence was limited because it was crammed with advertisements, and after the Civil War it became, as Frank Luther Mott described it, merely "an old-fashioned Republican paper with small circulation" (*American Journalism, A History: 1690–1960,* 3d ed. [New York: Macmillan, 1962], 448; see also 181, 184, 339n2). In 1891 it was purchased by Collis P. Huntington, who held it through the Cahan years.

At that time, the *Advertiser* was published six days a week for two cents a copy on weekdays and three cents on Saturdays, when a photographic supplement doubled its usual length of eight to twelve pages. The paper published national and international news, giving excellent coverage to such historic episodes of the day as the Spanish-American War and the seemingly endless Dreyfus issue, which was in and out of the courts for years. It included special sections on sports—especially cycling and horse racing—social and cultural news, religion, "Women's Interests," education, and editorials, though not all of these items appeared daily. The financial and commercial interests, including abundant advertising, always covered the last several pages. Topics in the weekly supplements varied from photographs of the social elite and war heroes to life among the Sioux. In short, it was a praiseworthy, well-edited newspaper, diversified in its coverage, tasteful in its presentation of news and features.

4. Lincoln Steffens, *The Autobiography* (New York: Harcourt, Brace, 1931), 321.

5. Howells, too, had a similar advantage, as he discovered to his great surprise when he read Morris Rosenfield's Yiddish poems in *Songs from the Ghetto* (1898), printed in German rather than the usual Hebrew script (Rudolf and Clara M. Kirk, "Abraham Cahan and William Dean Howells: The Story of a Friendship," *American Jewish Historical Quarterly* 52 [September 1962]: 40n16).

6. Moses Rischin, ed., introduction to *The Spirit of the Ghetto* by Hutchins Hapgood (1902; Cambridge, Mass.: Harvard University Press, 1967), ix; further references are from Hapgood's writing and are hereafter cited in the text as Hapgood.

7. In 1985 Moses Rischin gathered a varied selection of more than 160 of Cahan's short journalistic pieces, including human interest articles, biographical sketches, and light, entertaining stories, nearly all first published in the *Commercial Advertiser,* and brought them out with an illuminating historical and analytical introduction under the title *Grandma Never Lived in America: The New Journalism of Abraham Cahan.* Because copies of the *Commercial Advertiser,* even in microform, are difficult to obtain, Rischin's collection is invaluable, a treasure trove of items under such topics as the waiting room for immigrants at Castle Garden, the nearby Barge Office (explained below), and Ellis Island; day-to-day issues and commerce in the East Side streets and tenements; ideological squabbles; translations and discussions of prominent realists; interviews with newsworthy people; labor controversies; and courtroom and station house scenes. (The Barge Office was used to process immigrants while the buildings at Ellis Island were being rebuilt after their destruction in a devastating fire in 1897.) In most cases, Rischin provides his own titles, but apart from that difference the pieces are identical to the originals.

8. Abraham Cahan, "Tailors at Peace," *New York Commercial Advertiser,* 13 August 1898, 2; also in *Grandma,* 371. Pieces from the *Commercial Advertiser* hereafter cited in text under *CA* with article title and date of publication.

9. Abraham Leon Sachar, *A History of the Jews,* 5th ed. (New York: Alfred A. Knopf, 1964), 320–21.

10. Leon Stein, introduction to *Education,* vi.

11. See also *Forward,* 22 May 1893, 23, and Jules Chametzky, "Abraham Cahan," in *Twentieth-Century American-Jewish Fiction Writers,* ed. Daniel Walden, vol. 28 of *Dictionary of Literary Biography* (1984), 30.

12. Gus Tyler, "Guarding the Memory of the Gift of the Magid," in "The Forward Century," special section of the *Forward* (English ed.), 22 May 1992, 24.

13. David Remnick, "News in a Dying Language," *New Yorker,* 10 January 1994, 40–41.

14. Joseph Gollomb, "Abraham Cahan," in "Interesting People," *American Magazine,* October 1912, 672.

15. For information on Zhitlovsky, see Goldsmith, 161–81.

16. Moses Rischin, "Abraham Cahan: Titan of East Broadway," in "Forward Century," 23.

17. Quoted in Howe, 543; Howe quotes from Villard, "America's Most Interesting Daily," *Nation,* 27 September 1922, 301–2.

18. Ellen Kellman, "Love and Death in Weekly Installments," in "Forward Century," 20.

19. David M. Fine, *The City, the Immigrant and American Fiction, 1880–1920* (Metuchen, N.J.: Scarecrow Press, 1977), 125.

20. Rachel M. Brownstein, *The Tragic Muse: Rachel of the Comédie-Français* (New York: Knopf, 1993), 66.

21. In Isaac Metzker, ed., *A Bintel Brief: Sixty Years of Letters from the Lower East Side to the Jewish Daily Forward* (Garden City, N.Y.: Doubleday & Co, 1971), 60–61; hereafter cited in text as *Bintel Brief.*

22. Titles of the individual volumes are *From the Old World to the New (Fun der alter velt tsu der nayen),* vol. 1, and *Discovery Journeys after Columbus (Entdekungsraysen nokh kalumbusen),* vol. 2.

23. "Chadwick Heads Team at *Forward,*" *Forward* (English ed.), 9 September 1994, 5; "*Forward* Promotes Mahler to Key Post," *Forward* (English ed.), 16 February 1996, 4.

24. Motl Zelmanowicz, "Philologos' Crocodile Tears for Yiddish," *Forward* (English ed.), 5 January 1996, 6. Yiddish programs have emerged recently in the curricula of such major universities as Yale, Harvard, and Oxford.

Chapter Three

1. Edwin H. Cady, *The Light of Common Day: Realism in American Fiction* (Bloomington: Indiana University Press, 1971), 13.

2. Abraham Cahan, "Tolstoy, the Artist" [Rischin's title], *CA,* 2 February 1901, and *Grandma,* 523–25; Cahan, "The Mantle of Tolstoy," *Bookman* 16 (December 1902): 332, and *Grandma,* 535.

3. Everett Carter, *Howells and the Age of Realism* (Philadelphia: J. B. Lippincott Co., 1954), 96.

4. Abraham Cahan, "Realism," *Workmen's Advocate,* 6 April 1889, 2.

5. Edwin H. Cady, *The Realist at War: The Mature Years, 1885–1920, of William Dean Howells* (Syracuse, N.Y.: Syracuse University Press, 1958), 28–55.

6. Alexander Kahn, eulogy for Cahan, quoted in the *New York Times,* 6 September 1951, 31.

7. Ernest Poole, "Abraham Cahan: Socialist—Journalist—Friend of the Ghetto," *Outlook* 99 (28 October 1911): 478.

8. Emma Lazarus, "Barnay as 'Mark Antony,'" *Century* 26, N.S. 4 (June 1883): 312.

9. A. H. Fromenson, "Amusements and Social Life (A) New York," in *The Russian Jew in the United States*, ed. Bernheimer, 228.

10. American realism is approached from this perspective in "Romance and Realism: Children of the New Colossus and the Jewish Struggles Within," my contribution to *American Realism and the Canon*, ed. Tom Quirk and Gary Scharnhorst (Newark: University of Delaware Press, 1994), 102–26.

11. W. D. Howells, "New York Low Life in Fiction," *New York World*, 26 July 1896, 18.

12. Abraham Cahan, *Yekl and The Imported Bridegroom and Other Stories of the New York Ghetto*, intro. Bernard C. Richards (New York: Dover Publications, 1970), 26; references hereafter cited in text as *Y&IB*.

13. Mike Fink was a folk hero among the river and canal boatmen in early nineteenth-century America, an outrageous rough-and-tumble Yankee, as portrayed in many popular tales from that era.

14. Edward S. Shapiro, "Jews and Americans," {*American Jewish*} *Congress Monthly*, September–October 1988, 4.

15. Elsa Nettels, *Language, Race, and Social Class in Howells's America* (Lexington: University Press of Kentucky, 1988), 98.

16. "An East Side Romance" [review of *Yekl*], *New York Times*, 12 July 1896, 31.

17. Nancy Huston Banks, "The New York Ghetto" [review of *Yekl*], *Bookman* 4 (October 1896): 158.

18. *Hester Street*, a film based on *Yekl*, was brought out by Midwest Film Production in 1975 to generally favorable reviews. Written and directed by Joan Micklin Silver, it was produced by Rafael D. Silver and starred Carol Kane as Gitl, Steven Keats as Jake, and Dorrie Kavanaugh as Mamie.

Chapter Four

1. W. D. Howells. *Criticism and Fiction* (New York: Harper & Bros., 1891), 99.

2. W. D. Howells, [Review of] *The Imported Bridegroom*, *Literature*, 31 (December 1898): 629.

3. Like *Yekl*, "The Imported Bridegroom" has been adapted into a film. Written, produced, and directed by Pamela Berger in 1990, *The Imported Bridegroom* stars Eugene Troobnick as Asriel, Avi Hoffman as Shaya, and Greta Cowan as Flora. Though set in Boston instead of New York, the film generally adheres to Cahan's novelette until the end, when his melancholy conclusion is transformed into a double-wedding farce.

4. Abraham Cahan, "The Apostate of Chego-Chegg," *Century* 59 (November 1899): 94; hereafter cited in text as "Apostate."

5. Abraham Cahan, "Rabbi Eliezer's Christmas," *Scribner's* 26 (December 1899): 661–62; hereafter cited in text as "Rabbi."

6. Abraham Cahan, "The Daughter of Reb Avrom Leib," *Cosmopolitan* 30 (March 1901): 53; hereafter cited in text as "Daughter."

7. In Jewish mysticism, the Sabbath is traditionally welcomed as a bride, as in the *Daily Prayer Book: Ha-siddur ha-shalem,* trans. and ed. Philip Birnbaum (New York: Hebrew Publishing Co., 1949), 244. Shortly after the evening Sabbath service opens, reader and congregation join in reading or singing a poem that begins, "Come, my friend, to meet the bride; let us welcome the Sabbath," a line that becomes a refrain.

8. Abraham Cahan, "A Marriage by Proxy: A Story of the City," *Everybody's Magazine* 3 (December 1900): 569; hereafter cited in text as "Marriage."

9. Letter to Alexei S. Suverin, 27 October 1888, quoted in Ronald Hingley, *Chekhov: A Biographical and Critical Study* (1950; New York: Barnes and Noble, 1966), 95.

10. Abraham Cahan, "Tzinchadzi of the Catskills," *Atlantic Monthly* 88 (August 1901): 221; hereafter cited in text as "Tzin."

Chapter Five

1. A[braham]. Cahan, *The White Terror and the Red: A Novel of Revolutionary Russia* (New York: A. S. Barnes & Co., 1905), 321–29; hereafter cited in text as *WT&R.*

2. Sachar's account in *A History of the Jews* confirms that this peak period of Russian anti-Semitic rampage was initiated by V. K. von Plehve on being appointed minister of the Interior by Nicholas II in 1902. Although the Czar favored reform, his leading advisors did not, and the reactionary von Plehve joined them. Their counsel prevailed, and instead of negotiating with the radicals, which Cahan believed could have worked, the government imposed further restrictions and force, provoking more revolutionary violence in response. Von Plehve was assassinated by revolutionaries in July 1904, but his policies were continued.

The earlier of Cahan's two English articles on the pogroms, "The Diabolical Massacre of Jews in Kishinev" (as titled in *Grandma,* 43–49), was published in the *Commercial Advertiser* on 23 May 1903, within two months of the incident. The other, "Jewish Massacres and the Revolutionary Movement in Russia," appeared about six weeks later in the *North American Review* (177 [July 1903]: 49–62). Although both highlight von Plehve's nefarious role in victimizing the Jews, the latter is more substantive.

In it, Cahan compares the hostile situation of the day between the government and the radicals with that in existence a little more than two decades earlier, when von Plehve was head of the imperial police under Alexander II. Like Nicholas, Alexander had also wanted to consult the revolutionaries and to work out an acceptable solution without actually going so far as to support a democratic form of government under a constitution. Had he attempted it, Cahan believes he would have been successful ("Jewish Massacres," 50). This was the aim proposed early in 1881 by one of Alexander's principal advisors, Count Loris Melikoff, minister of the Interior, and approved by the Czar, but because reports of this initiative never reached the radicals, they assumed he had no intention of listening to them, and a few days later he was slain by members of the Will of the People Party who bombed his carriage. (Ironically, von Plehve was assassinated in the same manner.) Cahan states that this group had become "practically a thing of the past" by 1901, though two decades earlier it had comprised "fifty or seventy-five fearless and able leaders, backed by a few thousand of more or less active propagandists" ("Russian Nihilism of Today," *Forum* 21 [June 1901]: 416, 419).

Early in the twentieth century, "the Fighting League of the Social-Revolutionists" replaced the Will of the People Party, but whereas the former group was largely integrated with the other revolutionaries, the Fighting League was a small, detached terrorist arm that maintained only a tenuous link with the rest through one or two liaisons. Although Cahan dealt specifically with their activity as that of the nihilists in *The White Terror and the Red,* the "proclamations of the new terrorists read almost exactly like [those] of the Will of the People" (Cahan, "The Russian Revolutionists," *World's Work* 8 [September 1904]: 5311–12, 5313; hereafter cited in text as "Russian Revolutionists").

By comparing the two periods, in both of which von Plehve's animosity was central, Cahan perceived "a most interesting connecting link between the present situation and the situation of 1881" ("Jewish Massacres," 50). He noted, for example, that after the assassination of Alexander II, a riot broke out in Elisavetgrad because of a general anti-Semitic attitude, which created a feeling among the people that the stability of the empire was in jeopardy. This was only the beginning, however, for it provoked a series of other riots that were politically supported; within about a year and a half some 200 Jewish towns and villages were destroyed ("Diabolical," *Grandma,* 43; "Jewish Massacres," 52).

As if anticipating what was to come in the next two years, Cahan also pointed out that about two months before the Kishinev attack a massacre of Gentiles had occurred in Zlatoust; he believed that the two incidents were "linked by ties of logical affinity," which he identified as revolutionary developments and prevailing Russian anti-Semitism ("Jewish Massacres," 49). Moreover, he indicated that as in previous pogroms, the Kishinev riot occurred chiefly in the slums, as if the poor working Jews had squeezed money from the Gentiles.

Indeed, in his earlier article for the *Advertiser,* Cahan had quoted von Plehve as informing the governor of Bessarabia, where Kishinev is located, that the rioters should not be held back because the Jews are "the principal fleecers of the region," so he should "let our boys have some fun with the Jews," whom the police restrained from self-defense ("Diabolical," *Grandma,* 44–45). Cahan said that the army and police were encouraged by their officers to squelch socialism and harass the Jews whether or not they were socialists, and he illustrated this policy by referring to the Kishinev riot ("Jewish Massacres," 59–60; "Russian Revolutionists," 5311–15).

3.   Cahan quotes Ralph Waldo Emerson, "The Fortune of the Republic," in *Miscellanies,* vol. 11 of the *Complete Works* (Boston: Houghton Mifflin, 1903–1904), 536.

4.   Abraham Cahan, "The Share of Count Brantsev: A Story," *Ainslee's Magazine,* March 1901, cited from *Grandma,* 490–96; discussed in the concluding pages of this chapter.

5.   "The Share of Count Brantsev" is not listed in Pollock's bibliography.

6.   Edwin Lefevre, "Abraham Cahan's *The White Terror and the Red,*" *Bookman* 21 (April 1905): 187–88.

7.   [Review of] *The White Terror and the Red, Critic* 46 (February 1905): 108–9.

8.   All three reviews were anonymous: "A Revolutionary Novel of Russia," *New York Times Book Review,* 22 April 1905, 258; *Outlook* 79 (11 March 1905): 654–55; and *Reader* 5 (May 1905): 784.

9.   Hutchins Hapgood, "A Realistic Novel," *Critic* 46 (June 1905): 561.

Chapter Six

1.   Jules Chametzky, introduction to *The Rise of David Levinsky* (New York: Penguin Books, 1994), vii–viii; hereafter cited in text as Chametzky 1994.

2.   Anonymous editorial epigraph for Abraham Cahan, "The Autobiography of an American Jew: The Rise of David Levinsky," *McClure's* 40 (April 1913): 92–93; hereafter cited in text as "Autobiography."

3.   Isaac Rosenfeld, "America, Land of the Sad Millionaire," in *Breakthrough: A Treasury of Contemporary American-Jewish Literature,* ed. Irving Malin and Irwin Stark (New York: McGraw-Hill, 1964), 259.

4.   Jules Zanger, "David Levinsky: Master of Pilpul," *Papers on Language and Literature* 13, no. 3 (Summer 1977): 294.

5.   John Higham, introduction to *The Rise of David Levinsky* (New York: Harper & Bros., 1960), x.

6.   Abraham Cahan, *The Rise of David Levinsky* (New York: Harper & Bros., 1917), unnumbered contents page; hereafter cited in text as *RDL.* The plates and therefore the pagination in the paperback Harper and Penguin editions are the same as in the first edition, the one here cited.

7. Although Chametzky correctly observed that Cahan's female characters are not types but individuals (Chametzky 1977, 113), Levinsky's mother is a clear exception.

8. See also Leslie A. Fiedler, "Genesis: The American-Jewish Novel through the Twenties," *Midstream* 4, no. 3 (Summer 1958): 29.

9. Ralph Waldo Emerson. "Self-Reliance," in *Essays: First Series,* vol. 2 of *Complete Works* (Boston: Houghton Mifflin, 1903), 55.

10. Crane wrote to Garland: "If one proves that theory [i.e., that 'environment is a tremendous thing regardless'], one makes room in Heaven for all sorts of souls (notably an occasional street girl) who are not confidently expected to be there by many excellent people" (*The Portable Stephen Crane,* ed. Joseph Katz [New York: Viking Press, 1969], 1).

11. For reference to Dickens as a source for the novel, see David Green, "The Price of Success: Use of the Bildungsroman Plot in Abraham Cahan's *The Rise of David Levinsky,*" *Studies in American Jewish Literature* 12 (1993): 19–24.

12. M. M. Carlin, "The Rise of David Levinsky," *University of Cape Town Studies in English* 9 (1979): 59.

13. Rischin's title for the article is "Women of Valor."

14. Bonnie Lyons, "David Levinsky: Modern Man as Orphan," in *Essays in American Literature in Memory of Richard P. Adams,* ed. Donald Pizer, *Tulane Studies in English* 23 (1978): 90–91.

15. Sanford Pinsker, *Jewish American Fiction, 1917–1987* (New York: Twayne Publishers, 1992), 4.

16. Everett Carter, "Realists and Jews," *Studies in American Fiction* 22, no. 1 (Spring 1994): 85.

17. W. D. Howells, letter to F. A. Duneka, in *Life in Letters of William Dean Howells,* ed. Mildred Howells (New York: Doubleday Doran, 1928), 2:375. Frederick A. Duneka was vice president of Harper & Bros. at the time. I acknowledge that Howells's use of "autobiographical" is ambiguous; he might have meant it in reference to Cahan's representing his own experiences through his narrator, as suggested here, or to the *type* of novel that Cahan was writing: an *autobiographical* novel, which employs a first-person narrator, in contrast to a *biographical* or *historical* one. He may well have meant the term to be understood in both ways.

18. Richard S. Pressman, "Abraham Cahan, Capitalist; David Levinsky, Socialist," *Studies in American Jewish Literature* 12 (1993): 2–4.

19. Joan Zlotnick, "Abraham Cahan, A Neglected Realist," *American Jewish Archives* 23 (April 1971): 45.

20. Jules Chametzky, "Notes on the Assimilation of the American-Jewish Writer: Abraham Cahan to Saul Bellow," *Jahrbuch für Amerikastudien* (Yearbook for American Studies) 9 (Winter 1964): 175.

21. H. L. Mencken, "Abraham Cahan, The Novelist," *Forward,* 7 June 1942; reprinted in the English edition of the *Forward,* 23 April 1993, 9; further references are to the 1993 edition.

22. Cushing Strout, "Personality and Cultural History in the Novel: Two American Examples," *New Literary History* 1, no. 3 (1970): 425, 433, 436.

23. Phillip Barrish, "'The Genuine Article': Ethnicity, Capital, and *The Rise of David Levinsky*," *American Literary History* 5, no. 4 (Winter 1993): 660n4.

24. Sam B. Girgus, "A Convert to America: Sex, Self, and Ideology in Abraham Cahan," in *The New Covenant: Jewish Writers and the American Idea* (Chapel Hill: University of North Carolina Press, 1984), 74.

25. Lothar Kahn, "*The Rise of David Levinsky:* Fifty Years After," *Chicago Jewish Forum* 26, no. 1 (Fall 1967): 4.

26. Cahan seems to have drawn the name (Mr. Even) of this apparent philanthropist from a location in First Samuel 7:12, though Mr. Even has shortened and Americanized it. After Israel had defeated the Philistines with God's help, Samuel memorialized a stone at the site of the victory and he called the place "Ebenezer." Mr. Even helps the Jews as God does, but Levinsky emphasizes that his assistance is more a *mitzve* (a divine obligation) than an act of love (*RDL,* 98–99, 102).

27. As noted in *Yekl and the Imported Bridegroom,* 25.

28. David Singer, "David Levinsky's Fall: A Note on the Liebman Thesis," *American Quarterly* 19, no. 4 (Winter 1967): 697.

29. In *Maggie,* a beer-hall singer requests the national anthem, and "[i]nstantly a great cheer swelled from the throats of the assemblage of the masses. There was a heavy rumble of booted feet thumping the floor. Eyes gleamed with sudden fire, and calloused hands waved frantically in the air" (Stephen Crane, *Maggie: A Girl of the Streets,* in *The Portable Stephen Crane,* ed. Joseph Katz [New York: Viking Press, 1969], 29–30).

30. Ronald Sanders, "Up the Road to Materialism," *New Republic* 144 (6 March 61): 18.

31. David Engel, "The Discrepancies of the Modern: Reevaluating Abraham Cahan's *The Rise of David Levinsky*," *Studies in American Jewish Literature* 5, no. 2 (1979): 90.

32. Karen Horney, *Neurosis and Human Growth: The Struggle toward Self-Realization* (New York: Norton, 1950), 111–12.

33. Diane Levenberg, "David Levinsky and His Women," *Midstream* 26, no. 7 (August–September 1980): 53.

34. Jules Chametzky, "Focus on Abraham Cahan's *The Rise of David Levinsky:* Boats against the Current," in *American Dreams, American Nightmares,* ed. David Madden (Carbondale and Edwardsville: Southern Illinois University Press, 1970), 92.

35. Milton Hindus, "Abraham Cahan: Early American Realist," *Jewish Heritage* 7 (Fall 1964): 44, and Higham, xi. A discrepancy exists on the year the Grosset and Dunlap edition was taken out of print; whereas Higham (xi) says it was 1943, Charles Angoff cites the date as 1939 ("Dusting off the Bookshelf

IV—*The Rise of David Levinsky,* by Abraham Cahan," *{American Jewish} Congress Weekly,* 20 January 1950, 15.

36. R. B., "Americans in the Making," *New Republic,* 2 February 18, 31–32.

37. John Macy, "The Story of a Failure," *Dial* 63 (22 November 1917): 522–23.

38. "Abraham Cahan and David Levinsky," *Call,* 7 October 1917, 15.

39. H. W. Boynton, "A Stroll through the Fair of Fiction" [review of *RDL,* etc.], *Bookman* 46 (November 1917): 338; "Outstanding Novels of the Year" [review of *RDL,* etc.], *Nation* 105 (29 November 1917): 601.

40. Kate Holladay Claghorn, "*The Rise of David Levinsky*" [review], *Survey,* 1 December 1917, 260, 262.

41. "Glimpses of Reality: *The Rise of David Levinsky,*" *Nation,* 18 October 17, 432.

Chapter Seven

1. Lewis Fried, "American-Jewish Writing: Then and Now," *Ethnic Forum* 13–14, nos. 1–2 (1993–94): 21.

2. Hector St. Jean de Crèvecoeur, "Letter from an American Farmer: III," in *Norton Anthology of American Literature,* 4th ed., ed. Nina Baym et al. (New York: Norton, 1994), 1:660.

Glossary

For the convenience of the reader, in addition to Yiddish and a few Hebrew words, all italicized, this glossary includes unitalicized terms from these languages that have recently been naturalized into English, often with modified spelling.

Am olam: "Eternal People." Idealistic immigrants from Eastern Europe who attempted to establish new Jewish settlements in America and Palestine.

bar mitzvah: Ceremony marking a Jewish boy's maturity at thirteen.

"Bintl briv": "Bundle of Letters" feature in the *Forward;* a personal advice column.

erev . . .: The day before a holiday, as in *erev yom kipur.*

kaddish: Prayer over the dead in praise of God.

kheyder: Beginning Hebrew school for boys (pl.: *khadorim*).

kosher: Clean, pure, especially pertaining to food.

landsman: Jew from the homeland (pl.: *landslayt*).

loshn-koydesh: Hebrew; the language of holiness, or biblical Hebrew.

luftmentsh: Impractical dreamer, usually between jobs.

maged: Preacher (pl.: *magidim*).

mame-loshn: Among Ashkenazic Jews, Yiddish, the mother-tongue.

melamed: Hebrew teacher (pl.: *melamdim*).

mezuzah: A small container holding a sacred inscribed scroll, usually attached to the doorpost of the family home as a sign and reminder of the Jewish faith.

nar: A fool.

olraytnik: A showy immigrant with new money and no taste; parvenu (Cahan's coinage from "all right").

pilpul: Analytical debate, often hairsplitting, especially on Talmudic commentary.

Rosh Hashana: Jewish New Year; commemorates the anniversary of original creation.

schlemiel: Perpetual victim, accepting all without complaint.

sedre: The weekly Torah portion read during Sabbath service in shul.

shabes: The Sabbath.

shatkhn: Professional matchmaker.

186

shtetl: Small Jewish community in Eastern Europe, especially in the Pale (pl.: shtetlekh, or sometimes shtetls).

shul: Synagogue.

shund: Tawdry, sentimental, escapist popular fiction—strictly commercial.

Simchas Torah: Holiday celebrating the conclusion of one annual cycle of weekly Torah readings and the commencement of another.

Talmud: Compilation of rabbinic commentary on Jewish scriptural law.

Torah: The Five Books of Moses; first five books of the Jewish Scriptures.

tref: Not kosher.

yenta: A crude female busybody.

yeshiva: A seminary for study of the Talmud and training of rabbis.

yeshive bokher: Yeshiva student.

Yidishkayt: Yiddish culture of Eastern Europe brought into the United States with the immigrants.

Yom Kippur: Day of Atonement; the holiest day of the Hebrew year.

Selected Bibliography

PRIMARY SOURCES

Novels and Collections in English

"The Autobiography of an American Jew: The Rise of David Levinsky,"
McClure's 40 (April 1913): 92–106; 41 (May 1913): 73–85; (June 1913):
131–32, 134, 138, 141–42, 145, 147–48, 151–52; (July 1913):
116–28.

*A Bintel Brief: Sixty Years of Letters from the Lower East Side to the Jewish Daily For-
ward.* Edited by Isaac Metzker. Garden City, N.Y.: Doubleday & Co.,
1971.

Grandma Never Lived in America: The New Journalism of Abraham Cahan. Edited
and introduced by Moses Rischin. Rischin's comprehensive introduction
is valuable for information on both Cahan and the *Commercial Advertiser.*
Bloomington: Indiana University Press, 1984.

The Imported Bridegroom and Other Stories of the New York Ghetto. Boston:
Houghton Mifflin, 1898; later published as vol. 7 of the American Short
Story Series, New York: Garrett, 1968. Also published in *Yekl and The
Imported Bridegroom and Other Stories of the New York Ghetto.* Introduced by
Bernard C. Richards. New York: Dover Publications, 1970.

The Rise of David Levinsky: A Novel. New York: Harper & Bros., 1917. Reprint.
New York: Grosset & Dunlap, 1928. With introduction by John
Higham: New York: Harper & Bros., 1960. With introduction and
notes by Jules Chametzky: New York: Penguin Books, 1994.

The White Terror and the Red: A Novel of Revolutionary Russia. New York: A. S.
Barnes & Co., 1905.

Yekl, A Tale of the New York Ghetto. New York: D. Appleton and Co., 1896.
Also published in *Yekl and The Imported Bridegroom and Other Stories of the
New York Ghetto.* Introduced by Bernard C. Richards. New York: Dover
Publications, 1970.

Short Fiction in English

"The Apostate of Chego-Chegg." *Century* 59 (November 1899): 94–105.

"Circumstances." *Cosmopolitan* 22 (April 1897): 628–40. Also in *The Imported
Bridegroom.*

"A Ghetto Wedding," *Atlantic,* 81 (February 1898): 265–73. Also in *The
Imported Bridegroom.*

"The Daughter of Reb Avrom Leib," *Cosmopolitan* 30 (March 1900): 53–64.

"Dumitru and Sigrid," *Cosmopolitan* 30 (March 1901): 493–501.

"The Imported Bridegroom." In *The Imported Bridegroom* only.

"A Marriage by Proxy: A Story of the City." *Everybody's Magazine* 3 (December 1900): 569–75.

"A Providential Match." *Short Stories* 18 (February 1895): 191–213. Also in *The Imported Bridegroom.*

"Rabbi Eliezer's Christmas." *Scribner's* [?] (December 1899): [?].

"The Share of Count Brantsev." *Ainslee's* 18 (March 1901): 191–213. In *Grandma*, 490–96.

"A Sweat-Shop Romance." *Short Stories* 19 (June 1895: 129–43. In The *Imported Bridegroom.*

"Tzinchadzi of the Catskills." *Atlantic* 88 (August 1901): 221–26.

Autobiography

The Education of Abraham Cahan. Vols. 1 and 2 of *Bleter fun Mayn Lebn.* Translated by Leon Stein, Abraham P. Conan, and Lynn Davidson. Introduced by Leon Stein. Philadelphia: Jewish Publication Society of America, 1969.

Chapters, Essays, and Articles in English

"Hear the Other Side." In *Hear the Other Side: A Symposium of Democratic Socialist Opinion,* edited by Abraham Cahan, 7–26. New York: Forward Publishing Assoc., 1934.

Introduction to *Socialism, Fascism, Communism,* edited by Joseph Shaplen and David Shub, 9–10. New York: American League for Democratic Socialism, 1934.

"Jewish Massacres and the Revolutionary Movement in Russia." *North American Review* 177 (July 1903): 49–62.

"The Mantle of Tolstoy." *Bookman* 16 (New York) (December 1902): 328–33.

"The New Writers of the Ghetto." *Bookman* (New York) 39 (August 1914): 631–37.

"Realism: Lecture Delivered before the N.Y. Labor Lyceum, March 15." *Workmen's Advocate,* 6 April 1889, 2.

"The Russian Jew in America." *Atlantic* 82 (July 1898): 128–39.

"The Russian Jew in the United States." In *The Russian Jew in the United States: Studies of Social Conditions in New York, Philadelphia, and Chicago, with a Description of Rural Settlements,* edited by Charles S. Bernheimer, 32–40. Philadelphia: John C. Winston Co., 1905.

"Russian Nihilism of Today." *Forum* 21 (June 1901): 413–22.

"The Russian Revolutionists." *World's Work* 8 (September 1904): 5311–15.

Social Remedies. New York: New York Labor News Co., 1889. (A pamphlet comprising two articles previously published in the *Workmen's Advocate.*)

"The Talent and Personality of William Dean Howells: The Renowned American Author Who Died This Week." *Forward,* 16 May 1920. Translated

from the Yiddish by Curt Leviant and published as an appendix to Rudolf
and Clara M. Kirk, listed below in Secondary Sources under Articles.
"Younger Russian Writers," *Forum* 28 (September 1899): 119–28.
Note: See also the selections in *Grandma,* listed above under Novels and Collections.

Dramatic Adaptations

Berger, Pamela, dir. *The Imported Bridegroom.* With Eugene Troobnick, Greta
   Cowan, and Avi Hoffman. Adapted from "The Imported Bridegroom."
   A Lara Classics film, 1990.
Sheffer, Isaiah, book and lyrics. *The Rise of David Levinsky.* With Larry Kert and
   Avi Hoffman. Music by Bobby Paul. A play with music, adapted from
   The Rise of David Levinsky. First produced by the American Jewish The-
   atre, 92nd Street YMHA (Young Men's Hebrew Association), New
   York, 1983. Also produced by the George Street Playhouse, New
   Brunswick, N.J., April 1986, and the Houseman Theatre, New York,
   December 1986. See *Playbill,* 29 December 86, 2.
Silver, Joan Micklin, dir. *Hester Street.* With Carol Kane and Steven Keats.
   Adapted from *Yekl.* Produced by Rafael D. Silver. Distributed by Mid-
   west Film Productions, 1975.

Selected Works in Yiddish

Bleter fun mayn lebn (Pages from My Life). 5 vols. New York: Forward Publishing Assoc., 1926–1931. Autobiography.
*Historye fun di fareynikte shtatn mit eyntselhaytn vegn der entdekung un eroyberung fun
   amerike* (History of the United States, with Details Concerning the Discovery and Conquest of America). 2 vols. New York: Forward Publishing
   Assoc., 1910, 1912. History.
Palestine. New York: Forward Publishing Assoc., 1934. Travel with commentary on Cahan's trips to Palestine in the 1920s.
Rafael naritsokh. New York: Forward Publishing Assoc., 1894. A novel origi-
   nally serialized earlier in 1894 in *Arbeter tsaytung* as *Rafael naritsokh iz
   gevoren a sotsyalist* (Rafael Naritsokh Became a Socialist).
Rashel. New York: Forward Publishing Assoc., 1938. Biography.
Note: See the chronology for an accounting of the editorial posts Cahan held
   with Yiddish papers.

SECONDARY SOURCES

Books and Parts of Books about Cahan

Chametzky, Jules. "Abraham Cahan." In *Twentieth-Century American-Jewish Fiction Writers,* edited by Daniel Walden, 29–35. Vol 28 of *Dictionary of Lit-*

erary Biography. Detroit: Gale Research, 1984. Valuable complement to *DLB* entries by Engel and Stovall (listed below).

_____. "Focus on Abraham Cahan's *The Rise of David Levinsky:* Boats against the Current," In *American Dreams, American Nightmares,* edited by David Madden, 87–93. Carbondale and Edwardsville: Southern Illinois University Press, 1970. *Levinsky* anticipated the "spiritual malaise" felt by American Jews, partly a result of the loss of Old World traditions.

_____. *From the Ghetto: The Fiction of Abraham Cahan.* Amherst: University of Massachusetts Press, 1977. The only critical monograph published on Cahan before the present one. Emphasizes matters of language and analyzes the Yiddish fiction as well as Cahan's writing in English.

_____. Introduction and notes to *The Rise of David Levinsky,* vii–xxxi, 531–38. New York: Penguin, 1994. Excellent on the way anti-Semitic tactics in the contemporary publishing milieu were employed to influence the reception of Cahan's serialized novel in *McClure's.*

Dembo, L. S. "Levinsky and the Language of Acquisition." In *The Monological Jew: A Literary Study,* 84–92. Madison: University of Wisconsin Press, 1988. Levinsky's loneliness is largely explicable by Martin Buber's "I-Thou" relationship through communion rather than competition.

Engel, David. "Abraham Cahan." In *American Novelists, 1910–1945, Part 1: Louis Adamek-Vardis Fisher,* edited by James J. Martine, 117–22. Vol. 9 of *Dictionary of Literary Biography.* Detroit: Gale Research, 1981. General biocriticism emphasizing cultural change in Cahan's fiction.

Epstein, Melech. "Abraham Cahan." In *Profiles of Eleven: Profiles of Eleven Men Who Guided the Destiny of an Immigrant Society and Stimulated Social Consciousness among the American People,* 49–109. Detroit: Wayne State University Press, 1965. Portrait by a fellow journalist highlighting Cahan's role in labor relations and his feud with Jacob Gordin.

Fine, David M. "Success as Failure: Abraham Cahan's Fiction." In *The City, the Immigrant and American Fiction, 1880–1920,* 121–138, 160–62. Metuchen, N.J.: Scarecrow Press, 1977. Refers to Cahan throughout and devotes chapter seven to an overview of his fiction in English.

Girgus, Sam B. "A Convert to America: Sex, Self, and Ideology in Abraham Cahan." In *The New Covenant: Jewish Writers and the American Idea,* 64–91. Chapel Hill: University of North Carolina Press, 1984. Cahan exposed the dark side of "the American Dream" with its "conformity, dehumanism, and materialism." Compares Levinsky with Fitzgerald's Gatsby as representatives of "a people, a generation, and a culture."

Greenspan, Ezra. *The "Schlemiel" Comes to America,* 30–43. Metuchen, N.J.: Scarecrow Press, 1983. Gives special attention to the characteristics of the schlemiel, notably in *The Rise of David Levinsky.*

Guttmann, Allen. *The Jewish Writer in America: Assimilation and the Crisis of Identity,* 28–33. New York: Oxford University Press, 1971. Emphasizes the predominant identity theme in Cahan's fiction.

Hapgood, Hutchins. "A Novelist." In *The Spirit of the Ghetto,* edited by Moses Rischin, 230–53. 1902. Reprint. Cambridge, Mass.: Harvard University Press, 1967. Appreciation of Cahan's fiction; praises Cahan as a major realist with true insight into East Side life.

Harap, Louis. *Creative Awakening: The Jewish Presence in Twentieth-Century American Literature: 1900–1940s.* Westport, Conn.: Greenwood, 1987. Refers to *The White Terror and the Red* as an effective depiction of prerevolutionary Russia and to *The Rise of David Levinsky* as the best of the "acculturation novels."

———. "Fiction in English by Abraham Cahan." In *The Image of the Jew in American Literature from Early Republic to Mass Immigration,* 485–524, 567–71. Philadelphia: Jewish Publication Society of America, 1974. Traces Cahan's career, with special attention to his allegedly questionable ethics in socialism and journalism. Treats the fiction chiefly as documentation for biographical criticism, with the character of David Levinsky representing Cahan's similarly divided consciousness.

Higham, John. Introduction to *The Rise of David Levinsky,* v–xii. New York: Harper & Bros. Harper Torchbook, 1960. Valuable commentary on the period of mass immigration by the author of *Strangers in the Land* (listed below).

Maurice, Arthur Bartlett. *New York in Fiction,* 69–74. New York: Dodd, Mead, 1901. Describes a few East Side streets that Cahan used as settings.

Miller, Gabriel. "Jews without Manners." In *Screening the Novel: Rediscovered American Fiction in Film,* 1–18. New York: Frederick Ungar, 1980. Compares *Yekl* with *Hester Street,* its film adaptation.

Nettels, Elsa. *Language, Race, and Social Class in Howells's America,* 97–99. Lexington: University Press of Kentucky, 1988. Perceptive on Howells's appreciation for Cahan's realistic use of English with characteristics of Yiddish.

Pinsker, Sanford. *Jewish American Fiction, 1917–1987,* 1–7. New York: Twayne Publishers, 1992. *The Rise of David Levinsky* presents a "compelling vision" of the change faced by immigrants wrenched from traditional backgrounds. The central theme of Cahan's novel is "unfulfillment."

Sanders, Ronald. *The Downtown Jews: Portraits of an Immigrant Generation.* New York: Harper & Row, 1969. A brilliant analytical history of the Americanization of East European Jewish immigrants in New York City that centers on the American career of Abraham Cahan to about 1920.

Steffens, Lincoln. *The Autobiography of Lincoln Steffens,* 314. New York: Harcourt, Brace, 1931. Good biographical context for Cahan with the *Commercial Advertiser.*

Stovall, James Glen. "Abraham Cahan." In *American Newspaper Journalists, 1901–1925,* edited by Perry J. Ashley, 32–38. Vol. 25 of *Dictionary of Literary Biography.* Detroit: Gale Research, 1984. A standard *DLB* entry giving most attention to Cahan's journalism.

Articles

Barrish, Phillip. "'The Genuine Article': Ethnicity, Capital, and *The Rise of David Levinsky.*" *American Literary History* 5, no. 4 (Winter 1993): 643–62. Familiar insights reconstituted from a current cultural-studies perspective.

Carlin, M. M. "The Rise of David Levinsky." *University of Cape Town Studies in English* 9 (1979): 54–70. Levinsky's problems originate with the early death of his mother. The novel demonstrates Cahan's masterful handling of English.

Carter, Everett. "Realists and Jews." *Studies in American Fiction* 22, no. 1 (Spring 1994): 81–91. Cahan is mentioned, but the principals are Howells and James, who opposed prejudice but were affected by the prevailing anti-Semitism among American literati. Exposes the ambivalence of Cahan's literary contemporaries toward Jews.

Chametzky, Jules. "Notes on the Assimilation of the Americn-Jewish Writer: Abraham Cahan to Saul Bellow," *Jahrbuch für Amerikastudien* 9 (1964): 173–80. Analyzes samples from the works of three generations of Jewish American writers to show how the literary style of the narrators may reflect the authors' unconscious sense of assimilation as Americans.

Engel, David. "The Discrepancies of the Modern: Reevaluating Abraham Cahan's *The Rise of David Levinsky.*" *Studies in American Jewish Literature* 5, no. 2 (1979): 68–91. A new-historicist reading of *Levinsky,* centering on "what it means to be modern." Levinsky's denial of his past and his Judaism manifests "self-betrayal" and leads to perpetual alienation. His dilemma is attributable to his own limitations.

Fiedler, Leslie A. "Genesis: The American-Jewish Novel through the Twenties." *Midstream* 4, no. 3 (Summer 1958): 21–33. Levinsky's alienation and dissatisfaction are seen in relation to his eroticism as a secularized immigrant in materialistic America.

Fried, Lewis. "American-Jewish Writing: Then and Now." *Ethnic Forum* 13–14, nos. 1–2 (1993–94): 17–33. A scriptural basis in covenantal Judaism accounts for the strong linkage among Jews as "a chosen people" historically represented by Jewish-American authors in "a chosen country." An identity quest is central in much Jewish-American fiction, where it is often depicted by "the idea of orphanhood."

Hindus, Milton. "Abraham Cahan: Early American Realist." *Jewish Heritage* 7 (Fall 1964): 38–44. On Cahan's relations with Howells as recalled in volume 4 of *Bleter fun mayn lebn.*

Howells, W. D. "New York Low Life in Fiction." *New York World,* 26 July 96, 18. Howells's laudatory review of *Yekl* with Crane's *George's Mother,* in which he greets Cahan in large print as "a New Star of Realism."

———. "Some Books of Short Stories." *Literature,* 31 December 1898, 629. Praises *The Imported Bridegroom* collection for its combined humor, tragedy, and realism.

194   SELECTED BIBLIOGRAPHY

Kahn, Lothar. "*The Rise of David Levinsky:* Fifty Years After." *Chicago Jewish Forum* 26, no. 1 (Fall 1967): 2–5. Levinsky symbolizes "emerging Jewish American values"; through him, Cahan implicitly proposed socialism as the only alternative to his "barren spiritual existence." With lost traditions replaced by materialism, Levinsky represents the dilemma of many immigrants on the East Side.

Kellman, Ellen. "Love and Death in Weekly Installments." In "The Forward Century," special anniversary section of the *Forward* (English ed.), 22 May 1992, 20. Surveys the popular fiction serialized in the Yiddish *Forward* under Cahan's editorship.

Kirk, Rudolf, and Clara M. "Abraham Cahan and William Dean Howells: The Story of a Friendship." *American Jewish Historical Quarterly* 52, no. 1 (September 1962): 25–57. The best account of Cahan's association with Howells.

Kress, Susan. "Women and Marriage in Abraham Cahan's Fiction." *Studies in American Jewish Literature* 3 (1983): 26–39. Discusses the bleakness of marriage in Cahan's fiction.

Levenberg, Diane. "David Levinsky and His Women." *Midstream* 26 (August–September 1980): 51–53. Levinsky's sustained dissatisfaction and longing evolve directly from the death of his mother, for whom he constantly seeks a surrogate. He courts, seduces, and rapes America but gains no satisfaction.

Lyons, Bonnie. "David Levinsky: Modern Man as Orphan." In *Essays in American Literature in Memory of Richard P. Adams,* edited by Donald Pizer. *Tulsa Studies in English* 23 (1978): 85–93. *The Rise of David Levinsky* prophesied the detachment and malaise that characterize American life more than half a century after it was published.

Marovitz, Sanford E. "The Lonely New Americans of Abraham Cahan." *American Quarterly* 20, no. 2 (Summer 1968): 196–210. Most of Cahan's characters are lonely and dissatisfied because of their own limitations, not America's failure to provide for their needs. Those immigrants who retain their Jewish ties find satisfaction through community despite their poverty.

———. "The Secular Trinity of a Lonely Millionaire: Language, Sex, and Power in *The Rise of David Levinsky.*" *Studies in American Jewish Literature* 2 (1982): 20–35. The recognition of Levinsky's interrelated drives to acquire fluency in English, dominate competitors, and conquer women leads to the conclusion that a lifelong egocentricity explains his alienation and dissatisfaction.

Michel, Sonya. "*Yekl* and *Hester Street:* Was Assimilation Really Good for the Jews?" *Literature/Film Quarterly* 5, no. 2 (1977): 42–46. Unlike Cahan's novel, a feminist theme and an overworked ghetto setting dominate Silver's film.

Novick, Paul. "Abraham Cahan and the *Forward.*" *Jewish Life* 6, no. 1 (November 1951): 14–16. Condemns Cahan's allegedly destructive impact on

American Jewish life. Sees the *Forward* as sensationalistic and superficial in promoting socialism and Jewish tradition. A personal attack that represents the hostile reactions of Cahan's opponents.

Poole, Ernest. "Abraham Cahan: Socialist—Journalist—Friend of the Ghetto." *Outlook* 99 (28 October 1911): 467–78. Praise by a fellow socialist and future author of *The Harbor* (1915), one of the most popular radical novels of the decade. Chiefly biographical. Admired Cahan as a realist.

Pressman, Richard S. "Abraham Cahan, Capitalist; David Levinsky, Socialist." *Studies in American Jewish Fiction* 12 (1993): 2–18. *The Rise of David Levinsky* is better understood as a contemporary novel than a historical one because the period of composition marked a transformative stage in Cahan's life.

Rich, J. C. "60 Years of the Jewish Daily *Forward*." *New Leader* 40 (3 June 1957): sec. 2, pp. 1–38. An appreciative history of the Yiddish daily by a writer who had been a member of the *Forward* editorial staff since 1922.

Rischin, Moses. "Abraham Cahan and the *New York Commercial Advertiser:* A Study in Acculturation." *Publication of the American Jewish Historical Society* 43 (September 1953): 10–36. Anticipates by three decades aspects of his introduction to *Grandma Never Lived in America* (listed above in Primary Sources).

Rosenfeld, Isaac. "America, Land of the Sad Millionaire." *Commentary* 14 (August 1952): 131–35. Levinsky's yearning is typically Jewish; it originated in his youth and remains insatiable in America because the hunger itself is a sustaining force within him. His voice is authentic, but he seems devious. Structurally, the novel has a Talmudic quality: "it consists of an extended commentary on a single text."

Singer, David. "David Levinsky's Fall: A Note on the Liebman Thesis." *American Quarterly* 19, no. 4 (Winter 1967): 696–706. Having forsaken his piety before leaving Russia, Levinsky typifies most East European immigrant Jews, according to the Liebman thesis, because they retained their ethnic traditions without their orthodox faith.

Strout, Cushing. "Personality and Cultural History in the Novel: Two American Examples." *New Literary History* 1, no. 3 (1970): 423–38. A historicist analysis in which *Levinsky* and Henry Adams's *Esther* exemplify how novels can help reveal "the complex transactions between the self and its culture."

Vogel, Dan. "Cahan's *Rise of David Levinsky:* Archetype of American Jewish Fiction." *Judaism* 22, no. 3 (Summer 1973): 278–87. Cahan created two archetypal themes in Jewish literature: (1) the conflict of cultures arising when traditional East European Jewish immigrants are confronted by materialistic American values, and (2) the secularized Jewish anti-hero who cannot elude his linkage with Judaism. Levinsky's alienation became thematic in later Jewish-American fiction.

Zanger, Jules. "David Levinsky: Master of Pilpul." *Papers on Language and Literature* 13, no. 3 (Summer 1977): 283–94. Develops Rosenfeld's theme (listed above) that *The Rise of David Levinsky* structurally resembles the Talmud. Levinsky's early training as a Talmudist leads to the complexities and technicalities in Cahan's strategic representation of the past.

Zlotnick, Joan. "Abraham Cahan, A Neglected Realist." *American Jewish Archives* 23, no. 1 (April 1971): 33–46. Praises Cahan as a "literal realist" whose fiction is "comic in spirit" but "sometimes tragic in implication."

Books, Parts of Books, and Articles on the Cultural Context in which Cahan Lived

Bernheimer, Charles S., ed. *The Russian Jew in the United States: Studies of Social Conditions in New York, Philadelphia, and Chicago, with a Description of Rural Settlements.* Philadelphia: John C. Winston Co., 1905. A chapter by Cahan on New York and more than thirty others by various hands provide a valuable contemporary overview of economics, social conditions, demographics, and the state of arts and letters among East European Jews in the United States.

Cady, Edwin H. *The Realist at War: The Mature Years, 1885–1920, of William Dean Howells.* Syracuse, N.Y.: Syracuse University Press, 1958. Portrays Howells among his many literary associates, including Cahan, and thereby presents a cross-section of American realism.

Chyet, Stanley F., ed. "Forgotten Fiction: American Jewish Life, 1890–1920." *American Jewish Archives* 37, no. 1 (April 1985): 5–232. Useful introduction and selection of fiction not easily available elsewhere.

Cohen, Israel. *Vilna.* Jewish Community Series. Philadelphia: Jewish Publication Society of America, 1943. History of Vilna is good background for Cahan's early years and Russian anti-Semitism through the post—revolutionary period.

Epstein, Melech. *Jewish Labor in {the} U.S.A.: An Industrial, Political, and Cultural History of the Jewish Labor Movement, 1882–1952.* 2 vols. in 1. 1950. Hoboken, N.J.: KTAV, 1969. Volume 1 (1884–1914) presents Cahan as a major figure in the development of organized labor among the Jewish immigrants.

Heinze, Andrew R. *Adapting to Abundance: Jewish Immigrants, Mass Consumption, and the Search for American Identity.* New York: Columbia University Press, 1990. A revisionist view of the ghetto economy, with emphasis on spending to realize the American Dream.

Higham, John. *Strangers in the Land: Patterns of American Nativism, 1860–1925.* New Brunswick, N.J.: Rutgers University Press, 1955. A history of the immigration period, emphasizing the increasing hostility toward the millions of newcomers.

Howe, Irving. *World of Our Fathers.* New York: Harcourt, Brace, Jovanovich, 1976. The best general cultural history of mass Jewish immigration and the first place to turn for information. Abundant references to Cahan and the *Forward.*

Howells, W. D. "An East-Side Ramble." In *Impressions and Experiences,* 127–49. New York: Harper and Bros., 1896. Howells's ambivalent response to wandering among the streets and tenements of New York's Lower East Side.

James, Henry. *The American Scene.* London: Chapman & Hall, 1907. James was astonished and bewildered after visiting the Jewish district because the city appeared so different from the way he had known it; like Howells, he was ambivalent, not hostile.

Marovitz, Sanford E. "Romance and Realism: Children of the New Colossus and the Jewish Struggles Within." In *American Realism and the Canon,* edited by Tom Quirk and Gary Scharnhorst, 102–26. Newark: University of Delaware Press, 1994. Jewish-American realism is distinguishable from, yet a part of, the broader realistic movement in the United States. Provides an American literary context for Cahan.

Riis, Jacob. *Jacob Riis Revisited: Poverty and the Slum in Another Era.* Edited by Francesco Cordasco. Garden City, N.Y.: Doubleday, 1968. An exposé of the slum and ghetto with a selection of Riis's photographs. Includes his three books on the subject: *How the Other Half Lives* (1890), *Children of the Poor* (1892), and *A Ten Years' War* (1900). A provocative revelation.

Rischin, Moses. *The Promised City: New York's Jews, 1870–1914.* Cambridge, Mass.: Harvard University Press, 1962. A detailed history of the impact of Eastern European Jewish immigration on the social and economic development of New York City, especially the Lower East Side.

Dissertations

Pollock, Theodore Marvin. "The Solitary Clarinetist: A Critical Biography of Abraham Cahan, 1860–1917." Ph.D. diss., Columbia University, 1959. A thorough account of Cahan's life and career drawn from sources in Yiddish and English. Although the readings of the fiction are unimaginative, the biographical and historical data are valuable. With the autobiography (*Bleter*) and Sanders's *The Downtown Jews,* this dissertation is an essential source for information on Cahan.

Waldinger, Albert. "Abraham Cahan as Novelist, Critic, and Folk Advocate." Ph.D. diss., Boston University, 1971. Covers Cahan's auctorial career from a socialistic and realistic perspective, emphasizing Russian realism.

Bibliographies

Cronin, Gloria L., Blaine H. Hall, and Connie Lamb. "Abraham Cahan: 1860–1951." In *Jewish American Fiction Writers: An Annotated Bibliography,* 89–111. New York: Garland, 1991. A basic list of the major novels and stories in English with good coverage of the secondary material, including selected reviews.

Jeshurin, Ephim H. *Abraham Cahan Bibliography*. New York: United Vilner
     Relief Committee, 1941. A valuable unannotated compilation of primary
     and secondary material in Yiddish, Hebrew, Russian, and English;
     includes full-page photographs of title pages from Cahan's publications.
Marovitz, Sanford E. "Abraham Cahan." *American Literary Realism, 1870–1910*
     8, no. 3 (Summer 1975): 206–8. Identifies and briefly describes the six
     dissertations all or partly on Cahan that had been accepted to date since
     Pollock's in 1959.
_____, and Lewis Fried. "Abraham Cahan (1860–1951): An Annotated Bibli-
     ography." *American Literary Realism, 1870–1910* 3, no. 3 (Summer
     1970): 196–243. Though now dated, this is still the most inclusive pri-
     mary and secondary bibliography of works by and about Cahan in Eng-
     lish published through 1969.
Polster, Karen L. "Abraham Cahan: An Annotated Bibliography of Criticism,
     1970–1988." *Studies in American Jewish Literature* 12 (1993): 25–35.
     Largely duplicates the post-1970 items in the Cronin, Hall, Lamb bibli-
     ography (listed above) but brings it up to date and includes some fuller
     annotations.

Index

Aleichem, Sholem, 53; *Fiddler on the Roof,*
2
Alexander II, Czar, 12, 172n. 13, 181n.
2; assassination, 118, 126, 129, 172n.
13, 181n. 2
Alexander III, Czar, 13, 34, 172n. 13
American in the Making, An (Ravage), 163
Americanization: Cahan's role, 165
American Minerva, The, 41, 176n. 3
Am olam (Eternal People), 14–15, 17
Anti-Semitism, 12–13, 44, 118–19,
172n. 13, 181–82n. 2; among socialists, 12, 23; Vilna environs, 5
"Apostate of Chego-Chegg, The," 168;
bleakness, 104; moral ambivalence,
106; publication, 104; summary,
105–6
Arbeter tsaytung (Worker's Newspaper), 23,
25, 36; Cahan's role, 36, 38
Arbeter Tsaytung Publishing Assoc., 36,
38
Asch, Sholem, 53
"Autobiography of an American Jew,
The," 30; alienation theme, 138; comparison with *The Rise of David Levinsky,* 137–38; composition, 52,
135–36; implicit anti-Semitic context,
136–37; initiates Cahan's self-exploration, 137; publication, 135–36

"Back to Dear Old Russia/The Disillu-
sionment of Sonia Rogova," 121;
duality in, 48
"Bake Shop Count, The," 46
Bakunin, Mikhall A., 23
Barge Office, The, 111–12, 177n. 7
Barondess, Joseph, 22
Beach, Erasmus Darwin, 35
Beiliss, Mendel: trial in Kiev, 154
"Bintl briv," 28, 169; beginning, 55–57;
success, 55–57
Black Hundreds, The, 119
Bleter fun mayn lebn (Pages from My Life,
Ab. Cahan), 2, 15, 59, 127

Bogoraz, Natan, 130
Bronstein, Aniuta, 17; *see also* Cahan,
Anna (wife)

Cahan, Abraham: Americanization, 1, 14,
124; birth, 1; and communism,
23–24; in the countryside near New
York, 117–18; crossed eyes, 8–9, 14;
didacticism, 43; duality, 1, 7, 47,
65–66, 92, 121; early schooling, 5, 7;
in Europe (as Socialist delegate), 23;
final years and death, 27, 31–32; flees
from Russia, 14–16; as "Hester Street
Reporter," 40; humor, 44–46; as a
Jew, 6–7, 166; on Jews and Judaism,
65, 165–66; keen memory, 2–3, 5,
33; on language, 8, 18, 33; legacy of,
170; marriage, 17, 100, 173nn.
19–20; marriage theme, 100; music,
affection for, 33; naturalization, 23,
175n. 26; and the *New York Commercial Advertiser,* 101–4; opposes Communism, 58; and organized labor, 22;
pseudonyms, 25; on realism in art,
63; on realism in drama, 67; as realist,
8, 44, 60–70, 166–67; relations with
father, 7; on romanticism, 64–65; and
Russian authors, 7–8; Russian publications, 34; on socialism and art,
61–62; as socialist, 19–25, 27–28,
119; as teacher, 18–19; at Vilna
Teachers' Training Institute, 9–10;
writing style, 8; and Zionism, 30–31
Cahan, Anna (wife), 34, 39, 118, 154
Cahan, Isaac (brother), 4, 7
Cahan, Sarah (mother), 4, 7
Cahan, Shakhne (father), 3, 6–7, 19–20;
language, devotion to, 33
Chagall, Marc, 96
"Chasm, The," 115; description, 117–18
Chekhov, Anton, 8, 60, 86, 114
Chernishevsky, Nikolai, 10–11; *What Is
to Be Done?,* 10–11
Chmyelnicki, Bogdan, 128

199

The Author

Sanford E. Marovitz is Professor Emeritus of English at Kent State University, where he taught from 1967 to 1996 and where he chaired the English department from 1987 to 1992. He earned his B.A. with honors at Lake Forest College and his M.A. and Ph.D. at Duke University. He has been a Woodrow Wilson Fellow (1960–61), a Fulbright Instructor at the University of Athens, Greece (1965–67), and a Visiting Professor of English at Shimane University, Japan (1976–77). In 1985 he received the Distinguished Teaching Award at Kent State and the Distinguished Service Citation from Lake Forest College, where he is a member of the Board of Trustees. Coeditor of *Artful Thunder: Versions of the Romantic Tradition in American Literature in Honor of Howard P. Vincent* (1975) and coauthor of *Bibliographical Guide to the Study of the Literature of the U.S.A.,* 5th ed. (1984), Professor Marovitz has published widely in critical collections and professional journals, mostly on nineteenth- and twentieth-century American literature.

The Editor

Nancy A. Walker is Director of Women's Studies and Professor of English at Vanderbilt University. A native of Louisiana, she received her B.A. from Louisiana State University and her M.A. from Tulane University. After receiving her Ph.D. from Kent State University in 1971, she taught American literature, American studies, and women's studies at Stephens College, where she also served as Assistant to the President and Chair of the Department of Languages and Literature.

A specialist in American women writers, Walker is the author of *A Very Serious Thing: Women's Humor and American Culture* (1988) and *Feminist Alternatives: Irony and Fantasy in the Contemporary Novel by Women* (1990), which won the first annual Eudora Welty Prize. She has published numerous articles in such journals as *American Quarterly, Tulsa Studies in Women's Literature, American Literature,* and *American Literary Realism,* and several essays on women's autobiography. With Zita Dresner, she edited *Redressing the Balance: American Women's Literary Humor from the Colonial Period to the 1980s* (1988).

Walker is general editor for the period 1800–1914 for Twayne's United States Authors Series.

DATE DUE

GAYLORD			PRINTED IN U.S.A.